## *About the Author*

PAT MONTANDON was reared in Oklahoma, the daughter of Nazarene ministers. In the 1960s she fled Oklahoma for the excitement and glamour of San Francisco, where she created a life as a newspaper columnist, television host, and writer. Her books include *How to Be a Party Girl*, *The Intruders*, *Making Friends*, and *Celebrities and Their Angels*. She has been interviewed extensively by the media, including the *New York Times*, the *Los Angeles Times*, the *Washington Post*, *USA Today*, *The New Yorker*, *Esquire*, *People*, the *San Francisco Chronicle*, and the *San Francisco Examiner*. She has appeared on *Today*, *The Tonight Show*, NBC News, and CBS News. She lives in Beverly Hills, California.

# WHISPERS FROM GOD

**ALSO BY PAT MONTANDON**

*How to Be a Party Girl*
*The Intruders*
*Making Friends*
*Celebrities and Their Angels*

PLAYS

*Patience Patient*
*Them Oklahoma Hills*
*Family Album*

POEMS

"Black Silence"
"The Banner"
"Testosterone Drums"
"Ghosts"
"Tiananmen Square"
"The DMZ"
"American Dream"
"The Children of Chernobyl"

# WHISPERS FROM GOD

## A Life Beyond Imaginings

## PAT MONTANDON

HARPER

NEW YORK · LONDON · TORONTO · SYDNEY

HARPER

All interior photographs courtesy of the author's personal collection.

A hardcover edition of this book was published under the title of *Oh the Hell of It All* in 2007 by HC, an imprint of HarperCollins Publishers.

HarperCollins books may be purchased for educational, business, or sales promotional use. For information please write: Special Markets Department, HarperCollins Publishers, 10 East 53rd Street, New York, NY 10022.

FIRST HARPER PAPERBACK PUBLISHED 2008.

*Designed by Kris Tobiassen*

Library of Congress Cataloging-in-Publication Data is available upon request.

ISBN 978-0-06-137392-3 (pbk.)

08  09  10  11  12  DIX / RRD  10  9  8  7  6  5  4  3  2  1

FOR MY SON, SEAN,
AND
MY DAUGHTER, STAR,
AND
FOR THE HUNDREDS OF BRAVE
CHILDREN WHO TRAVELED
THE WORLD WITH ME

# CONTENTS

# PROLOGUE

On my fifty-first birthday—December 26, 1979—my dearly loved husband Al, and our nine-year-old son Sean had awakened me with an armful of white Moondance roses, a steaming cup of French Roast coffee, and a three-pound tin of Beluga caviar. "This is just for you, Patsy," Al said. He put the breakfast tray over my legs and then kissed me. "We know how much you love caviar."

"I'll share," I said, laughing. Sean climbed up on the bed next to me but when I spooned the glistening gray eggs into his mouth, he made a face. "That tastes awful Mom, why do you like that stuff?" he asked. "I just do, Sean-Sean," I said, amused.

Al said, "Sweetheart, Sean has a surprise for you, right Sean?"

"Yeah," Sean said, scrambling off the bed. He fished a small box from Al's jacket pocket and handed it to me. "I made this for you at school," he said. "It's a ceramic cross on a string so you can wear it."

"Oh, Sean-Sean," I said, putting the cross around my neck and hugging him. "What a beautiful present. I'll treasure it forever."

Having my adored family around me was a delicious way to begin a milestone birthday—every bit as good as our extravagant eighth wedding anniversary when Al had taken me on a whirlwind trip to Paris.

In the City of Light, my handsome husband had put on a tuxedo, looking more handsome still, and I had donned a Dior evening gown for a gastronomic feast at the famous La Tour d'Argent. We dined on roast duckling with orange sauce and drank vintage Chateauneuf du Pape while enjoying a killer view of Notre Dame Cathedral from across the Seine. At the end of the evening, Al gave me a pair of emerald and diamond earrings. "Al darling, you are too good to be true," I had said, kissing him.

"I've told you many times that you saved my life, Patsy," Al said. "I was just sitting up there in that penthouse waiting to die until I met you."

On this day of my fifty-first birthday, we were in our San Francisco penthouse with its twenty-three-foot tall glass walls enhanced by furniture of beige travertine by the famous interior designer Michael Taylor. Our dining table seated fourteen and was so huge that it had had to be lifted by crane up to our thirty-third-floor aerie. The view was spectacular, too, and included the entire San Francisco Bay, from the Faralon Islands thirty miles in the Pacific to the Port of Oakland, and the hills and water and three bridges in between.

Al would fly us over that view in his jet helicopter to our beautiful country home, River Meadow Farm in Rutherford, California, in the famed Napa Valley, the day after my birthday. River Meadow was my dream home and the place where we relaxed, and swam, and dug in the earth and grew grapes.

After growing up poor, I appreciated all the material things Al provided, but my happiness was more deeply rooted than that. The true joy of my life was my husband and son. Growing up I had been blessed with a kind and gentle father who had taught me to care about those marginalized by society and not to be impressed by possessions. My father's "It can be done" motto, along with my mother's insistence that I be able to speak out in public had stood me in good stead. Mother's sense of humor and her ability to handle adversity—including hunger—were gifts I hoped to pass along to Sean. In spite of the fact that she had twelve pregnancies and eight living children, she always expected us to be clean, properly dressed, and insisted we were to be educated. But she could also be a rigid taskmaster and I could never please her. I was determined that I was going to be a different kind of mother to my child.

Al and I lived a grand life with grand friends and grand parties. There was the house blessing at River Meadow Farm where Benny Goodman serenaded Alex Haley, Danielle Steel, and two hundred other friends, the '40s Sentimental Journey party where Clint Eastwood, Ethel

Kennedy, and Valentino danced to the music of Les Brown and His Band of Renown.

Since marrying Al I had enjoyed an endless stream of happy surprises. We flew to Florida in a Gulf Stream jet to attend the space launch of Apollo XIV. We relaxed aboard a yacht in the Florida sun with Cary Grant and John Wayne after attending the moon shot. At a dinner in our San Francisco home, astronaut and fellow Oklahoman Tom Stafford, the commander of Apollo X, gave me a gold pin that spelled "Okie" that he had taken to the moon.

On the night of my half-century mark, Al threw a dinner party for me at Trader Vic's—THE restaurant in San Francisco. Among the guests were our closest friends—Danielle Steel, Alex Haley, Cyril Magnin, Ann and Gordon Getty, and our Napa Valley neighbors John and Dede Traina. Dede was not only my best friend but Sean thought of her as his "best friend ever" as well. He was smitten with the woman, and although her two sons, Todd and Trevor, were his age, Sean always preferred Dede's company. She seemed to enjoy Sean's company, too.

Touched by Al's thoughtfulness and very much in love, I toasted my husband. "To Alfred Spalding Wilsey, the most wonderful husband that ever was. You've made my life into a flower garden." With tears sliding down my face I raised my glass, "Here's to the love that produced our beautiful son Sean and to the rest of our lives together."

Eight days later, on January 4, 1980, as we prepared for bed, Al said so casually that I might have missed it had I not been listening, "I want a divorce." My world collapsed.

# PART ONE

# TROUBLE IN PARADISE

# I.

# PREACHER'S DAUGHTER

Almost everything was considered a sin while I was growing up as a preacher's daughter in Texas and Oklahoma in the '30s: makeup, dying one's hair, funny papers on Sunday, movies, short-sleeved dresses, and jewelry. Tent revival meetings with sermonizers exhorting sinners to confess dotted the landscape, which stretched mile after mile across the flat plains of the Lone Star State and throughout the rolling hills of Oklahoma.

As a child my world was family, school, friends, and church. Church came first. It permeated my youth. As the seventh of eight children born to a West Texas fundamentalist minister father, I was constantly exhorted to be good. Goodness was enforced according to the rigid tenets of my parents' faith.

My strict father was often warm and kind, although he could fly off the handle, scaring us kids half to death. He loved all humanity, advocating equality between races at a time when it was dangerous to do so. His friendship with Negroes was the one point of contention between my father and mother. She would often tell him he would rue the day he allowed "Coloreds" to attend his services.

Mother was severe and unsympathetic, yet she loved music and played the piano, taught us poetry, and emphasized the importance of being able to read and speak in public. She could also be quite humorous, but that was rare.

One of my sisters, Betty Ruth, had died from a mastoid infection when she was two, shortly before I was born on December 26, 1928. The ghost of my dead sister haunted me. Knowing I could never replace her I would try to be more accomplished than my older siblings and then maybe, someday, my family would love me too, I thought. My six surviving siblings—three sisters and three brothers—were usually in Mama's good graces, because they never dared to disagree with her. But she and I were constantly at war. I wanted to listen to The Pepper Cadets, a kids' radio show, play dress-up using lipstick, and go to a Shirley Temple movie—all sinful things in my parents' view.

One Sunday morning when I was eight, I refused to go to church.

"I'm not going. I'm not!" I yanked off the pink ribbons just tied onto my pigtails and threw them on the floor. Mother's sharp slap was like a gunshot. My face stung, but I would not allow myself to cry.

"No eight-year-old girl will tell me what she's going to do, and not going to do." Collecting her Bible, Mama commanded me to follow her and my cooperative older siblings to the church house. In her shapeless print dress (pink roses against a blue background), face, eyebrows, and lashes covered with Rachel Number One, a face powder deemed okay by God, I thought Mama looked like an albino.

"I hate her," I dared whisper to that secret inner self where all my real thoughts went.

Our battle raged almost every Sunday. I rebelled at going to church and hearing about the Mark of the Beast, Seven-Headed Monsters, The End of the World, and all those folks burning in hell, because God, a man with a beard sitting on a throne in the sky, said they were sinners. God scared me. Of course I always had to go, no matter how mightily I professed to having a stomachache, or even once when I pretended to have broken my leg.

One Sunday before we trooped off to church, Daddy sat us down and told us that he had invited his "Colored" friends to the service that day and that we were to be kind and welcoming to them. Mama had frowned and said under her breath that Daddy would be sorry.

At church I tuned out the preaching so I wouldn't have to think about the screams of sinners being burned in hell. I thought instead about the fried chicken dinner we would enjoy later, and our beautiful white Victorian parsonage, which had a flourishing flower garden and indoor plumbing. It was the most beautiful house I had ever seen, much less lived in.

"Hallelujah! Glory to God!" someone shouted. The sermon over, everyone rose for the final hymn and altar call. "Please turn your songbooks to page forty-five," Daddy said. "As we sing the last song, remember this may be your final hour on earth. You had better think about that, Brothers and Sisters. You had better march up here and give your hearts and souls to God. This could be your last opportunity to make things right with your Maker." As the fervor of his emotional pitch for heaven became more intense, Daddy's voice became thunderous, only to stop and then resume, as quiet as a whisper.

"Mother, while you play," he said, indicating the black upright piano, "and the choir sings, I want those of you who are burdened with sin to come forward." Mama took her place at the keyboard. She banged away as the men and women of the choir, wearing the mournful expression of career saints, sang.

"Softly and tenderly, Jesus is calling,

Calling for you and for me . . .

Come Home, Come Home. O-o-o-h sinner,

Come H-O-O-O-me."

What if I died today, I thought, as I often did: Would I be saved? No—I would go straight to hell for sure. Remembering my past sins . . . how I lied about breaking Daddy's watch and how I stole a penny from the church collection plate once—I wailed "O-o-o-h . . ." as tears began to slide down my face, "I don't want to die a sinner."

At the first O-o-o-h, several of the devout, sitting nearby, enveloped me as if they had found a genuine diamond on a kid's treasure hunt. They propelled me to the mourners' bench, where I fell on my knees, sobbing. "Here's little Patsy Lou, Lord Jesus, a sinner," intoned the supplicants. "Only you know what dark deeds she's done, what evil thoughts she's had. Oh dear God, we pray for her deliverance." In the background, I could hear shouting, "Amen, Glory to God, I've got religion!"

My mind wandered from my own sins long enough to peek through my fingers to see if one of the Elders was going to throw a songbook like he sometimes did when spiritual enthusiasm overcame him. Sure enough, he was winding up. Daddy ducked as the book, its pages fluttering, sailed toward him.

My trespasses forgotten, I addressed more immediate concerns, such as the onion breath of one of those praying for me. Taking advantage of the songbook diversion, I crawled to a side door and escaped into the warm summer air.

"That was a good meeting," Daddy said, spooning up gravy at the supper table that night. "Lots of people prayed through to salvation." Then he pulled his gold-rimmed spectacles down on his nose and caught me dead center in his gaze. "But, little Chik-a-lik," he said, using my nickname, "if you keep running to the altar every Sunday, folks are going to think you're a professional sinner." He scowled, then smiled, reaching out to pat my cheek. I knew my Daddy loved me, even if I was corrupt.

The following night I half awoke from a deep warm sleep, sensing that something was wrong. Then a scream, as if Satan had poked a transgressor with his pitchfork, caused me to come fully awake. Someone was yelling, "The church is on fire! The church is on fire!"

My sister Glendora, five years my elder, and I crouched at our bedroom window and watched, transfixed, as flames enveloped the small chapel, lighting up the night sky. In spite of efforts to save it, before long the structure was nothing more than a blackened, smoldering ruin.

The next day Daddy called a family meeting. "Children," he said, "that fire was set on purpose." We stared in disbelief. "It's because of the Colored folks." His voice sounded scratchy. "Now the Deacons don't want me as a preacher anymore. We have to vacate the parsonage." In the shocked silence, my father cleared his throat and then made a final statement. "But I want you children to know that I did the right thing. Remember to always do the right thing, no matter what others say or do. You do the right thing. Understand?"

We nodded yes.

"It's that old Depression that causes people to act like that, Daddy," I said, "isn't it?"

"Well, you could be part right, Patsy." Daddy always answered my questions. "Poor folks act from fear, not logic. The dust storms, no rain, makes it hard for everyone." He rubbed a hand across his face and fought to catch his breath. "The farmers can hardly get a weed to grow. Just a little cotton here and there."

After Daddy's church was burned down, our lives, too, lay in shambles. There was no money, no insurance. We were destitute. It was 1936 and times were hard for everyone, Daddy said, but he thought it would get better now that President Roosevelt had been re-elected.

When we were told we would have to go on Relief, a new government agency established to help those in need during the Great Depression, it was an added blow. Soon bags of powdered milk were hauled into our house, their sides split, leaving a trail on the floor. Cans of black strap molasses and tins of lard arrived from the Relief Office. We were given stiff black corduroy overalls that were uncomfortable and didn't fit us.

"I'm not wearing these ugly ole things." Glendora held her nose, tears streaking her face. "It's like . . . an poor white trash sign."

"Glendora, you don't need to talk like poor white trash. Say, 'a' poor white trash sign, not 'an' poor white trash sign." Mama made knots out of a corner of her apron as she talked. "And don't you ever let me hear tell of you saying such things again. We just need time to get back on our feet, that's all.

She continued, "Now children, Brother Connors has some tag-end-of-the-season cotton up near the Grover place. Charles, you and Patsy Lou are to go there tomorrow morning, bright and early, to help pick."

The next day my brother and I slunk around the alleyways to get to the cotton patch on the outskirts of town. I prayed we would not run into schoolmates. Picking cotton was considered the depths of abasement. Only "darkies" picked cotton, and in spite of Daddy's attitude, associating with them was regarded as contamination.

We were given long canvas sacks with wide straps that fit over our shoulders and told to pick as much as we could. The contents would be weighed and then dumped into a slatted wagon parked at the edge of the forlorn acreage. I looked around, pigtails brushing my shoulders. There were eight Negroes but no other whites. Charles and I were sent to one side of the field, the Negroes to the other, segregated even in the cotton patch.

Not long after I started picking, I wanted to give up. The sharp bolls made my fingers bleed. I pulled the heavy sack along, like a freakish snail, leaving a dusty trail in my wake. Soon I stopped picking and began to play tic-tac-toe in the dirt.

"You'd better stop that," Charles said. He was keeping an eye on me from two rows away. "Mama will git you for sure if you don't make some money."

With that threat in mind, I bent to work again. The relentless sun burned my face and arms. Every muscle ached. Eternity came and went before it was time for lunch. I looked over the distant rows and saw that the Negroes had picked much more than I had. They had been to the weighing-in scales, time after time, their earnings recorded in a notebook by a skinny white man in a straw hat and overalls. He used the stub of a pencil, wetting it in his mouth before each entry.

A hot breeze periodically shimmered the leaves of a lone cottonwood tree. The Negroes were soon clustered under it. They opened newspaper-wrapped hoecakes and passed around bottles of soda pop. Charles and I sat apart, half in sunlight, munching on dry biscuit sandwiches, furtively watching the dusty group under the tree.

"Ya'll want a swig, gal?" a black-skinned woman held out a bottle of Orange Nehi Crush.

"No, thankee," I replied.

Charles pinched my arm. "Scaredy cat," he whispered. "Go ahead, drink it—it'll turn you into one of them and then I can git rid of you!"

"Shut your mouth, Charles, jist you wait 'til I tell Daddy." I looked away, across the sun-baked field. Waves of heat conjured up the mirage of a lake.

"I was jist kiddin'. We've gotta stick together." His words made me cry. I was not used to anyone being sweet to me.

"Ain't I seen you chillun' hereabouts afore?" asked a skinny black man. He was dressed in a sweat-soaked undershirt and bib overalls. The Negro's smile revealed empty spaces between crooked ivory teeth. "Don't your Pa preach at the Holy Roller Church?"

We shook our heads up and down in assent while munching on our dry sandwiches; our eyes round with fear. "He-uns a good man, the

Preacher," the man said. Seven dark heads nodded agreement. "You'uns sure ain't much of a picker." The man pointed to my limp cotton sack. "I'se got a lot of extry bolls and seein' as how I don't rightly need 'em, why don't I jist give 'em to you'uns?" It was more of a statement than a question. Even as he talked he was filling my sack.

All the way home, I skipped the dirt into iridescent arcs, unmindful of anything but the twenty cents clasped tightly in my hand. That was the nicest thing anyone had done for me in my whole entire life, I thought. The very nicest thing.

But even the extra money from picking cotton wasn't enough to make ends meet—we would have to leave our home. The lines from Mama's nose to her mouth suddenly seemed deeper. Her face was grim. "Y'all start putting things into boxes and no dillydallying either." A new preacher and his family would be coming the very next day, she said. They were to have our beautiful house, the flower garden, my secret hiding place, everything. My insides hurt as if I had caught the appendicitis Glendora had almost died from.

We moved into a dilapidated brown shingle house on the edge of the little town of Chillicothe, Texas. The appearance of our new home was not enhanced by the weeds growing rankly around it.

We were accustomed to moving about every two years, or whenever Daddy found new pastures to till for the Lord. A carpenter as well as a preacher, he would build the church house, find the sinners, convert them, and then move on. But it was different this time. The energy Mama displayed on previous moves was missing. She did not read the morning paper to us or teach us poetry, like she used to. Daddy sat for hours on the broken-down porch, looking at his outstretched fingers, opening and closing them, labored breathing keeping him company. "My visions have ended," he told us one evening after prayers. "God has finished with me. My work's done."

How could that happen? Daddy's visions had led to the founding of churches all over Texas and Oklahoma. They couldn't just end. I lay awake all night thinking about Daddy and asking God to give him back his gift.

Hearing a commotion after we had all gone to bed in that drafty old house one night, I peeked out the window and saw white forms outlined against a flaming cross. The smell of acrid smoke drifted through cracks in the window jamb. "Nigger lover!" someone shouted. The words bounced around the walls, reverberating, echoing, and scaring me so much I wet myself. Then others outside took up the chant, "Nigger lover, Nigger lover!" I crawled under the bed with Glendora, stirring long dormant dust mites. We lay there not daring to speak, staring at rusted bedsprings, trembling for the whole of the dark hours.

The following day, we children were sent to live with friends and relatives for a while. I was to stay with the Hammers, sympathetic people who lived on a farm thirty miles away. "It's right nice of Brother and Sister Hammer to take you," Mama said in her company voice. "Now mind your manners, Patsy Lou."

Daddy gave me a quick hug before I climbed into the waiting Model A Ford. Waving to my family out the back window of the car, I kept it up, even after they disappeared from view. I waved and waved until my wrist ached. Then a much deeper pain took hold. I slid down between the cardboard boxes containing my meager possessions, feeling such loneliness that each breath was an act of will. "I'll never see my Daddy again," I moaned. "Never again."

I did see him again. We were reunited two months later when my parents decided to move to Waurika, Oklahoma, a place where we had lived before and where we had friends. Daddy had sold our most prized possession, a black upright piano, so we would have the money to be together again.

In Waurika a church member loaned us a Philco radio so we could listen to news reports about Hitler's Luftwaffe bombing Poland. Every night our family knelt and prayed for "the poor people in Poland." I was scared silly that Hitler would come skidding down the electric wires and kill us. After the Japanese bombed Pearl Harbor on December 7, 1941, and the United States declared war, it seemed like every boy I knew went off to fight for our country. Most of them never returned. I was deeply troubled by so many of my friends being killed in war.

Daddy was sick with Bright's disease and heart trouble and was taken to the hospital two days after Christmas in 1941. He died on December

31, 1941, twenty-four days after Pearl Harbor was bombed and five days after I turned fourteen. Daddy was fifty-six.

Lying in bed the night after my beloved father's funeral, I began to shiver. I was so cold that the bedsprings shook. Finally I got out of bed and put a piece of wood in the pot-bellied stove and sat thinking about Daddy and shivering until dawn. After that, whenever I was traumatized, I would have what I called the shakes. I wondered if my brothers and sisters felt as sad as I did.

Three of my siblings were married and making their way in the world: My oldest brother, Carlos Morrison (a name Mama saw in the *Herald of Holiness*), was eighteen years older than I; he was "the smart one." Nina Aileen was sixteen years older, "the beautiful one." Minnie Faye was fourteen years older, and "the tiny one." Charles Clay, nine years my senior, "the stubborn one," was working his way through college. What was left of our family were Vivien Glendora, "the good one," with five years on me; I was known as "the rebellious one," and James Taylor, Jimmy, "poor Little Jimmy raised without his father," born seven years after I had gotten used to being the youngest.

Our transition, living in Waurika without Daddy, was hard, but made worse when I accidentally burned down the little house friends and family had bought for us. It happened, Mama said, because school friends had given me playing cards while she was away visiting a sick uncle. Even in all the rubble, Mama had found the evil pasteboards hidden under my waterlogged mattress.

The truth was I had filled a five-gallon kerosene tank for our living room heater and had not placed it in the receptacle correctly. It overflowed and the house caught on fire when I lit it. I had run down the street to find a phone and call the fire department but the house was engulfed in flames before they could get there. I couldn't find my little brother Jimmy, whom I was caring for, but neighbors held me fast preventing me from searching for him. When I heard my little brother cry out for me from the outhouse, I almost fainted from relief. That night Mama arrived home on the Greyhound bus and I had to tell her we no longer had a home.

Mama fell on her knees right there in the Greyhound bus station and loudly prayed to God for help. And he did. So did the community, and in a few months we had a better house in a better part of town and furnished from top to bottom by the bighearted citizens of Waurika, Oklahoma. They even included a supply of bobby pins for me and my sisters.

But guilt became my companion. I was never again free of the knowledge of what I had done. Like the arsonist who set fire to Daddy's church, I was unredeemable.

When I was fifteen, I got a job as a waitress at the Waurika Café to earn money for school supplies. I also got my first sense of independence. My real goal, however, was to be a model, after learning the art of the model walk and pivot from a book. I also had big dreams of being a movie star like Betty Grable or Greer Garson, whom I had seen when I was able to sneak off to the movies.

Risking Mama's wrath when I was seventeen, I told her I was going to Dallas, Texas to work for the summer. She simulated a heart attack (her usual method of responding to hearing something she didn't want to hear) and fell on her knees, praying for my lost soul. I went anyway. I was going to be a model, come hell, high water, or Mama. To my own astonishment, I was hired by the posh Neiman-Marcus department store as a junior model. Friends in Waurika had told me I was tall enough to be a model, so with that in mind I walked into Neiman's and asked for a modeling job. My timing was perfect, as their junior model had just fallen ill. Knowing that my mother thought modeling was the next best thing to prostitution, I told her I was selling hosiery. At least, Mama wrote, I was living at the God-approved Young Women's Christian Association.

Neiman's was the brightest star in the retail firmament. The store was like a fairy tale to me: thick gray carpets, crystal chandeliers, salesladies wearing elegant black dresses, and the hushed tone of a paging device. I kept changing from one pretty skirt and sweater outfit to another. Self-consciously, I would walk through the salon to fitting rooms, where I would show young girls and their sweet-smelling mothers what I was wearing.

Church sisters dropped by the "Y" whenever they came to Dallas. I tried to visit with them, and was always polite, just as Mama had taught me, even though I knew they reported directly to her like a payroll of spies. Shortly after one of these visits, I was at work parading around the divine (as I learned to say) Neiman-Marcus salon, when lo and behold, there stood Mama.

"Mother," I gasped, "What are you doing here?"

"You're coming with me, young lady," she hissed, pretending to smile. "You're doing an evil thing. You told me you were selling stockings, not displaying your body around for everyone to see. Vanity will be your downfall, Patsy Lou."

"I won't go!"

"Your Grandpa Taylor drove me all the way here to get you and I intend to do just that. We're taking you to visit your Aunt Maudie in California for the summer until school starts. I've already told the Young Women's Christian Association to pack your things up." With her black oxfords firmly planted in the luxurious Neiman-Marcus carpet, she grabbed my arm. Her eyes flashed fire and brimstone. She would not leave without me. I was beaten.

Leaving the aesthetic paradise that was Neiman-Marcus was like being cast out of heaven. I wished time could be tied off like an umbilical cord, allowing me to stay in that aromatized paradise forever.

Grandpa Taylor, who drove us to California, was my mother's father, part Irish and part—the part mother refused to acknowledge—Comanche Indian, or so he claimed. Six feet tall, thin, Grandpa was a model for good posture. With thick white hair and a hooked nose, he was an imposing figure; ninety years old and licensed to drive only during the day. Our trip to California took so long it seemed to rival Around the World in Eighty Days.

"There's Californie," Grandpa declared when we eventually crossed into the Mojave Desert. Where were the fountains of orange juice, Lana Turner, Betty Grable, Gregory Peck, and Bob Hope? Movie stars leading us into the Promised Land? There was only sand, rocks, and tired-looking cactus, their prickly arms outstretched as if crucified by the burning sun. "It's different in Oakley where your aunt lives," Grandpa insisted. "You'll like it there."

I hated it there. My mother's sister lived with a raft of cousins in a converted school bus, parked in a cherry orchard. They were migrant fruit pickers. Mama and I quickly moved in with another of her sisters who lived in a sweet little house in Brentwood. We would stay there until the end of summer when Grandpa would take us back to Oklahoma, so I could start college.

"I'm getting a job so I can go back to Dallas and be a model," I told Mama.

"You go right ahead, Miss Priss." She did not believe for one minute that I could get a job. But trudging up a busy road to a bus station coffee shop, I got my second job as a waitress.

It was unlike the Waurika Café. Customers in California were different, not gentle and mannerly like people at home. Many of them called me an "Okie," and I learned firsthand about prejudice. I tried to eradicate "y'all," "jist," and "git" from my vocabulary and to get rid of my drawl, by copying radio announcers.

"Say 'y'all' again, honey," a customer would bait, or "How many mattresses did you all have on top of your car when you left the dustbowl for California?" I was told that a rich Okie was someone with two mattresses on top of the car. Occasionally someone would plunk a nickel into the jukebox, and the nasal voice of a country singer filled the café. "Hey, Arkie, if you see Okie, tell him Tex has a job for him out in Californie, picking prunes and squeezin' the erl out of olives," were the words to one ditty.

I would go right on mixing thick chocolate shakes, pretending I didn't hear. But it hurt like an open sore rinsed with alcohol. I wanted to beat my tormentors until their ugly California heads fell off and rolled under the counter.

Then one day a man I thought looked just like Gregory Peck walked in and asked for a cup of coffee. Twirling the mug around on the red Formica counter, stammering, he asked me for a date. "I'll have to ask Mama," I said, "and she'll want to meet you."

"Okay," Howard said, looking moony-eyed. "It's good to have a mother who looks out for her little girl."

When I took Howard to meet Mama she was entranced with the twenty-seven-year-old rancher who brought her red roses, and asked permission to take her daughter out. "He's a nice boy," she whispered, smiling.

Howard Groves lived with his family on a large, desolate wheat and cattle ranch in Farmington, a small community in California's San Joaquin valley. He wasted no time in asking me to marry him. His proposal made me sweat. I stalled. I had been taught never to hurt anyone's feelings. I liked him, but I was not ready for marriage.

"Mama says I can't get married until I'm eighteen. Besides, I'm leaving for college in September."

"I'll wait until you're eighteen. That's just a year," he said. "And I'll call you on the telephone every week."

We returned to Oklahoma shortly thereafter. During my medical entrance exam for the Oklahoma College for Women, the doctor discovered I had a heart condition. She said I might not live long. I didn't believe her. I felt fine, and besides, a woman doctor could not really know anything, I thought. But now I had a good excuse to leave home and get away from Mama. When Howard came to see me at Christmas time, knowing about my heart condition, he said he wanted to marry me and take care of me. He backed his proposal up with a real diamond ring, and I accepted it.

My entire family had traveled to my sister Nina's house in Little Rock, Arkansas for the holiday when Howard gave me the blue-white-and-perfect half-carat diamond.

Nina had been playing love songs on the piano and serenading us with tunes like "Oh Promise Me." "Y'all should get married on *Bride and Groom*, that radio show in Hollywood," she said, inspecting my ring.

"I've never heard of it," I said, intrigued by the word Hollywood. "Sounds like fun, doesn't it, Howard?" Howard, never one to speak if a shake of his head would do, nodded his head in assent.

"The couples get all kinds of things, refrigerators, luggage. Oh, it's wonderful." Nina acted as if it were her wedding. "I'll write the producer for you." She mailed in our application the next day. They replied with a questionnaire.

After answering the questions and sending photographs of ourselves along with the story of Howard's proposal ("Dancing under a full moon reflecting off a lake . . .") we were accepted for the show. Good Friday was the only date available, they said, so we agreed even though the idea of being married on the day Jesus was crucified seemed inauspicious.

Before trekking to Los Angeles for the nuptials, Mama and I stayed at the Groves family ranch in Farmington. All of Howard's family was there—his mom and dad, his sister Edith and brother Wally. Mrs. Groves ("Call me Mom") gave me "something blue" to carry during the ceremony. It was a handkerchief with the initials, embroidered in blue, of her great-great grandmother. "Patsy, we're really happy to have you in our family," she said, patting me on the back.

The next day we left for Los Angeles where Howard and I were to be united as one on the *Bride and Groom* radio show.

I was eighteen and this was not what I had planned for my life.

# 2.

# TEA FOR TWO

Howard and I were married in Hollywood on *Bride and Groom* on an April morning in 1947. "HOLLYWOOD, MOVIE CAPITAL OF THE WORLD," proclaimed a billboard. I expected a gold curtain to rise, fairy godmother Billie Burke to wave her magic wand, and Gene Kelly to come tap dancing along the pavement.

What a disappointment! The streets were gray and dirty. Not a movie star in sight. Oh! There was the Brown Derby restaurant, shaped like Charlie Chaplin's hat, with a door right under the brim. Things were looking up. "We're almost there, honey," Howard said, referring to the Chapman Park Hotel from where *Bride and Groom* was broadcast. We were to be married in an hour.

My stomach fluttered. Married? No. I wanted to be a model. I glanced at Howard. I did love him, I told myself. Anyway, at eighteen, I was supposed to be married. Most of my girlfriends had already tied the knot.

Except for my mother, none of my other family members were present. But I knew they would be clustered around the radio, listening. I was surprised that Mama was not only going along with this plan, she seemed to be enjoying it. Wearing a new navy blue hat with red cherries hanging off the side, she actually smiled at me. "You be good to him, young lady, you hear?" was her offering for my future happiness.

Dressed in a white satin gown seeded with pearls and a filmy nylon veil, made from a McCall's dress pattern by an Oklahoma neighbor, I followed a clipboard-carrying woman who told us what to do. "Are you ready, dear?" she asked.

My stomach fluttered, again. Surely God won't let this happen, I thought. Someone from Neiman-Marcus will step forth and say, "I object!"

I could hear applause coming from the studio, and then the announcer: "And now, from Hollywood, *Bride and Groom*." Loud clapping segued to the wedding march. Howard and I walked into the hall as a baritone sang, "Here comes the bride, with her the groom. They aren't married n-o-o-w, but they w-i-l-l be soon."

Women in flowered hats cheered. The host, John Barbor, gushed into the CBS microphone, "Here's our handsome couple, ladies. What a beautiful bride. Now don't be nervous, just come right up here with me, we're going to pry," he said with a wink, followed by a laugh carried on the airwaves across California to Arizona and New Mexico, gathering speed through Texas and Oklahoma, and finally in a burst of static, right into my big sister's house in Little Rock.

My future husband looked as if he had been embalmed and was about to be buried standing up. "How many in your family?" asked the radio host, thrusting the microphone in his face.

"Uh—would you mind—repeating that, sir?" The question was restated, but there was no verbal response, only four shaky fingers held up.

"Well, the groom is supposed to act that way," said a perspiring John Barbor, breaking for a commercial.

"Use Philip's Cleansing Cream for a beautiful skin. Look like a bride every day of your life . . ."

Back on-air, the host was working hard to elicit excitement. "Now Patsy, what are you going to do on your wedding night?" he inquired, smirking.

I could feel a stinging blush spread from my neck to my face. "Well, goodness, Mr. Barbor, I reckon I'll go to sleep, just like any other night." The audience detonated in laughter.

Feigning sincerity, John Barbor cooed, "And now our beautiful bride and handsome groom will walk down the tree-shaded path to the little Chapman Park Chapel where they will be joined in holy matrimony by a minister of their choice. We'll talk to them later, but now a word from our sponsor:

"Philip's, the finest . . ."

Mother and the Groves family trailed us down a walkway and into the church where a minister waited.

"You only have five minutes," hissed the clipboard woman.

"We are gathered together in the sight of God . . . Do you Patsy Lou Montandon, promise to love, honor and obey?"

"Hurry," urged the woman. The parson gave her a sour look and pronounced us man and wife. Scurrying back, we entered the CBS studio to thunderous applause. Some of the women were crying, as if we were related to them. Some reached out to touch my gown. All of them were beaming.

Describing our gifts, John Barbor's ecstasy increased with each item: "A Max Factor makeup kit. A year's supply of Ivory Soap. A Lilly Daché hat. Luggage by Amelia Earhart. A four-day honeymoon with all expenses paid at the playground of the Stars . . . PALM SPRINGS! Their accommodations will be at the beautiful DESERT RETREAT. They will dance at the DOLL HOUSE and dine in sumptuous splendor at the DESERT INN." And finally, with his lungpower exerted to capacity, "A BEAUTIFUL TAPPAN GAS RANGE WITH THE VISULITE OVEN. WHEN OUR BRIDE IS COOKING FOR HER HANDSOME HUSBAND, SHE WILL BE ABLE TO SEE EXACTLY THE PROGRESS HER BAKING IS MAKING!" I was led to the stove for a photograph.

"Congratulations." John Barbor shook our hands. "And now," conspiratorially, "what is your special love song, Mrs. Groves?"

"Symphony," I answered. A popular song, but not our first choice, which was "Oh Promise Me." Told it had been used on the show too often, we had to choose another.

"Isn't that lovely, folks?" (Folks clapped dutifully.) Sanctimoniously, our host concluded, "And now as our *Bride and Groom* soloist sings your favorite love song, you may leave for your Palm Springs honeymoon, knowing you will be taking with you the good wishes of the entire United States."

There was a trill on the organ. I clasped Howard's black-suited arm, careful to bend my fingers so my bitten-off nails wouldn't show, listening.

"Symphony, Symphony of Love, Music from above. How does it start . . . ?"

We ran from the studio as the assembled body of women pelted us with rice.

En route to Palm Springs, I flipped on the car radio. Arthur Godfrey with his Lipton tea bags, Oxydol's Ma Perkins, and Our Gal Sunday entertained us all the way to Palm Springs. Looking at my groom driving our new 1947 Plymouth, I wondered how I could have thought this pimply-faced man with the prominent Adam's apple looked like Gregory Peck. He was a farm boy, not a movie star, just as I was a small-town girl, not a Neiman—Marcus model. I felt like crying.

Nervous, virginal, I was glad I could delay sex. Before leaving for Hollywood, and while staying with his parents, Howard had taken me to his physician to be fitted for a diaphragm. The doctor cut the hymen, tissue I didn't know I had. So, until I healed, I couldn't be fitted for a diaphragm. We also could not have intercourse for several days, the doctor said.

On the third day, my husband indicated it was time. The sun was shining, I did not know that people "did it" during the day. Howard said he had "protection" in the drawer beside the bed. When he went to the bathroom, I opened the drawer but could only see a small orange packet and a Bible. What protection? I wondered.

"I love you, Little Okie," Howard said, pressing his appendage into me with such force I wanted to scream. Trying to divert my thoughts, I looked at the glitter-flecked, cottage cheese ceiling. A glamorous touch, I thought. Clenching the pillow in pain and fright, I wondered where the "moonlight and roses" feeling was. In movies, lovers were suffused in a glow, they kissed, and the camera panned away as one's imagination continued the rhapsody. It was not that way at all. I did not like "doing it."

"Oh, my God," my husband exclaimed, rolling off me. "The rubber broke, you'll get pregnant. We've got to find a doctor." He began thumbing through the Yellow Pages while yelling for me to get dressed. I fled into the bathroom. "Okay, I've found a doctor who will see us," he said when I emerged from the bathroom, pulling on his beige cords. I had never seen him move so fast.

The physician kept adjusting his glasses, playing with a plaster cast of the female body. "The chances of you getting pregnant from this one incident, Mrs. Groves, are virtually nil." (I later learned that plenty of women get pregnant the first time.) The doctor looked as if he was trying to suppress a smile as he thrust the plastic figure forward. "Now, this represents the uterus." His pencil tapped a pink area on the model. Humiliated, I could not look, as he described the female reproductive system.

Later, as we were leaving, Howard whispered, "That doctor is a Jew." The tone of my husband's muted comment sealed the fate of Jews.

A day later, I packed my Palm Springs honeymoon things: frothy nightgowns, feathered mules, pink rubber douche bag. It had taken a while to figure out the contraption, but I had been told it was necessary for married life. Each time we had intercourse (I could not call it "making love") I would douche, letting vinegary water cleanse me of the sin of sexual contamination.

We drove from Palm Springs to the Groves ranch in Farmington. We lived there for a few months until we found a small house of our own in Stockton, twenty minutes from the ranch. The empty days started to stretch out in front of me. Married life was not the end in itself I had expected. Life did not begin and stop with that walk down the aisle. "Down the aisle and into a pan of dirty dishes," I was fond of saying. Everyday I poured a tablespoonful of Dr. Miles Nervine, an over-the-counter nerve tonic, in a glass of water and drank it to try to calm what Howard called my "nerves."

"You let your nerves rule you, Patsy. Try to be more like other girls." There was something abnormal about me. I hated ironing, mending, cooking, and sex. All day while I cooked and cleaned, I would listen to the radio: *Stella Dallas*, *Our Gal Sunday* ("Can a girl from a little mining town in Colorado find happiness as the wife of England's richest, most handsome Lord?"), and the inevitable Arthur Godfrey, whose charm and easygoing manner dominated the air waves with his unscripted monologues and interviews with movie stars.

I prayed for something to relieve the deadly boredom. Our social life consisted of an occasional movie and dinner at a third-rate Chinese restaurant on Sunday night. Howard always ordered pork chow mein and sweet and sour spareribs. When we finished our meal, he would fortify himself with a handful of toothpicks from the roller dispenser near the cash register. "Gonna build?" I asked. Emily Post would not approve of my husband, I felt sure.

Mama wrote brief, almost illegible letters reminding me of the pitfalls of the Devil. She wrote on the backs of envelopes, wrapping paper, the edges of newspapers, although we kept her supplied with boxes of nice stationery. Trying to read one of her missives was tantamount to working a crossword puzzle without a word clue. Except I knew exactly what her message was, even if I could not read it. She always included enlightening mottoes or an article from the *Herald of Holiness*. She never signed her letters with anything other than her title, "Mama."

Forlorn, I would telephone her. "Mama, this is Patsy."

"What's wrong, Patsy Lou? Why are you calling long distance?" Our conversation never lasted beyond my asking about Jimmy, "He's fine," and Glendora, "She's fine," and Mama: "I'm (sigh) as well as can be expected." She never said good-bye but always dropped the receiver back on its hook in the same abrupt way she ended her letters. She was living on a small church pension and donations from her children. Every month I sent Mama four dollars, all in ones that I had saved from the allowance Howard gave me to pay bills.

One morning after I fixed my husband his usual three fried eggs, six slices of bacon, a slab of ham, toast with lots of butter, and coffee with cream and sugar, I braved a question. "Howard, I want to get a job," I said.

He stood up, towering over me, his hands on his hips. "I support you well enough."

"Yes, but, uh, well, it isn't that, honey, I'm bored." It would be nice to have money of my own too. Whenever I wanted to buy something I had to ask and have a good reason for needing it. I felt as if I was on welfare.

"What do you think you can do?" he asked with a grin. "Wait tables?"

"No, I'll get something good."

"Well, if you can get a good job, I'll allow you to work until you get pregnant."

After he kissed me good-bye and left for his day, I rushed to get the dishes done. I already had a job. I had gotten it two days earlier and I was due to start work that very morning as a doctor's receptionist and secretary. After getting the job I had opened a charge account at a specialty store, forging Howard's permission, and bought a white nurse's uniform, white stockings, and white shoes that I had hidden under our bed.

I looked like a real nurse, I thought, as I greeted patients, found their charts, and placed them in the proper sequence on the doctor's desk.

One week later, the glow of my new job faded. Having lied about my nonexistent secretarial skills, I found myself face-to-face with a shorthand notebook and Doctor Langley Collis, my employer. He looked exasperated. "O-B-E-S-E," he spelled for the second time. "Patsy, don't you know what that means?"

"No sir."

"Fat, it means fat! Let me see your notes," he said, holding his hand out for my steno pad.

Following Mama's example of feigning a heart attack when anything went wrong, I clutched my chest. "My heart," I gasped. Having told him previously about my potential heart condition, the ruse worked. He called his nurse and they half carried me into the examining room.

"Strip from the waist up," the doctor said. I complied, hiding the shorthand book under my pile of clothes. After completing the examination, he told me to get dressed, and come to his office.

He looked serious. "Patsy, you do have a heart condition," he said, scribbling in a chart. "You have a murmur and your pulse is much faster than normal." He looked up at me. "You have a very serious condition. I'm prescribing digitalis to slow your heart down." He handed me the prescription. "Take the digitalis pills twice a day and come back in two weeks for tests."

"Am I fired?" I asked, trying to suppress my fear.

"You need complete bed rest so you really can't work." Standing up, he dismissed me.

Numbed, I collected my Hershey candy bars from the desk and got my white purse, all the while trying to control the old familiar shakes that had begun when my father died. I'm going to die, I thought. I'm going to die and I'm only eighteen. I haven't done anything with my life yet. My only solace was the picture of my mother bent in sorrow over my untimely demise. That image soothed my nerves as I climbed aboard a city bus to go home and tell Howard that he was married to an invalid.

# 3.

# YOU'VE GOTTA
# HAVE HEART

Two weeks later, Howard had to carry me in his arms to Dr. Collis' office; the doctor checked my heart and immediately had me admitted to the hospital. After dozens of tests, Dr. Collis determined that a hole between the aorta and pulmonary arteries of my heart had not closed at birth. My heart had to beat much faster than normal to supply enough blood to my lungs. The digitalis slowed my heart down, making the cure worse than the disease. The condition was medically known as patent ductus arteriosis.

Filled with pride by his diagnosis, Dr. Collis stood at the foot of my hospital bed, and bluntly gave me the word. "Without corrective surgery, you will die by the time you're twenty-five. Your heart will wear out," he said.

Surgery? I had never heard of a heart being operated on. I began to tremble. I am going to die, I thought.

"Only three people in the United States are qualified to perform the surgery you need," he said, continuing. "But there are two places in the West where you can have it done: Stanford or the University of California in San Francisco."

"The operation takes eight or nine hours. They give you curare, an Indian poison, to stop your breathing. You'll need blood transfusions too."

As Dr. Collis continued telling me the bloody details, I tried not to listen because he was scaring me half to death.

"Which hospital do you think you would like to go to?" he asked.

"Howard's sister Edith is a nurse at UC so I guess I'll go there," I said, trying to act casual.

While waiting to be admitted to UC, we lived in Farmington at the Groves ranch where I tried to forget the gory details my former employer had supplied. But every night I would awaken from a nightmare of death and get up and pace back and forth across the bedroom floor. Stopping in front of a large oval mirror in a Victorian dresser, I stared at my emaciated self. I had lost weight and deep shadows hollowed my cheeks and eyes. I'm already dead, I thought.

One afternoon, propped up in the old-fashioned walnut bed on big white pillows, staring through the bedroom windows at the never-ending rain, I was told I had company.

"There's someone to see you," Mom Groves said, beaming.

"Who'd come all the way out here on a day like this?" I asked, smoothing my tangled hair.

"I would, Chicken Liver," came a happy cackle.

"Grandpa," I yelled. Grandpa Taylor warmed the room with his presence. "Oh, Grandpa," I cried, hugging him around the neck when he bent over the bed.

"I heard you were sick so I came to see you." Grandpa pulled a brown leather rocking chair up next to the bed. He held my hand. "Your Mama told me you were going to have your heart operated on so I just got into my tin Lizzie and came to see you. Been traveling for twelve days."

I could envision Grandpa chugging across a vast expanse of the United States, from Texas to California, just to see me. My throat closed. I did not know that anyone loved me that much.

"I'm scared I'm going to die, Grandpa," I whispered, plucking at the coverlet with my free hand.

"You're too mean to die, Chicken Liver. Besides, I have half the state of Texas praying for you."

"What about the other half?" I asked, smiling.

"They won't matter. I'm going to pray my special prayer for you myself." He slid to the floor and knelt at the side of the bed, his spine erect, his eyes closed.

"Now God," he prayed conversationally, "you take care of my little granddaughter. She's going into a time of trouble and I know you well enough to ask you for a favor. You take care of her, God." He opened his faded blue eyes and winked. "God said he would, Patsy Lou."

Twenty minutes later, Grandpa jammed his old felt hat on his head and walked toward the door. "I've gotta get going, Chicken Liver, it's a long ways to home."

"I love you, Grandpa," I yelled, knowing his hearing was bad.

"I love you too, Chicken Liver," he yelled back to me.

A car door slammed and then above the dense sound of rain, I heard the rasping motor of his automobile. I could imagine Grandpa's long, gnarled fingers clutching the steering wheel. He would be sitting ramrod straight, giving no indication of his ninety-two years.

Mom Groves loaned us her new Chrysler, roomier than Howard's Plymouth, for the three-hour drive from Farmington to San Francisco and the UC Hospital. A comfortable nest of blankets and pillows was made into a bed for me in the back seat. I curled up in the blankets for the hundred-fifty-mile drive to the City by the Bay. At least I'm not bored, I thought, as we rode along.

I loved the city: the bridges, the fog, the rain-slicked hills and the cable cars. The whole atmosphere was alive and romantic. When we approached the medical center, at the top of a steep hill, I wondered what lay ahead. There had been long discussions on the phone between Howard and a hospital administrator. The operation would cost over eight thousand dollars, they said, but because it was such a rare procedure and UC was a teaching facility, I could go through the clinic as a semi-charity patient. We would only have to pay for medication and blood transfusions.

I was in and out of the hospital for a year, going back and forth between San Francisco and Farmington, undergoing tests, before my surgery was scheduled.

A month before my operation, Mama descended on us at the ranch, protesting mightily that I was not to undergo such a radical, unheard of procedure. She was disruptive, praying, carrying on, and causing me intense emotional pain. I asked Howard to tell her to leave, to go stay with her sister in Oakley, although my guilt over doing so was almost unbearable. I was afraid God would punish me for dishonoring my parent and I would not survive the operation. I was so afraid I would die that I closed my eyes when we drove past cemeteries.

Finally, I was back in the hospital awaiting the knife. My surgeon, Doctor Brodie Stephens, kept a chart of heart surgery patients prominently displayed on a wall in his office. It had a horrifying attraction for me. I noted the names that had been scored through, the ones who had died, and I always looked for my own name, as if to reassure myself that I was still alive.

When he examined me, Dr. Stephens distracted me by talking about catching the longest football pass in the history of the University of California. A week before my operation, Dr. Stephens came to the ward where I was one of twenty-six patients, to reassure me. "You are a very lucky girl," he said, after listening to my heart. "The human heart has been a forbidden organ, thought too delicate to tamper with until this very year." It was the end of 1948 and I was nineteen.

"Am I a guinea pig?" I asked, afraid it was so.

"No, Patsy. You're a pioneer. The fellows hit by shrapnel in World War II were the guinea pigs. It was experiments with ways to remove shrapnel from beating hearts that led to closed-heart surgery. Like what you'll have."

"Closed-heart surgery? How can you do that?"

"Well, it's called that. But, I'll make a nice incision across your back, cut a rib and rejoin it with a silver wire when I sew you up. You'll have a very long but very fine scar from the nape of your neck to the bottom of your ribs." He smiled, "It's not as bad as it sounds, Patsy. Your operation will take about seven hours and you'll be right as rain within three months."

"I'm . . . I'm afraid I'll die." I fought back tears.

He put his stethoscope in the pocket of his white coat, and then held my cold hands in his warm clasp. "Patsy, you are not going to die. Early results from this surgery were disastrous, but now with improved techniques and procedures, it's quite safe. Not many can claim, as you can, to be the tenth person in the world to have heart surgery and live." He smiled. "You'll live and do good things with your life, I've no doubt."

The days became a countdown: Five, four, three . . .

A new patient about my age came to the ward. A frail brunette, she was given the bed next to mine, and like prisoners we began to talk.

"What are you in for?" I asked.

"Tests," she replied. "And you?"

"Heart surgery." I felt infinitely superior to "tests."

Her name was Debbie, and we quickly became friends. Debbie's home was near Fremont, California. She was engaged to her high school sweetheart, and they were planning a spring wedding. He came to visit her, bringing boxes of chocolate-covered orange sticks.

The night before I was to "face the knife," I lay awake, staring holes into the ceiling. "Oh God," I prayed, "please don't let me die."

Debbie leaned over the side rail of her bed. "I'll be praying for you," she said. There was caring in her voice, and a sympathy that reached through my loneliness and helped me feel brave about the morning ahead. Deep down, though, I was scared, scared, scared.

Daylight arrived in a haze of shots and pills: "Just to make you drowsy, Patsy." White, balloon-like leggings were slipped on me. "Please remove your ring, and take all the bobby pins out of your hair." A white cap covered my head, and in a state of grogginess, I signed a permission form for surgery.

I was wheeled out of the room on a gurney, past a distorted mirage of shapes and soft good-byes from beds far, far away. I tried to reply but only slurred sounds came forth. At the end of the hallway, a small group of people clustered around the gurney. It was Howard, his mother, and my sister Fay. I was surprised that they were there so early in the morning. "Patsy, Mama is praying for you," Fay said. They kissed me good-bye, and I felt the dampness of tears. Theirs or mine? I didn't know.

There was an enormous white light overhead and then a shot of sodium pentothal and then nothingness.

I awoke when I felt someone pressing on my stomach. "What are you doing?" I whispered.

"She's awake."

It had been ten hours since they had taken me to the operating room. I was to experience long days and nights under an oxygen tent: shots of morphine, intravenous feedings, and blood transfusions. And prayers. My left arm was paralyzed from nerve damage. And the nerves connecting my vocal cords had been pulled. I couldn't talk above a whisper.

"The Lord is my Shepherd, I shall not want." I looked through the cellophane of the oxygen tent. It was Debbie. She had come to my newly assigned private room to see how I was doing.

"I'm supposed to switch the lights on and off if you're okay. They're all waiting to see," Debbie said flicking the lights. "I'm so happy you are going to be well." She squeezed my hand. "See you later."

Doctor Stephens came to see me several times a day. He was warm and sympathetic. His genuine interest in me, and his unflappable attitude, helped stem the shivers of panic I would sometimes feel as the nerves in my chest and arm began to heal.

Just as the doctor said, the thin red scar curved from the nape of my neck to the bottom of my ribs—one of which had been cut and rejoined with a permanent silver wire. Periodically, a hollow needle would be inserted through my back to draw fluid from my lungs. "We don't want you to drown," the doctor said, as liquid from my lungs gurgled into a container.

Debbie visited me every day. Her tests had determined that she, too, had a heart condition and needed immediate surgery.

"It's my turn to pray for you," I said.

"I'm not afraid. If you can make it, so can I," Debbie said.

"Just the same, I'll say a prayer," I whispered.

Fourteen hours had passed and Debbie hadn't returned from surgery. I kept pushing the call button to ask about her. The nurses stopped answering.

Still weak, although I was walking a little bit everyday, I got slowly out of bed, pulled a robe over my useless left arm, and shuffled down the corridor. Opening the door to Debbie's room, I peered inside. A nurse standing in the shadows told me to go back to bed. Debbie had not survived, she said.

I went down the hall to my room as fast as I was able. I crawled into the bed and covered my head with a pillow, trying to deny what I had heard. That night I cried myself to sleep.

When I left the hospital I took with me the memory of Debbie's encouraging voice, her kind smile and her personal courage.

It took me several months to recover and to regain the use of my arm and my voice. But as I grew stronger, Howard became more accepting of my ambitions than he had been before my surgery. He owned me, he said. It was because of him that my heart had been repaired and so now he didn't have to be concerned that I might leave him, which seemed an odd notion to me. I would never consider doing such a thing. Marriage was for better or worse in my view. But he didn't own me, I thought, no one would ever own me.

In the spring of that year, I was asked to model for Market Week, which was the time designers showed their latest fashions. Howard was relaxed enough to let me go to the city and stay at the Y. A short time later I approached the local college with the idea of teaching grooming and modeling classes. The idea was a huge hit as more than two hundred girls signed up. As a way of saying thanks and using my students as models, I put on a benefit for the American Heart Association. My career as a party giver was underway.

In 1952, during the Korean Conflict, Howard was recalled back into the Air Force from earlier service. He got an instant promotion from First Lieutenant to Captain, the highest rank he ever achieved. When Howard was sent to Lajes Air Force Base in the Azore Islands, I went along as his dependent. I had to obey the stringent rules of a military wife, but it was a blue sky of newness to me.

A world that included dances and big band entertainment was made even more exciting when I was elected program chairman for the Officers' Wives Club and continued to put together successful events. I wrote and produced a musical, "Them Oklahoma Hills," as a benefit for a local orphanage. The island was only fifty miles around, and the nearest fashion store was thousands of miles away. My friends and I were starved for fashionable clothes so I wrote to Rich's, a well-known store in Atlanta, Georgia, asking them to send us the latest styles. They sent us six boxes

of beautiful clothes, which I used in a musical fashion show. It never occurred to me that Rich's would say no.

Everyone appreciated my creativity except Howard, who became jealous of my popularity. "You're not such hot stuff," he said, "in fact, you're
ugly." After his airplane hit a pile of gravel at the end of the runway and
almost fell into the ocean, Howard was grounded. My success com-
pounded his failures. He took his frustration out on me. After that he was
not only dictatorial, he became abusive. He insisted that I stay at home. I
was not to put on plays. I was to iron his shirts, and clean, and cook for
him. Howard was depressed over being grounded and not promoted like
his peers. When he hit me, I decided then and there to divorce him the
moment we returned to the U.S. I had had enough.

Back in the States, I tried to give our marriage one more try. But
things only got worse. Once, when I asked to buy a Frank Sinatra
record—I was a married bobby-soxer fan of the crooner—Howard went
ballistic. Whether it was his dinner being late or me asking him to take
me to a movie, I never knew what was going to set him off. I'll never forget his huge hand, black hairs bristling across knuckles, clenched in a fist,
slamming into my face, leaving me crying and bruised. And anything that
would require Howard to spend even the littlest amount of money would
enrage him. "We're saving for furniture, don't you remember? I'll bet
you would prefer to sit in a stinking movie house pretending Gregory
Peck or Frank Not-So-Hot-Ra is kissing you? Making you come? Huh?
Huh? Huh?" Slam. I could feel my eyes swell shut almost at once.

"Why can't you be normal, like other girls?" Howard said. "You're
full of grandiose ideas, doomed to fail."

He's right, I thought. I wasn't like other girls. There was something
wrong with me. When I asked for a divorce, Howard cleared his throat, a
half-smile on his lips. "Someday, Patsy, you'll beg me to take you back."

I didn't think so. I would miss Mom Groves, though. She had always
been kind to me, and had taught me so much I had never learned at
home.

My marriage to Howard Groves lasted twelve years. We had no children. Howard, we later learned, was sterile because he had caught
mumps from my nephew a few months before our wedding.

Thinking I had made no contribution to our financial status because I had earned no money, I did not ask for my share of our community property. That was fine with Howard. The judge, however, granted me one hundred dollars a month for one year and instructed Howard to give me a car. That's how I ended up with a purple-and-white, secondhand Chrysler that I hated, and with a total sum of $400 to live on. But I wasn't concerned, I was actually joyous as I drove that ugly purple-and-white car Howard had dumped on me, and headed for San Francisco, the city I had fallen in love with during trips to UC Hospital.

I was thirty-one.

# 4.

# OLE BLUE EYES

The glamour and sophistication of San Francisco in the 1960s was like water on parched earth after growing up in Waurika, Oklahoma. Suddenly my life was touched by magic. From a temporary home at the YWCA, I went to work as a junior trainee for Joseph Magnin, a progressive career girl department store. "You can sink or swim here," I was advised by Cyril Magnin, the company president. "It's up to you, Pat. You either have what it takes, in which case you'll be promoted, or you don't, in which case you'll be fired."

My energy and eagerness to work paid off. In four months, I became the manager of a branch store in San Francisco's financial district, and I was able to rent a nice apartment on the famous Lombard Street hill, "The Crookedest Street in the World." Knowing nothing of the nuances of society, or the "right" location in which to live, I had stumbled into the perfect spot.

Mama called. "Young lady, you had better find yourself another good husband. Otherwise you'll never be able to support yourself," she said.

"You have no faith in me, Mama. It makes me feel bad," I said, hanging up.

I loved San Francisco and my job but having been married for the whole of my adult life I was so lonely that I sometimes cried myself to sleep. When I was introduced to bachelor Eddie Wise, a friend of the Magnin's, who asked for a date, I gratefully accepted. Eddie bombarded me with attention. We hadn't even kissed when, at a party for Cyril Magnin's influential daughter Ellen and her husband Walter Newman,

Eddie slipped a ring on my finger and announced that we were getting married. Incredibly naïve, I didn't realize Eddie was gay until after the ceremony. I figured it out on our wedding night when we slept in separate beds and Eddie didn't make love to me. Sex had never been discussed in my family and being married to Howard had not enlightened me either, but I knew something was wrong. I knew immediately that I'd made a huge mistake and quickly got an annulment. But I felt like a fool and vowed that I would never again allow loneliness to overcome my good judgment.

Prompted by my desire to meet new people and expand my circle of friends, I began giving parties, like the church socials I knew so well from growing up a preacher's daughter. My work mates pitched in with food and wine and decorations so I was able to manage just fine on my limited budget. I invited coworkers, their friends, the grocer, or anyone else who seemed interesting. Soon I decided to try costume parties. Everybody loved fantasy, I quickly learned. My guests dressed as movie stars, the Maharishi, or characters from *A Midsummer Night's Dream*. Neighbors craned their necks for a glimpse.

Frances Moffatt, a legendary society reporter for the *San Francisco Chronicle*, came to one of my shindigs with a photographer in tow. She wrote a story about my party that appeared, along with four large photographs, in the *Chronicle* a few days later. Reporters for the three other local newspapers, the *Examiner*, the *Call Bulletin*, and the *Oakland Tribune*, took notice and also began writing about my parties.

Because of my social success in a town usually thought of as closed and snobbish, people just assumed I came from money. I was labeled a socialite, a word I hardly knew. This is wild, I thought, thinking about my humble beginnings.

Whenever I was presented with a new challenge, I reminded myself of my dad's motto—It Can Be Done—emblazoned on a hand-lettered sign he carried to church each Sunday. Every day brought proof he was right. Thanks to Frances Moffat, *Esquire* magazine took notice and named me one of the top hostesses in the United States. Soon after that McGraw-Hill asked me to write a book about party giving.

When my photograph appeared on the cover of a San Francisco

Sunday magazine, with more pictures and a story inside, the caption read, "The New Golden Girl Jet Set Queen." I laughed, thinking others would recognize the joke. Jet Set Queen, indeed. The fact was that I did not drink more than an occasional glass of wine, I worked hard, and I did not stray far from the godly principles I was taught as a child. But, for the first time in my life, I was dating and having fun. Men asked me out, if for no other reason than to get their picture in the paper. My social calendar was full.

"Will you go to the Waltzing Society Ball with me?" a well-to-do San Franciscan beseeched.

"I'd love to but I don't know how to dance," I said.

He was so surprised, he stuttered, "Didn't . . . you go to dancing school?"

"My mother didn't believe in dancing. I was very protected," I said.

"Of course, you're a Southerner. It doesn't matter though. I'll teach you to dance." He was right. It didn't matter, and I did learn to dance.

Three years had passed since I first moved to San Francisco as a single woman and I had loved every minute of it. In 1963, I leapt at the chance when Cyril Magnin asked me to go to Lake Tahoe for the summer to manage the store there at the Cal Neva Lodge. The Cal Neva was owned by Frank Sinatra and a guy named "Skinny" d'Amato and was located half in California and half in Nevada. Gambling was legal on the Nevada side and Cal Neva had become the playground for celebrities. This was going to be a good summer, I thought.

Sinatra had made a huge comeback, having been written off by almost everyone until he won an Oscar for *From Here to Eternity* in 1953. Now, ten years later, he was the most famous entertainer in the world.

I sublet my San Francisco apartment and began to pack for a summer at Lake Tahoe. With a Sinatra song on my record player, I danced while I packed, singing along with Frank. "I'll be seeing you; La de da de da . . ."

I decided to unload the hated purple-and-white Chrysler and use my savings to buy a new car. A baby-blue Buick Skylark convertible with baby-blue upholstery and a white canvas top screamed out my name. "PATSY LOU, HERE I AM, THE CAR YOU ALWAYS DREAMED OF. PICK ME, PICK ME!" I fell in love with that sexy, high-powered

Skylark. Driving it in the mountains of the High Sierra en route to Crystal Bay and Lake Tahoe made me feel sexy, too.

I was as happy as I had ever been in my life. I imagined the sinners who prayed for salvation during one of my dad's sermons and then rose from the altar to shout praise felt as I did. A stone of guilt had rolled off my shoulders. I felt light and joyful.

Religious music had defined my childhood so it was not surprising that the song of Easter, the "Hallelujah Chorus," came surging through my gray matter. I let it all out, singing at the top of my voice, as I rolled along in my sunshine-washed car, with a sunshine spirit.

After I got settled in the little mountain house that Joseph Magnin rented for me, and got acquainted with Kaiser, a Great Dane I was to dog-sit as part of my house-renting deal, I set up a table where I could work on my party book for McGraw-Hill. And then I drove to Cal Neva where the store was located.

Four salesgirls (we were called girls regardless of our age) soon arrived from their living quarters to help with the store opening. Laura Straun, Scottish and a top-notch salesperson, had worked at the Cal Neva Lodge the year before. So when we decided to take a look around, Laura led the way. Laughing and giggling like kids who had been let out of school, we gawked at the rustic "Lady of the Lake," as the place was called, and talked about celebrities.

"Girls, look down there," our guide Laura said, interrupting our chatter. She pointed toward cabins on a white-boulder and pine-tree-dotted hillside at the edge of the pristine lake. "Marilyn Monroe stayed in bungalow number 3 when she was here last year, just before she died. Bungalow number 5 belongs to Frankie," she said.

We were impressed.

Inside the rustic Lodge, with its massive stone fireplace, was the Circle Bar with windows overlooking the lake and snowcapped mountains. Laura, wearing a rakish straw hat on top of her graying hair, was in her element. "Girls," she said, "every day after work we can park our tushes on these stools at the Circle Bar and have ourselves a wee nip." The bartender, his white shirtsleeves rolled up, looked up from polishing glasses and grinned. "Well if it isn't my old friend Scottie," he said.

"Hi Ralph, meet this year's crop of salesgirls," Laura said.

"Hiya gals," Ralph said. "Hey, Scottie, you better make reservations if you want to see the shows this year. Ole Blue Eyes will be here and probably Dino and Sammy too. And," he added, "the Maguire Sisters and Juliet Prowse." Ralph laughed. "The whole Rat Pack. Can you believe it? The whole Pack will be right here at the Circle Bar this year."

Ole Blue Eyes was the Chairman of the Board and leader of the Hollywood Rat Pack. I tingled at the thought of Frank Sinatra being in such close proximity.

"This place will be hopping," Laura said. "We'll do big business selling to the Ladies of the Night who hang around gambling casinos. Ralph," she said, "remember to send the Ladies to me." Ralph nodded, said okay, and went back to setting up his bar.

When a "Lady" came in to buy a dress, Laura would drape a fox or mink stole across her shoulders and say in her inimitable brogue, "You need a wee bit of pussy to frame your face, sweetheart." More than once, a Lady would ask Laura to hold the fur for an hour or two until she had made enough money to buy it.

A week had passed since we'd arrived and unpacked the merchandise and the store sparkled. It was June, too early in the season for many customers.

One day while we were lollygagging, giggling and talking, rearranging things and dusting as usual, Frank Sinatra himself, accompanied by two buddies, opened the glass door to our store and walked inside. My sales staff was dumb struck. Even Laura couldn't utter a word. It was left for me to approach him.

I remember exactly what I was wearing that day: a blue-and-white silk shantung Pierre Cardin sheath dress with high heel black patent opera pumps. At 5 foot eight, Frank and I were eye to eye. Young blue eyes met Ole Blue Eyes.

"May I help you?" I said.

His eyes held me captive. He grinned. He's cute, I thought.

"I'm looking for a couple of nightgowns. Something filmy and pretty. In blue," he said.

To match her eyes, I thought.

"We have just the thing." I shepherded Frank and his buddies toward the lingerie counter. Laura, never one to lose a sale, had recovered sufficiently to wait on them. Passing near by, I whispered to her, "Do not try to sell him a wee bit of pussy."

When two nylon nightgowns, one blue and one white, had been purchased with cash from a large roll carried by one of his friends, Frank asked that we mail the package to a woman in a hospital in Reno. "She's a fan. I want to cheer her up," he said, giving Laura the name of the woman and the address of the hospital.

"Well," I said, after the three had left, "how about that!"

That evening, while Laura and the sales staff were at the Circle Bar having their wee nip, I went home to feed Kaiser, the Great Dane, and to call friends in San Francisco to tell them about Sinatra. I had been home about forty-five minutes when the phone rang. I answered.

"Hello Patty?"

"Yes."

"Patty, I'm calling for Frank."

"Frank?"

"Frank Sinatra."

"Oh."

"He would like to invite you to have dinner with him."

"He would?"

"Yes."

"Well, then he should call me himself."

"Okay, I'll tell him."

An hour had gone by and Frank hadn't called. Laura and the girls at work were playing a practical joke on me, I thought. The caller was probably Ralph the bartender and right now they were laughing about putting one over on me.

The phone rang. I swallowed. "Hello."

"Patty baby, this is Frank. How about going to dinner with me tomorrow night?"

"How did you get my phone number?"

"It was easy, Patty. I asked Laura."

"Okay. What time?" I said.

"How about eight o'clock?"

"Okay. I'll meet you at the lodge."

"You don't want me to pick you up?"

"No. I'll drive myself." I was a bit awed by Frank's celebrity and concerned by his reputation for brawling. I wanted to be able to leave without being dependent on him.

"I'll be waiting for you in the parking lot in front of the lodge," Frank said.

After I hung up I realized how nervous I was. Perspiration stained the underarms of my dress. My hands were shaking. I had a date with the Chairman of the Board. "How about that, Howard Groves!" I thought, throwing myself on top of the bed and laughing until tears rolled down my face. How about that! Kaiser began to bark, keeping me company as I laughed.

I had expected to have a surprise for the staff the next day, but I was the one surprised. They already knew about my date. In fact, they were able to tell me what was happening on the other end of the phone during Frank's call.

The girls said they were at the Circle Bar when Herb, one of the men with Frank, asked Laura for my name and my phone number. Frank wanted a date with me but was shy about phoning so Herb made the call. "We were right there in the bar having our toddy when it happened," Laura said, with a long sigh. "He used a red phone they set on the bar counter for him."

"You're kidding. Frank Sinatra, shy? Please."

"No it's true." Another girl interrupted Laura, who grimaced.

"When the first fellow hung up, Frank said, 'She won't go out with me, will she? I told you she wouldn't,' and then he hit his hand hard on the bar counter."

"No!" I exclaimed.

"Yes, and then he called you and when he hung up he was smiling from ear to ear. He said, 'We have a date tomorrow night,' and then he bought us all drinks and left." She paused for breath giving Laura an opportunity to jump back into the conversation.

"What are you going to wear Patsy? You've got to look smashing. How about a fur?"

"No, Laura, no. But I'll wear something pretty, don't worry."

It was hard for me to believe that someone as famous as Frank could be insecure about a date. Especially a date with me, I thought.

At eight sharp the next night, I pulled into a parking space at Cal Neva. Frank was waiting for me. With a smile, he opened the car door, took my hand, and pulled me to my feet. "Patty baby, I'm glad you could make it," he said.

"Me, too."

"Patty," Frank took my hand, "I apologize, but before we go to dinner I've got to sign a few autographs. It won't take long. Comes with the territory."

"No problem," I said, smoothing the skirt of my peach silk dress.

"You're pretty," he said, "you look like a blonde Ava."

"Ava?"

"Ava Gardner, my former wife," he replied, just as we entered the Lodge where about twenty kids were waiting for him. They held out autograph books, eager smiles on their faces.

"Wait a sec," Frank said to the kids. "I want to see that my girl is taken care of." With that, Francis Albert Sinatra steered me toward the Circle Bar, introduced me to two men and their wives, and excused himself. I could see him talking to the kids and signing their books. He's sweet I thought, not at all like the reputation he has for punching people out.

Dinner was in a private room at Cal Neva with ten others. Everyone ordered Frank's favorite; a thick New York strip steak sautéed in olive oil with garlic and mushrooms, topped with a red wine sauce. Frank entertained us all evening, laughing and telling stories about *High Society*, a movie he had made in 1957 with Bing Crosby and Grace Kelly, and people I had never heard of like "Bones" and "Skinny" and "Wingy."

Red wine and Jack Daniels flowed freely. When Frank noticed that I had hardly touched my drink, he said, "Patty baby, I feel sorry for people who don't drink. When they wake up in the morning, that's as good as they're going to feel all day." Everybody laughed.

After dinner the crooner walked me to my car, kissed me lightly and said, "Tomorrow night Patty, same time, we'll have dinner together."

"Okay. I'll meet you here in the parking lot."

"The parking lot? It has a ring to it." Frank laughed. "You're on, Patty baby."

We dated all summer, but were never intimate; there were always other people with us. Frank was a raconteur of the first order, and he brought his audience along. When he was not at Cal Neva, he had instructed the staff never to let anyone bother me. The Lodge was the only place near enough to eat lunch, so every workday I ate there. Croupiers and waiters formed an informal aisle for me as I walked to the Lakeview restaurant and was seated in Frank Sinatra's favorite booth, third from the door.

The whole summer was like that. Frank was more protective than amorous, which suited me fine. He always walked me to my car, kissed me lightly, and watched as I drove off. One evening he said he would be away for a couple of weeks. He would call me when he returned.

"Okay," I said. "Frank, this is a different kind of world for me and I'm having a great time."

"Patty baby, this is a different kind of world for most people, and for this guy from Hoboken, well I nearly fell off my chair when this fame thing first hit. But, you'll get used to it, and don't ever let it throw you."

As the summer progressed, Cal Neva became a booming metropolis of intrigue and gossip. When Sam Giancana, a reputed Mafia boss, arrived with his girlfriend Phyllis Maguire, rumors began flying. The gossip seemed to spill over the mountains, across the water of the clear blue lake in a tsunami of speculation. Tourists were giddy and spending money as if the slots were paying off in ten-carat diamonds instead of nickels.

A week before Frank returned to the lake, he called to invite me to the show he and Dean Martin would be doing the next week in the Celebrity Showroom. "The maître d' will seat you at my table. I'll see you after the show," Frank said before ringing off.

Laura helped me pick my outfit—a black lace dress with a short black veil to go over my hair, a popular look at the time, and yes, a silver-blue mink stole, borrowed from our fur department.

The Celebrity Showroom held three hundred fifty people but there must have been four hundred on the evening of Frank and Dean's appearance. The place was packed. Jack Daniels with a splash, Frank's drink of choice, had plenty of company. Tables were a forest of booze and bottles and glasses and overflowing ashtrays. Everyone was laughing and drinking and telling jokes, slapping each other on the back, happy to have gotten tickets to the hottest show in America. Glamorous-looking women in low-cut dresses, their breasts looking like Pouter Pigeons, were scattered about the audience like confetti at a birthday party.

Seated ringside at a white-linen-covered table with eight other people I was up-front center. Just when I thought I could not stand another minute of anticipation, the band struck a chord, the crowd quieted, and then applause began like light rain and roared to a full-fledged torrent when Frank appeared.

Frank swaggered onto the stage looking as if he was born to wear a tuxedo. At that moment, with Frank Sinatra's aura drifting over me like heavy snow in the winter, some hidden spring within me clicked into place. I was transported back to my girlhood when every phrase of Frank's magical husky throbbing voice, "Night and Day," awakened in me a longing for romance, for love. The alchemy of his voice was pure gold. No doubt about it, I was in his spell and loving the spell I was in.

Dean Martin followed Frank on stage and the throng roared again. The two of them were debonair and witty, funny and relaxed. They sang and chatted and drank and horsed around, entertaining us effortlessly and having a better time than anyone. Dean was the "pizza pie in the sky that's amore" guy. Frank looked straight at me and sang, "When somebody loves you" from "All The Way," and well, I practically swooned

We stomped and clapped and rose to our feet, exhilarated.

Frank had said I was to meet him in a room at the back of the theater after the performance. When I arrived it looked like half the audience was there, too. Over the heads of his fans, Frank waved to me, and almost at once a bodyguard appeared at my side.

"Frank wants you to wait for him in his bungalow. I'm to take you there," the fellow said.

I looked at the crowd pushing toward Francis Albert Sinatra, hangers on, each one. As much fun as all of this was, I definitely did not want to go to Frank's bungalow, with all that going there implied. That summer, I had seen lots of women in diamonds and furs, hanging on to a guy just to be in his aura and to get to wear expensive clothes and jewels. They seemed to have no identity of their own. That was not for me. I didn't want to be a satellite to celebrity.

"Tell Frank I'm sorry but I can't stay," I said to the bodyguard.

"He's not going to like that."

"I don't want to be rude but I have obligations at home," I said. I had hoped to get to know the man, not the celebrity. "Please tell Frank I'm having a party next week and he's invited."

"What's the occasion?"

"It's my birthday," I blurted out. It was not my birthday. My birthday was in December, five months away. I had no idea why I said that.

"I'll tell him. Want me to walk you to your car?"

"No, I'm fine."

The next day I got a phone call saying Frank would come to my party. After giving him my address and the date and time, I called my friends in San Francisco and told them they had to come.

About fifteen of my pals were there as well as my sales staff, including Laura. One woman, the wife of a physician, was so nervous that she broke out in hives and her husband had to give her a shot to quell them. After an hour, when Frank had not arrived, people began to doubt that I really knew him.

Then the phone rang, and it was Frank. "Patty baby," he said, "I'm lost in these hills. How do I get to your place?"

When Frank arrived twenty minutes later with Paul, his lawyer, he handed me a gift-wrapped box. In it was a jade necklace. "For your birthday, Patty baby," he said.

"Oh, gosh, Frank, it's not really my birthday," I said with embarrassment.

"You'll have a birthday someday, won't you? Keep it," he said with a smile before spotting Kaiser, locked out on the deck. "Look at that dog," Frank said, heading toward the Great Dane. "I love dogs." Frank pulled the screen door to the deck open.

"Frank, no, he'll bite you," I yelled, trying to get to the door before Kaiser had a chance to realize he was free.

"Dogs love me," Frank said, just as Kaiser clamped his jaws down on the crooner's right hand. Paul and I raced to Frank. We pried the dog's mouth open, rescued the famous singer, and quickly locked the screen door. Frank laughed. "Well, I guess all dogs don't love me, just Hollywood dogs, maybe." Frank Sinatra sat on a stool in the center of my living room, and with a Jack Daniels in his unharmed hand entertained us as if we were paying customers. He was always so kind and respectful to me and I adored him. Deep down I knew we didn't have a future together but I just loved being close to him. At the end of the summer, after I returned to San Francisco, I got one last phone call from Frank. He wanted to send his plane to take me to Palm Springs for a party he was giving in his home there. I didn't go. By then, I was becoming involved in a volatile romance of my own.

# 5.

# THE KING
# OF TORTS

Back home, my life once again moved along at a steady and happy pace. My mother was now living in Modesto, California, two hours outside San Francisco. She'd finally given in to the urgings of my siblings to come to California, where three of us had settled. I sent her money and talked to her on the phone, but I didn't go to see her. The last time I visited mother I was surrounded by photographs of Howard and me. "You lost a fine man," she kept saying.

For the first time in my life, I was creating my own world. I had moved on from the retail world to CBS radio with a show called *Ask the Expert*. People could call in with questions about party giving and etiquette. I was so involved with all that I was doing, working on my McGraw-Hill party book, and teaching classes on customer service for Bank of America, that I paid little attention to what was going on in the wider world. When friends asked if Mel Belli could call me for a date, I did not know who he was.

"You don't know who Mel Belli is?" They were incredulous. "He's the lawyer who represented Jack Ruby, the man who killed Lee Harvey Oswald."

"Oswald, the man who assassinated President Kennedy?" I said, waking up. "I once read a story about Mel in *Life Magazine*. He was called the King of Torts."

"That's him! The guy loves publicity but he hasn't been in the limelight for ages. You're as well known locally as he is now, Pat. Date the guy. You'll have fun."

"Okay," I said.

Dating Mel was an exciting, crazy experience. I had never met anyone remotely like him. When I went to New York to meet with publishers at McGraw-Hill, Mel and his friend Alex Haley, who was writing *Roots* at the time, went with me. At the publishing house offices, Mel commandeered a desk and a telephone and drafted two secretaries to help him with a legal matter. The whole office was agog.

Alex and I were hard-pressed to keep up with Mr. Energy. One day, Mel got us up at four in the morning to go to the vibrant but smelly Fulton Fish Market. Afterward we had breakfast at a nearby cafe with some fishmongers. I loved the adventure, the grittiness, and the realness. And I was falling for Mel.

Alex and I bonded on the New York trip and he became the person who taught me how to write a book outline. In the dulcet tones of his native Tennessee, he encouraged me. "Honey," he said in front of Brentano's Fifth Avenue bookstore one day, "I can see your book in this window next year, right in front."

"Really, Alex, do you think so?" I asked.

"Why honey I know so," he had said.

My affair with Mel Belli was tumultuous. We were constantly being photographed—at the opera, symphony, film festivals—for magazines and newspapers from the East Coast to the West. It was fun for me and pleased Mel enormously. He loved publicity and made sure that our entrances and exits were timed to elicit the most coverage.

Mel's boundless energy was matched with a penchant for illegal mischief. He once put Plaza Hotel room service silverware in his suitcase and had the bellman carry it out to our taxi. When I protested, Mel had an answer that only a lawyer could think of. "I'm innocent," he said. "The bellman was the one who put the suitcase in the cab, I didn't."

After a three-day camping trip in the High Sierra where bears stole our food, we bathed in a lake using sand for soap, and cuddled in a sleeping bag, I decided that I had to break up with the King of Torts. He drank too much. Even allowing for my upbringing—where anything alcoholic was deemed to be a tool of Beelzebub—Mel Belli flat-out drank to excess and when he did, he became sarcastic and verbally abusive.

I was also beginning to notice that Mel had too much interest in other women to suit me. At a film festival party, Jayne Mansfield had flashed her breasts at him, and then the two disappeared together for almost an hour. Mel said he was introducing her to his associate Sam Brody (Sam later became Jayne's companion and attorney). I left the party but Mel followed me and convinced me he was blameless.

Breaking up with this charismatic man was difficult. I loved him and he said he loved me. Our twenty-five-year age difference didn't matter, but his drinking did. Two days after I told him I couldn't see him anymore, he called me at midnight.

"I miss you, baby," he said. Even though I was half asleep, there was no mistaking the mellifluent voice of the famous barrister.

"I miss you, too," I admitted.

"We should have a farewell drink, baby. I've got champagne on ice. Meet me in the courtyard of my building in fifteen minutes."

He knew I would come. Few could resist his charm.

The interior garden, adjoining his historic red brick office building in San Francisco's financial district, was cozy and softly lit. Nearby a fountain splashed. Red roses, more than two dozen, rested on a table in their cellophane cocoon, a gift for me. The scent of the flowers mingled with Mel's designer aftershave, aroused all my senses.

He greeted me with a flute of Perrier Jouet and immediately embarked on an extravagant toast. "French bubbly for the woman I love. The only woman I've ever loved, the beautiful girl who inspires me to ever greater acts of daring." He drained his glass in one sustained gulp.

"Mel, listen, please." Pent-up words came out in a rush of feeling. "Mel, darling, I really can't see you anymore. You aren't good for me . . . I . . . I . . ."

"Shush Patricia, shush." Warm kisses peppered my face as Mel pushed me gently down onto a red velvet love seat. "Don't talk. Listen to the tranquil silence, darling. Listen." He held me tightly against his body. "Stillness teaches us everything we need to know." Segueing from our moment of intimacy my swain launched into a poetry reading. As if playing to a packed house, his soulful voice created the illusion that every word originated with him.

"Out of the night that covers me, Black as the pit from pole to pole, I thank whatever gods may be, For my unconquerable soul."

Even when he was quoting William Ernest Henley, Mel was intoxicating. Following his recital, he knelt down and took my hands in his. "Baby, we're Scott and Zelda." His voice was yearning. "Marry me. I love you more than anything in life." Warming to the task, he embellished his proposal. "We'll do exciting things together, travel, write, make love under the stars, and have children. We'll have a wonderful time." Mel Belli knew how to appeal to me.

"I can't marry you, Mel. You drink too much. I love you, but I hate it when you're incoherent and start to get abusive."

"I'll never touch alcohol again," he said, leaping to his feet. Thundering across the walkway to his office, he threw open the doors to his liquor cabinet, and in a spray of broken glass and booze, sent bottle after bottle crashing across the courtyard. The aroma of scotch and wine mingled with the scent of roses like a bartender's bouquet.

"Now do you believe me?" Hands on hips, a bad-boy smile playing across his handsome face, he represented power, and reminded me, as unlikely as it seems, of my father. "I'm General Counsel for Japan Airlines, baby, and I'm going to Tokyo in three days. Come with me. We can be married in a Shinto ceremony there." His soul was in his eyes, I fancied, weakening.

"A Shinto ceremony?" Mama would have a wall-eyed fit. Reason enough to do it.

Mel was like a mischievous and egocentric child. Often broke, sometimes rich, moderation was unknown to him. Against my better judgment, I finally said yes with three caveats: First, he must promise not to tell the press. Second, he absolutely had to stop drinking. Third, he had to stop flirting. Mel agreed to all three.

Believing that he hadn't told anyone about our plans, I flew with him to Hokkaido, Japan, where the sacrament was to be performed. It was October 1966. Driving from the airport, I was calmed by the tranquility of the countryside. Mel, however, was far from calm. "Did you see that

caged bear back there? That's cruel and unusual punishment. I'm going
to liberate that animal!"

Addressing the hapless Japanese associate accompanying us, he or-
dered, "Buy that goddamn bear and see that it's sent to San Francisco.
Don't say it can't be done. Anything can be done if you have enough
money." Peeling bills from a large roll, he handed them to his friend.
The man scurried off to do Mel's bidding, unsuccessfully as it turned out.
Putting his arms around me, nuzzling, Mel laughed. "Baby, that god-
damn bear is your wedding present. I hope you know how to cook it."
Mel loved jokes, and I was a great audience.

We stayed at a Japanese inn overlooking a creek where water tumbled
over round white rocks, lulling any marriage fears I harbored.

"I want to give you a real wedding gift," Mel said. "I haven't much
money, but I do own that apartment house I live in. So, I'll write out a
deed, giving it to you." Mel scribbled on a piece of stationery he had
taken from a cloth-covered box in our room.

"I don't want your property." I laughed. "I don't want anything except
your love, and your commitment to our marriage."

"Here it is anyway baby, your apartment building," he said, handing
me the paper. I folded the document and put it in my jewelry box. It was
one of Mel's extravagant gestures and meant nothing, really. Or so I
thought.

That night I read a booklet in English, about the Shinto marriage
ceremony. I wanted to be able to follow the service.

The next morning we went directly to the wedding pavilion, a place
where brides were prepared for their nuptials. Five Japanese attendants
were waiting to dress me. My face was powdered stark white, brilliant red
lipstick was applied in brush strokes, and a towering black wig with two
long pins extending from it was placed on my head, supporting a white
cloth that stretched over my forehead "to hide horns of jealousy, cardinal
sin for wife," I was told.

Over three layers of silk kimono, white, purple, and red, I donned a
gold-embroidered brocade robe. It was cinched by a red obi into which a
tiny dagger was tucked. "To protect honor," an attendant explained. It
was part of the Shinto dressing ritual for brides.

Mel joined me. He was dressed in a swallow-tailed morning coat and white socks. Tabbies, the traditional Japanese cloth covering for the feet, were too small, he said. We walked arm in arm to the wedding shrine, which was built like a stage with one side open. Serene, beautiful, it was in a meadow surrounded by maple trees. A crowd of people waited there. "Who are they?" I asked. Mel shrugged and mumbled, "Press." Too horrified to speak, I continued on, feeling like Anne Boleyn walking to the guillotine.

We sat on big white cushions with our backs to the spectators in the meadow, as two priests, wearing stiff white robes and black lacquered headdresses, waved tassels over our heads. "Horses tails," my groom whispered. Actually, it was a purification rite. Japanese words poured forth in a recitation of an oath to keep faithful and obedient to each other in married life, so the booklet had said.

The priests presented us with three red lacquer bowls of liquid. "What's this?" I whispered to Mel. "Sake. Just keep drinking." He grinned and gave my hand a quick squeeze. It's going to be okay, I thought, as we solemnly exchanged the cups, sipping the sake three times, pledging marriage and a stronger connection. Mel placed a gold band on my ring finger. We kissed. A gong sounded.

"We're married, baby," Mel said as we turned to face our audience. Flashbulbs popped. Reporters surrounded us.

"They're all here, baby: *Time, Life, Newsweek,* Associated Press." Aglow, my good-looking husband disappeared into the swarm, leaving me stunned, and standing alone in my golden robes. Experiencing a sudden chill, although I stood in the warmth of an autumn sun, I wondered if Mel had married me to get more publicity. "Dear God," I prayed, "make it not so."

Alone, I was driven to a fish and sake reception for the press that I hadn't known about. Mel was already there, drinking, flirting with a female reporter, and playing to the journalists.

Our honeymoon was a booze-filled nightmare. He became abusive and threatening. I felt doomed. The fact that I had brought this on myself did not make it easier.

Topless dancers from clubs on Broadway, Mel's clients, greeted us on our return to San Francisco, throwing rice down my cleavage, mugging for television cameras.

"I can't be married to you, Mel," I said to him the next day. "Please, let's end this with whatever dignity we can summon."

He ignored my request, and asked me to go with him to Houston where he was to address a law conference. I refused but still drove him to the airport.

"I love you," he said.

"I love you too, Mel, but I can't live with you." We kissed good-bye.

The phone was ringing when I returned from the airport to my apartment. Abe Mellinkoff, city editor for the *San Francisco Chronicle* and a social acquaintance, was calling. I'd quietly sought Abe's advice on how to extricate myself from this horrific mistake. He said there was a story in that day's paper about a plane crash in Japan in which all the couples aboard were newlyweds who had been married in a Shinto ceremony. However, they weren't legally married because they hadn't signed certain documents. "Have you signed anything?" Abe asked.

"No, Mel said we didn't have to." He had written a book, *Life and Law in Japan*, so I thought he should know.

"Mel has an unsavory reputation, Pat. He's not for you. Now you can get out of this mess," Abe said. "Better act fast. Mel's talking to the press about this and there's already a story on the wire. He wants to marry you again, he says."

Instead of returning my phone calls to talk about a divorce, Mel sent messages through the press. "Pat has gotten lousy advice. Most lawyers couldn't attest to the validity of a dog license. We are legally married, but if it makes her happy, we'll get married again in a regular church." His protests grew louder until the lawyer I hired showed Mel his handwritten copy of the deed giving me his Telegraph Hill apartment building as a wedding gift.

"Give Pat a divorce and you'll get your building back," my lawyer said.

Mel changed his story and used our breakup for more publicity. He held press conferences and told reporters, although not me, that we would be married in Sonora and he would sign every paper in the book if

I wished. He didn't show up for legal hearings to decide if we were married or not, and was reported to be shooting hare in Belgium, but he finally gave in and our marriage was legally set aside. And Mel got his building back. In the eyes of the court, our marriage was an event that never happened.

It had happened though, and it left an indelible mark on my life. *San Francisco Chronicle* columnist Herb Caen dubbed the wedding "Thirty Seconds Over Tokyo." I became the butt of ridicule. Mel was treated differently, admired even. But when a former beau sent me a book, *Learning Japanese in a Hurry*, even I had to laugh.

Braving the negative publicity, I continued working at my radio job and writing my book about party giving. But I was ashamed that I'd "married" Mel although I confess that I missed the excitement he had brought into my life. One of the great things that happened from that saga was that Alex Haley and I became friends for life and I realized I liked adventure. Being "married" in a Shinto ceremony didn't seem at all odd to me.

Before the Belli debacle, I had arranged for a television audition, so I followed through but didn't expect to get the job. To my surprise I was hired by KGO, an ABC affiliate, as the hostess of a morning movie. My spirits revived when I encountered live TV. They told me I could do anything I wanted during the twenty minute "talk time," portion within the framework of a two-hour movie. I had a ball. Wearing evening gowns at eight in the morning, crying when the plot was sad, reading poetry—I was a hit.

Mama loved my celebrity. I was surprised to realize that she loved the spotlight as much as I did and was a performer at heart. Once, Mama appeared on my show dressed in my new white mink coat, her white hair a halo, her face powdered, looking for all the world like a polar bear. *Pat's Prize Movie* was the highest-rated television show in the Bay Area.

But even with my success in television, many people still referred to the Belli nonmarriage when talking to me, and about me. It was a huge embarrassment.

# 6.

# UNANSWERED PRAYERS

At least, I thought, I have my book to look forward to. But when *How to Be a Party Girl* was published, that too became a challenge. *TV Guide* published a notation regarding my upcoming appearance on the local *Pat Michaels Show* with the words "From Party Girl to Call Girl, how far can a party girl go before she becomes a call girl?" When I learned from concerned friends that a masked anonymous prostitute was to appear with me, I canceled my appearance and filed a suit for slander against *TV Guide*. Three years later, a jury agreed that as a public figure, I had been defamed, with malice, and awarded me two hundred thousand dollars. After that I was conservative in my dress and demeanor, fearful someone would think I really was a call girl.

The lawsuit and my relationship with Mel had been so traumatic that I did not accept a date for two years. My work became my life. I hired an assistant, Mary Lou Ward, who would prove to be my closest ally. The recent widow of an attorney, at forty-seven Mary Lou was a chic bundle of energy with a great sense of humor. She went on my book tour with me, scheduled speeches, and was my best friend in every sense of the word. She encouraged me to get out more and to date, but I was not interested.

At night I would scramble an egg for dinner, eat, and go to bed. I didn't usually answer my phone at night because of nutty callers, but on a fall evening in 1968 I did answer. It was Gerson Bakar, an acquaintance, saying that Alfred Wilsey, his business partner in real estate, would like a date with me. "He's a nice butter and eggs kind of guy. His wife Laurie died about a year ago. I think you'll like each other," he said.

Al called me three times before I accepted a date with him. Something about his voice reminded me of a male "fan" who called me and made sexual innuendos, but finally I said I would go to dinner with him.

Al was a young Burt Reynolds look-alike with a cleft chin and square jaw. He told me he had once been a boxer, which accounted for his muscular build. We had a good time on that first date and I was attracted to Al, but wary. I stalled when he asked for a second date. But Al was persistent. He sent huge bouquets of roses and pots of delicate orchids to the TV studio, along with notes inviting me to dinner. Slowly, my defenses weakened and I soon began to spend my free time with the handsome entrepreneur. One evening, while he was waiting for me to get dressed, Al marched into my little kitchen, rolled up his sleeves, and began washing the dishes I had left soaking in the sink.

"You need someone to take care of you." Al spoke softly. "And I'm the man who can do it." His muscled arms were covered with suds.

"Having you wash my dirty dishes embarrasses me."

"I do laundry, too," he laughed, as he stacked cups in the drying rack. "After divorcing my first wife Doris, I had custody of my two boys, and the PTA voted me the best mother in San Rafael," he said.

"Aren't you a widower? Didn't your wife die?"

"That was Laurie, my second wife. She died a year ago. Laurie was cute as a button, petite, tiny little thing. Wore a size four shoe. Before we were married, she was diagnosed with lung cancer. Her parents said I had to be the one to tell her." There was a faraway look in his eyes. "I crawled right into her hospital bed, put my arms around her and told her we were getting married." He gazed out the window. "Laurie died six years later."

Abruptly, finished with the dishwashing, Al rolled down his shirtsleeves and declared it was time for dinner. Al had invited me to his home for dinner and to meet his adult son Lad, who was living with him while recovering from a broken leg.

"I hope you like leg of lamb," he said. "I told my cook I was bringing the nicest girl in San Francisco home for dinner." His strong arms guided me out the door and toward my destiny. At forty-nine, his age was perfect, too, as I was nearing my fortieth birthday.

Mary Lou did not like Al. "He's too boring for you," she said. "Besides, I sense an undercurrent in him that I don't like. He seems stern."

"Oh, Mary Lou," I said. "You are too protective of me. Remember that it was you who insisted we go to that devil worshiper guy to get a love potion," I laughed.

"Yeah, but that was for a TV fan who asked for your help. She didn't want to be an old maid," Mary Lou reminded me.

"Well, I don't either," I said.

"Fat chance," she said. "It's been only two years since Belli."

"You've made a very good point. I'll find out more about Al," I said.

After making several phone calls to friends, I learned that not many people in San Francisco really knew Al because he had just recently moved to the city from Marin County. Finally, Elaine Untermeyer, a fashion coordinator friend said she knew a little about him. "Al runs a successful vegetable oil products company," she said. "He turned his dad's butter company into big business," Elaine continued. "I was told that during World War II he got a deferment because the government needed his product. He sold butter like gold bricks and at the same price. I don't think he's exactly rich, but you can be certain he's financially secure."

"What about his personal life?" I asked.

"I heard that he did a great job raising Mike and Lad, his two boys from his first marriage."

"I met Lad when Al invited me for dinner. He seemed nice. Al said Mike was in Singapore on a Fulbright scholarship."

"I think Mike is his favorite."

"What about his daughters Wendy and Susan?"

"They're grown now. But when they were kids they spent most of their time with their mom. She got custody of them," Elaine said. "Pat, I think you've finally met a genuinely good guy."

I reported what I'd discovered to my loyal assistant.

"So, Mary Lou." I smiled. "Maybe I've finally found a trustworthy man."

"He might be trustworthy . . . but," she broke off her sentence and smiled. "I only want your happiness, honey," she said. "You know that. I'm off to Italy in a few months and I want to be sure you don't get into trouble while I'm gone."

Although I felt I had allayed my concerns, one thing bothered me; I wanted to know why Al had divorced his first wife Doris. When I asked him about it he had laughed.

"Patsy, Doris was a harridan, not sweet like you are. One night she woke me up from a sound sleep and began sprinkling Babo, a scrubbing powder, all over me. She was totally nuts."

"Why would she do such a thing?"

"She's mentally sick, that's why I wanted my boys to stay with me. Anyway, I couldn't live like that. I got a divorce right after that. Does that set your mind at ease?"

I felt reassured. Al was the kindest man I'd ever met. He made me laugh. He loved me deeply. I loved him. What more could a woman want?

Four months after our first date, Al Wilsey asked me to marry him. I said yes. He said our real honeymoon would be a safari to Mozambique, East Africa, in September, with his two grown sons, but for now we would go to Hawaii.

My one regret was that Mary Lou would not be present. She was still in Italy and would not get back in time for the wedding. Al and I were married in a quiet and simple ceremony in the Pacific Heights home of Liza and Nappy McNaughton. Al's adult children, Wendy, Sue, and Lad, along with Pegi Brandley, Al's long-time trusted secretary, were our witnesses. At last I could relax, knowing I was truly loved. It was like surviving heart surgery and coming out of the anesthetic realizing I was alive, that my blood was pumping with renewed vigor, with life.

As we left for our Hawaiian first honeymoon, my groom whispered, "I know you've worked hard your whole life, but you don't have to work now. Give up your television job. I'll always take care of you and always love you. You can depend on me for the rest of your life."

I knew I could. His take-charge attitude and his calm personality convinced me that I could trust him.

I did not know how rich my husband was exactly until I moved into his six-thousand-square-foot penthouse and began living the high life. When he lived in Marin County he told me he had played a lot of golf and hung out with his old fishing and hunting buddies. Al seemed unassuming so I was not prepared for the opulence into which I was introduced. I had been taught that it was a breach of trust to discuss money, I had not done so in the past and I didn't with Al. Nor did he talk about finances with me, although we never lacked for anything.

During the week, when Al was at his office, I would prepare an afternoon picnic of hot tea and sandwiches. Even on foggy days we would sit in a nearby park, and eat and laugh and kiss.

"Patsy, no one has ever taken such good care of me," he said.

"I like taking care of you," I said. "It's fun."

"We're going shopping at I. Magnin next week, sweetheart. I want you to have the best there is. So get ready."

I laughed. "I think I can handle that. I love pretty clothes."

Shopping with my husband was an experience like none other. If I admired a scarf he ordered it for me in every color. One beautiful handbag wasn't enough so he bought six. He purchased cases of Moon Drops, the moisture cream I used, and as many as ten filmy nightgowns and matching peignoirs at one time. Salespeople loved Al Wilsey. I did too. Before long my walk-in closet sported designer gowns, furs, and racks of shoes and handbags. In time, Al also bought me major pieces of jewelry. But what truly mattered to me was our love and support for each other.

And only a month after we were married, I needed his support more than I could have ever imagined. With a year to go on the lease of my Lombard Street apartment, I did not hesitate when Mary Lou asked to stay there for a while when she returned from Italy. Her daughter had just gotten married and Mary Lou wanted to let the newlyweds use her house. On June 21, 1969, four days after Mary Lou moved into my apartment, and the day after I had had breakfast with her, I got an early morning call from the fire department. There had been a fire in my old apartment and they had found a female body in the charred remains of my former bedroom. It was Mary Lou.

I was inconsolable. An investigation and an autopsy revealed that

Mary Lou had not died from the fire. There was no smoke in her lungs. And there was no apparent cause for the fire. I was in shock. At that time I had not heard of survivor's guilt, but I felt as if I should have been the one to die in my bed, in my apartment, not Mary Lou. Had it not been for my husband, I don't know how I would have coped.

A month after Mary Lou's puzzling death, Al gave me a five-carat emerald ring. It was gorgeous but it did nothing to ease the pain I felt over the loss of my dearest friend. There were no suspects. Her death remained a mystery. I thought about Mary Lou and her strange death all the time, even on our African safari.

En route home from Africa, on a stop in Rome, I wasn't feeling well so Al took me to see a doctor. "Maybe you're pregnant," he said hopefully.

Thrillingly, I was pregnant. For the entire nine months of my pregnancy, we were giddy with excitement. Like all parents to be, we talked endlessly about what we would name our baby. We went shopping together for the nursery. At night I would dream about Al, our baby, and me doing all the things that families do. And I read every book on parenting I could find.

Cosseted in Al's love, I felt deeply cared for, and my pregnancy went well even though I had to spend the last five months in bed because of a bulge in my uterus. Al was in the delivery room when our son was born at 9:30 in the evening on May 21, 1970. We named our baby Sean Patrick Wilsey.

Tears were running down Al's face when he handed our newborn to me. I cuddled my baby close and looked into his eyes and ran my hands over his smooth head and inspected his perfect toes and tiny hands. When he closed his little fingers tightly around my finger and hung on, I felt a powerful emotion: one I had never before understood. Unconditional love.

"Fathers weren't allowed in the delivery room when my other children were born," Al told friends. "Seeing my son come into this world was the most moving experience in my life. When I looked at that miracle, I thought, boy am I going to do a good job for you."

I loved teaching Sean things, playing with him and showing him off to anyone who'd pay attention. The penthouse began to sprout framed photographs of Al and me, beaming with our baby Sean. My life was complete.

I had it all, I thought, a loving husband, a beautiful son, friends, and financial security.

But I was still burdened by the circumstances of Mary Lou's death. The fact that there was no cause for the fire in my old apartment and there was no smoke in Mary Lou's lungs and no cause for her death was so strange, and I was so plagued by it, that I wrote a book as a catharsis. *The Intruders* was published in 1975. The dedication read, "To Al Wilsey, who saved my life and then made it worth living, and Sean, an added dividend of love."

There was only one niggling issue. On the telephone I was often confused with Al's former wives, the other Mrs. Wilseys. It was as if Pat Montandon had been absorbed by Mrs. Wilsey. One day I asked Al how he would feel about me using my own last name instead of his.

"That is an unusual idea," Al said.

"Al, I love you so, so much, you know that," I said. "But if a good marriage had anything to do with a woman using her husband's name, then there wouldn't be so many divorces."

Al laughed, "Patsy, you are right." He leaned over and kissed me. "I'll think about it, okay?"

Four days later Al said he had thought about it and realized that it was unfair for a woman to change her name when her husband kept his. "I wouldn't want to change my name so why should you change yours?"

"You are a remarkable man, Al," I said, kissing him. "I'm so glad you aren't threatened by my sense of independence."

Soon after that, in 1972, I founded the Name Choice Center for California Women and issued a fact sheet endorsed by California Attorney General Evelle Younger. I traveled the state making media appearances to let women know of their right to use their own name after marriage without going to court. Al made appearances with me to support my stand.

Except for the sadness I felt about Mary Lou, my life was a fantasy.

We had maids; an old-world butler, Al Weidert, who insisted on serving in black tie and white gloves, while we were sometimes dressed in blue jeans; a chauffeur, Clifford Mooney, who was a Master Sergeant in the Marines; cooks Geri Crumpler and Verna Weidert, and two personal secretaries. Some days I just couldn't believe all this had happened to me—a preacher's daughter from Oklahoma.

I loved the people who worked for us. Because I'd been brought up in a large, rumble-tumble kind of family, I enjoyed having people around and I felt that our household employees were members of my extended family.

As Sean grew, we discovered that city life had its limitations, especially in foggy San Francisco summers. "We need a country house," Al said, "a place where Sean can learn to swim and play in the dirt."

I had thought life was perfect already, but this was the blush on the rose. It was the answer to a childhood prayer. Perhaps only someone who has grown up rootless and poor can fully understand what a real home, not just an apartment, however posh, meant to me.

"What kind of house?" I asked.

"Whatever kind you want."

"I've always dreamed of a house like the one in the movie *Enchanted Cottage*, with Robert Young and Dorothy McGuire. A cozy place with paned windows, cushy window seats, a fireplace, Priscilla curtains, lots of books . . ."

Al interrupted my headlong dreaming. "Is that all you want, Patsy?"

"Well, no, I would love to have acres of grass." Having had hard-packed dirt for a yard in Oklahoma, grass was the epitome of luxury to me. "Can we do that, have acres of grass? Can we afford it?"

"Sure we can," he laughed. "We're rich!"

A real home of my own. A lawn! I knew where it should be, too. I'd once been to a summer party in the Napa Valley just north of San Francisco, and the area had captured my heart. Al wasn't familiar with the Valley. So I planned a day in spring when the Valley was carpeted in wild mustard, to introduce him to it. I packed a picnic lunch, with thin-sliced leg of lamb, fresh asparagus, French bread, fresh strawberries, and a

Mondavi Cabernet. We drove out of the city, into the rolling hills and valleys until we came to a wildflower-strewn meadow in Rutherford near the Napa River.

The air was warm. Only a slight breeze ruffled the leaves of the oak trees at the crest of the meadow. The rippling sounds of water flowing over boulders floated up from the river. Al carried the picnic basket into the meadow, while I found the perfect spot to spread a blanket.

Sean began chasing butterflies and gathering wildflowers. He brought me a bunch of dandelions. "Mommie, for you," he said. I kissed him and put the flowers in a cup of water. Sean then took off to build something from twigs.

We ate slowly, saying little, savoring the food and balmy perfection of the day. Sated, Al and I lay side by side, holding hands and dreaming together. "You're right about this valley." Al rolled onto his side and kissed me. "We'll find land here, you'll have your acres of grass. I'll build you your Enchanted Cottage. I'm the happiest man on earth because of you and Sean. I want you to have everything."

"After you and Sean, everything else is icing," I said, "but I sure do like the icing." Our laughter skimmed across the grass like a stone skipped on water.

Al caressed me in a somnolent, married kind of way. We lay cuddled in each other's arms, Sean napping against my stomach, inhaling the fragrance of the field. Our Enchanted Cottage would be built on that very site.

Creating our country house was a labor of love for our entire family. Even little Sean had a say-so in deciding how his room would look and where he wanted to build a fort and a track for his go-cart. Al was excited about the heliport he was having built to house his Enstrom helicopter.

We began building our four-bedroom home in 1975 and completed it two years later. We named it River Meadow Farm. The two-story, Connecticut-style beige stone and white clapboard farmhouse on thirty acres included a slate-lined swimming pool and a pool house with a large playroom under the cupola; a tennis court, heliport, stone greenhouse, cutting garden; a fort for Sean, and acres of vineyard. Heaven could not be better, I thought.

Famed movie director Francis Ford Coppola and his talented wife Eleanor lived a few miles from us in a magnificent old white Victorian. Occasionally Francis's pilot would land an ominous-looking black military helicopter in our field and the Coppola children would pile out to swim while Francis sat on our terrace, saying little.

Dede and John Traina, whom I'd met when I was single but didn't know well, also had a country house, a small Victorian, about two miles from ours. Their sons, Todd and Trevor, were Sean's age. Before long, their whole family began hanging out at River Meadow Farm as if they lived there, swimming, enjoying bountiful lunches, and playing tennis.

Slowly Al's friendships began to change from his old buddies to those with country homes in the Napa Valley, like Charlie Crocker, whose grandfather made a fortune in the mid-1800s in gold, silver, and the Central Pacific railroad. My husband's desire to be part of San Francisco's "Old Money" set bothered me. I didn't fit in with that group nor did I want to. I knew it and they did too. They seemed closed-minded and narrow, only talking about the superficial things of their world. I told Al that he was becoming a snob. He laughed and said I could fit in if I wanted to, and to please try to for his sake. These people were good business connections, he said. "Okay Al," I said, "I'll try."

Every weekend we had long al fresco lunches and ate and ate and consumed bottles and bottles of Gewurztraminer, Chardonnay, Cabernet, and Merlot. I grew so weary of the Valley social scene that I organized a bicycle club of sorts. On Saturday mornings Pat's Insane Group, PIG, an ever-changing group of friends, would gather at River Meadow, bicycle through the vineyards with our kids, cementing the bond of family, and end with a picnic. Dede stood out from the others and was fast becoming a friend. She and John and their sons Todd and Trevor loved the bike rides, as did Sean. The boys also enjoyed the treasure hunts I arranged and were tickled that I was using their names, along with their mother's, for characters in a book I was writing. It was an idyllic existence.

One lazy Sunday afternoon when all the help was off and Sean was visiting Al's daughter and young cousins at Lake Tahoe, Al and I began to make love on our kitchen window seat when we heard a persistent tapping on the windowpane. It was Dede. With a hand shielding her eyes she peered inside. Tap . . . tap . . . tap . . . "Shit," Al said, as we quickly threw on our bathrobes. "That woman is such a snoop."

I opened the door and without apology Dede came inside. She was wearing pink short shorts, a tight sweater, and black high heel shoes. "Well, aren't you done up," Al said.

Dede giggled and wrinkled her nose. "I brought a present for Sean," she said, handing Al a box of Lady Godiva chocolates. "I forgot that he's not home this weekend." Dede hung around for the rest of the afternoon, but I didn't mind. She was fun, quick with witty remarks, and full of gossip about our Napa Valley community. She was my new trusted friend; Al seemed to enjoy her company, and Sean was besotted with her.

We cherished our weekends at River Meadow Farm and the days rolled by at a leisurely pace. Like all little boys his age, Sean wanted a dog. After laying down the rules of caring for a pet, we gave in. He selected two male fox terrier puppies and named them Foxy and Terry. As soon as we got home with the dogs, Sean called his buddy Dede to tell her about his pets. The next day Al and I were sitting by the pool when Dede arrived carrying a female fox terrier puppy. We watched, smiling, as she and Sean had a doggie love session.

"Sean," Dede had squealed. "Look what I've got. Now our darling little doggies can mate. We'll have puppies together. Isn't that wonderful?" She'd put the squirming animal on the grass next to Sean and his puppies.

My nine-year-old whooped in delight. He'd hugged Dede with exuberant affection and then they bestowed noisy kisses on the dogs. After their flurry of adoration, Dede had looked up at Al and me. "Well," she said, "I'll bet you two can't guess what I've named my darling little doggie."

"I can, I can guess." Sean was eager to play her game.

"No, Sean, sweetie, you'll never be able to guess." She turned to me. "Pat . . ." she said, talking to me but now looking at my husband, "I've named my darling little doggie" . . . her voice was a singsong, ". . . Ta . . . da . . . Mrs. Wilsey! After all, no one else is using the name." A chuckle underscored her pronouncement.

Al and Sean laughed as if the woman had displayed great wit. I laughed, too although I didn't think it was funny.

As soon as we went in the house I asked Al if he was attracted to Dede. I told him her antics were making me uncomfortable.

"Dede has nothing better to do. She's bored. I'll admit that she's fun sometimes but I'm not in the least attracted to her. Stop worrying." He kissed me. "Patsy, I love you and only you."

My husband was such a solid person, so grounded and trustworthy that I didn't think he would ever lie to me, but nevertheless I still felt prickly about Dede's "Mrs. Wilsey" joke.

Every evening, after tucking our son into bed, Al would lead me to the bedroom, select the nightgown he wanted me to wear, and help me undress.

"You're the best thing that ever happened to me," he said, brushing my hair, preparing me for bed. "You saved my life. After Laurie died, I was just waiting to die until I met you, my society Queen of the Jet Set." He chuckled. "I still have that *Chronicle* photo of you that I carried in my wallet before we met. I knew then that I would marry you someday." He laughed, and then changed the subject. "Hey darling, did you know that Dede is in the social register?" Al was impressed by high society.

"A social register is so silly," I said.

He hooted and then pinched me on the bottom. "Don't be too quick with your judgments, Patsy. Social position, giving money to the right causes, can get you what you want. Like it or not, my darling, it's the way the world works."

Al slipped a green chiffon nightgown over my head while caressing and kissing me. Our kisses turned to passion and once again, I was reassured.

My husband and I never argued. The only time I remembered us having a disagreement was after a crash in Al's helicopter. We were flying from our country house to our city home one Sunday afternoon when a bolt holding the helicopter engine came loose with a loud bang. Al put the machine into auto rotations and we landed with a hard bump in a saltwater marsh. Neither of us had a scratch but the accident scared me half to death. "I'll never ride in a helicopter again," I said, when we were securely on terra firma.

When Al bought a Hughes 500 jet helicopter to replace the Enstrom, I flew with him a few times, but I was bored with flying around the Valley, day after day, looking to see who was entertaining whom, something Al loved to do. When he asked me to fly to Lake Tahoe with him, I refused. He was angry with me and soon Dede was the one flying over the Valley with him.

When I said that I thought he was getting too chummy with our neighbor, Al laughed. "Are you nuts? Stop with the jealousy, Pat. Dede's a jabbering silly gossip, but I like company when I fly." He put his arms around me. "Let's get going on plans for our *Gone with the Wind* party," he said, kissing me.

At our annual summer party, three hundred guests wearing colorful antebellum costumes sipped mint juleps and listened to Dixieland music on our expansive lawn. A plethora of silver serving dishes gleamed from a twenty-foot buffet table set under moss-covered oak trees, smack dab in the middle of a vineyard. My husband, in the spirit of the occasion, had built a footbridge across the Napa River so guests could walk from our home to the site. It was a romantic and extravagant scene.

During the party planning stage, Dede had called me several times a day. She wanted to know every detail. "I bought the soundtrack from *Gone with the Wind* and keep the music on all the time, and I've been dieting like crazy," she said. "But my dress is a secret. I want to surprise you. But, tra-la, you'll hate me when you see it." She seemed giddy with excitement.

"Hate you? Why would I hate you?" I said, surprised by her choice of words.

Dede abruptly changed the subject. "Pat, does Al make you happy?"

"What a silly question. You know he does," I responded.

"Well, I'm not exactly thrilled with John," she said, "but I suppose he's the best I can do."

"I know you split up a few years ago, but I thought you had worked things out," I said.

"But John has no money," Dede said, sounding unhappy. "People think we're rich because I was a debutante and my mother is from the Dow family, but we're like church mice compared to you and Al."

Before I could answer, Dede's mood fluctuated once more. "Oh Pat, just you wait. You will hate me!" Her simulated drawl trailed off in paroxysms of laughter.

Arriving at River Meadow on the party day, my friend was an ersatz southern belle. She wore a dress in the exact green-sprigged fabric that Vivian Leigh had worn as Scarlett O'Hara for the barbecue scene at Tara. Somehow Dede had gotten the material duplicated and the dress copied in Hollywood. Eyelashes batting, she did a slow turn in a swirl of petticoats and green ribbons.

"Well, darlin,' I've outdone you this time," Dede said while taking a cursory look at my lavender hoop-skirted, off-the-shoulder dress and wide leghorn hat with pink roses tucked under the brim. "The hat is nice," she grudgingly admitted before turning toward Al, who was dressed like Rhett Butler in riding pants, shiny black boots, and a hunting jacket.

I was somewhat taken aback by the entire exchange with Dede and I was surprised that Al and Dede were dressed as a couple. But I was not truly uncomfortable until Dede smiled flirtatiously at Al, and took his arm to be escorted across the bridge.

"Honey chile," she said to me with a wink, "you just know I fit in here more than your ole' silly self. This should be my party, my barbeque, my lil' ole' house, and well, honey," she looked up at Al through a fringe of mascara, "my lil' ole' man, too."

Dede, and Al, laughed and I politely joined in although I didn't see the humor. Almost as a reality check, I glanced at John, dressed in a blue Civil War uniform complete with a shiny sword and white gloves, to see how he was reacting. But he didn't seem to be bothered by Dede's charade.

Still, this silly game of Dede's was no longer okay with me. "Why, Miss Scarlett," I said, keeping the tenor of the moment, "You're certainly getting carried away with your lil' ole' silly self, I do believe." I unclamped Dede's hand from Al's arm—while Al grinned at me in response. He then held out his arm to me and we sashayed across the bridge, with John and Dede three steps behind us.

Later, when I replayed the incident over and over in my mind, I realized that purposefully or not, the bridge Al had built over the Napa River was "the bridge of no return."

A few days later, Al said he was having business problems because of the huge cost overruns of a housing complex he and Gerson Bakar were building at Lake Merced.

"I'm losing a lot of money," he said. "Can you get along without Clifford and a cook until things get better?"

"Al, I can cook and drive and take care of the house. Of course, I'll help in any way I can," I said, concerned about my husband's health. Stress like this could cause a heart attack. "You can use my money, too. I have about three hundred thousand dollars that you invested for me."

"Thanks, sweetheart," Al said, looking worried. "I'm afraid I've already used it."

"You have? Without asking me?" I was outraged. "How could you do that?"

He put his arms around me. "I didn't think you would mind. I'll get all that money back for you and more, darling. But if you object I'll have it put back in your account."

"Not if you need it," I said. "But you should have consulted me." I thought I knew Al so well and I trusted him so wholly that I never doubted anything he said to me. If he had told me to jump off the top of a building and he would catch me, I might have entertained the idea, certain that he knew best.

In 1979, my mother had a stroke and was taken to a rest home. Shortly before her death, we went to see her. I massaged her hands while Al sat on the floor and read the Bible aloud to her.

"Mrs. Montandon," Al said softly, "I'm going to read to you from the book of Job." He cleared his throat and opened the black bound Bible, a Bible that had belonged to my father, "For then shalt thou lift up thy face without spot . . . And thine age shall be clearer than the noonday; thou shalt shine forth, thou shalt be as the morning."

"He's a saint," my sister Faye said, wiping her eyes, "an absolute saint."

"Yes, he is," I said in agreement.

A few days after Mama's funeral, Al broached the subject of our assets. We were in the kitchen at River Meadow. I was doing what I called my fried chicken number. Al was mashing potatoes. Sean had set the table and was outside playing with his dogs until dinner was ready. It was a family evening.

"I've been thinking. I'm ten years older than you are. We need to talk," Al said. I replied, "I know you're concerned about not being able to make love, lately. But sweetheart, I've read that all men go through phases like that. It's okay." He had been impotent for the past six months and I wanted to reassure him. "Perhaps you should see a doctor just to make sure you're okay."

"I'm tired, that's all." His lips were compressed into a tight line, his expression bland. "Sit down, Patsy. We need to talk about our estate."

"What's it all about, Alfie?" I sang, trying to make him smile.

"Seriously, sweetheart, we need to talk." Al put his arms around me. "We are extremely wealthy. When I die, you will be saddled with huge taxes. We need to start putting money into our tax-free Wilsey Foundation."

"But you said that we were going broke because of the Lake Merced project."

"Yes, but we still have paper assets, and other properties. I can salvage my business by selling things off, and putting the profits into the foundation."

"Al, I told you I would be happy to move to a lesser place if you need to cut expenses. We don't have to live like this, spending so much money all the time. You and Sean are what matter."

"Thanks sweetheart," he said. "I appreciate that you are willing to change your lifestyle. But . . . let's get on with signing off assets for now. We'll start with Woodlake," he said. Woodlake was a housing development we owned in San Mateo. "And the Oak Creek development and Newport, too. Okay?"

"Yeah, I guess so." I did not like thinking about Al's death, or my own for that matter. "What about Pool Sweep, the pharmaceutical company, the cut-flower company, Wilsey foods? Gosh Al, there's so much! It seems to me that unless someone has been mismanaging things you should definitely be able to save your business."

"My thoughts, exactly." He kissed my hands. "We'll start signing papers tomorrow."

None of this made sense to me, but as Al was quick to point out, I didn't have a head for business. I knew he would take care of everything.

And Al did take care of everything. Life continued as it had been. We had our busy active social lives in the city during the week and glorious relaxing weekends at River Meadow Farm with family and friends. Life could not have been any better. Just a few short months after our first conversation about our finances and eleven years after our wedding, Al gave me a surprise fiftieth birthday party in a private room at Trader Vic's in San Francisco.

Eight days later, January 4, 1980, as we prepared for bed, my husband casually said, "I want a divorce."

# 7..
# DANGEROUS
# LIAISONS

Everything I believed in came crashing down. I sat on the bed, numb, staring at my husband's face, his expression cool and remote as if he'd simply remarked about the weather.

"But . . . why? What have I done? Let's get counseling . . . I love you . . . Sean, our family . . . What have I done?" I heard my own incoherence, and in some remote corner of my mind, wondered at the litany of self-blame. But I must have done something wrong, otherwise Al would not have turned against me this way. He was a saint.

"Let's get counseling," I said. "Whatever the problem is we can work it out."

"I don't need counseling," Al said, continuing to undress. His utterly detached attitude convinced me of his seriousness more than any amount of shouting would have. He must be having an affair.

"Are you having an affair?

"Don't be silly."

I reached over to touch him, to make a connection with the man I loved. He pulled away from my touch.

"You've been acting odd lately, maybe you should see a doctor. I've read that a minor stroke, one you don't know you've had, can change a person's personality. Maybe you've had a little stroke."

"I have not had a stroke! You could damage my business by saying such a stupid thing." His face was flushed and his fists were balled. "I'm fine. I want a new perspective, that's all."

"You are having an affair!"

"I am not having an affair. If I were, you would have every right to be angry. But I'm not."

"What is it then? Why do you want to break up our family? Why?"

"I need time to sort things out, to get away from the great organizer."

"What do you mean by that?" I asked. "You always said you liked the dinners for your company, the parties, picnics,—sort out what things? Just last week you told me how much you love me." I felt as if I were on some strange planet, not in my bedroom with my husband.

"Loved you. Past tense."

"How can that be?" I asked, bursting into tears.

"It just is," Al flatly said, with no emotion.

"What about Sean? How can you do this to him?" Now I was sobbing.

"Stop crying! Sean will be okay. Might be good for him to have a dose of reality."

I was in a cloud of shock and denial as if I were anesthetized. That night we slept in the same bed together like a happy couple. I lay there rigid, not knowing what to do, hoping Al would come to his senses. He rolled over and made a half-hearted attempt to make love to me. I felt he was saying he was sorry, that he had not meant what he had said about leaving, so I tried to be inviting, but Al was impotent.

"You don't turn me on anymore," he said turning away from me. He yawned.

"You've gotten too independent. Writing books, and now a column in the *Examiner*, your picture in a full-page spread to announce it."

"You told me you loved my writing. You even went on my book tour with me and you helped me find items for my column. You said it was fun. Al, what's happened to you?"

"Pat, you don't know how to be married to a rich man. It's over." He turned his back on me and began snoring.

I shook him awake. "We need to talk, Al. Now."

"I have nothing to say to you. Go to sleep," he said, turning over and beginning to snore again.

I shook him awake again. "Al, you've got to tell me what's happening. I've never seen you like this. Are you sick?"

"No, Pat. Go to sleep and leave me alone," he said, pulling the blanket over his head.

I got out of bed and stumbled downstairs. The rest of that long night I sat staring at my reflection in the living room windows. A shadow self, an empty self, a phantom superimposed against the lights of San Francisco. I no longer felt as if I were a real flesh-and-blood person. Al had turned from Dr. Jekyll into a Mr. Hyde. I had never seen this side of him. My husband was now a stranger.

The next morning, Al left for work as if nothing had happened. I went through the day in a haze. That night, there was no conversation at the supper table, until Sean broke the silence.

"What's the matter Mom?" Sean asked.

"After dinner we have something important to tell you," Al said.

Sean's eyes widened, tears formed. "Did Dede die?" he asked. Her welfare was his first concern.

"No, Dede didn't die," Al, said. His face seemed chiseled from stone.

We continued to eat silently. I have no recollection of what was served for dinner or who served it.

I couldn't function. I was like a zombie, following Al's instructions. We sat at the table until he told us it was time to go upstairs. "Sean, put on your PJ's and come to our bedroom," Al said.

Somehow I got upstairs to our bedroom. Sean, in his blue cowboy patterned pajamas sat next to me on a chaise lounge. Al sat on a delicate French chair facing us. "Tell him, Pat, tell Sean what's happening," Al commanded.

"Your dad doesn't want to live with us anymore," I said, trying not to cry. "He's moving out."

"Is it because I didn't pull the weeds like you told me to, Dad?" Sean was curled over as if his stomach hurt. He looked so small and vulnerable.

Al did not respond to his son's painful question. I put my arms around my child's shaking shoulders as he began to sob. "No, Sean sweetheart," I said, "you had nothing at all to do with this."

Without a flicker of expression crossing his face, Al looked at us and said, "Stop the waterworks, Sean. I'll always be your father. Nothing will change that." I was stunned by Al's tone with our son.

"Come, Sean-Sean, I'll give you a bath in our big marble tub," I said, taking his hand and leading him into the bathroom. A bubble bath in our tub was always a treat for Sean and had soothed him through various childhood traumas.

Al was silent; his rugged good looks a mask of indifference. He didn't move as I shepherded our son into the bathroom and began to run warm water into the tub.

"Get undressed sweetheart, I'll give you a bubbly back rub," I said, composed for Sean's sake.

He let his pajamas fall in a puddle on the travertine floor. Naked, his ribs and the nodules of his backbone were sharply defined. He had stopped crying and was leaning against the wide ledge around the bathtub, his back bent, methodically smacking the palm of his hand hard against the flat marble ledge.

"What are you doing sweetheart?" I asked.

"I'm trying to find out if I'm having a bad dream," he said, slapping his tender skin against the inflexible surface over and over again.

"Oh, Sean sweetheart, I'm afraid this isn't a dream. I wish it were," I said. "Here, I'll help you into the water." I lifted him up and into the warm bath.

From the sudsy tub my son looked up at me, his eyelashes shiny with tears. "Mom," he said, "this must be the way you felt when Mary Lou died."

"I'll wash your back," I said, trying to control the tears that rolled down my face and dripped onto Sean's spine mingling with the bath water as I sponged his slender back. Wrapping him in a fluffy white towel, I carried Sean to his room even though he was nine years old and big for such cuddling. I began to rock him in an old green chair and sang softly to him.

"You are my sunshine, my only sunshine."

Eventually, Sean fell into a fitful sleep.

Dede called.

"I can't believe it Dede, Al's leaving me, he's moving out," I sobbed. "I feel as if I'm dying. I want to die." I was crying hysterically now.

"No, no, you mustn't say that," she said, then paused. "You must not think of killing yourself. Al would be very upset."

"He doesn't care."

"Of course he does, Pat. Al loves you. This is just a temporary thing." Dede paused once more. "Pat, I've got a great idea. While Al moves out, go to Mexico, to Puerto Vallarta, and take Sean. I'll come with you and hold your hand."

"You'll go with me?"

"I'll go with you. John, too, he loves PV."

My voice was a cry, "You will?"

"That's what friends are for," she said, and hung up.

Before I could leave for Mexico, I got a call from Pat Steger, the *San Francisco Chronicle* society reporter. "Pat, are you and Al splitting? That's the rumor."

"Who told you such a thing?" I asked, stunned that she knew about our rift. After all, this had only happened the night before in the privacy of our own home.

"Can't give away a source, Pat. People know, or think they do."

"We're temporarily separated. I'm sure we'll get back together," I said.

"Will you keep writing for the *Examiner*?"

"I don't know," I said. After I hung up, I barely made it to the bathroom where I vomited until there was nothing left. I lay, stretched out on the cool travertine floor, exhausted.

A day later columnist Herb Caen wrote a scathing item about me. It was another blow to my shattered sense of self. "That blond dumbshell," he wrote, ". . . too good to use her husband's name . . . is losing Mr. Nizeguy. He's going on to greener pastures . . . she's just going."

I felt as if I had fallen down the Alice in Wonderland rabbit hole. Overnight my world had turned upside down. I couldn't wait to get out of town.

Sean also seemed happy to be going away so long as it was with Dede. Once in Mexico, I couldn't stop crying. I didn't know I had that many tears inside me. Thankfully, John took charge of Sean. Sitting under a thatched umbrella on the beach one day, my face swollen, and reddened eyes hidden by sunglasses, my friend Dede comforted me. "Pat, do you know that I read cards? I can tell you what's going to happen."

"You can tell the future? You're kidding! How silly is that!"

"But I can," she nodded, her blonde hair falling over brown eyes. Her pink bathing suit matched mine. It was a private joke between Al and me that she copied whatever I did. But I didn't mind. I considered it flattery. "I'm really quite good at it."

My rational mind had deserted me. "Then tell me," I begged, grasping at the wind for an answer, any answer. "What's happened to Al? Is he having an affair? Is he in love with another woman?"

"I don't need cards to tell me that. Al is not having an affair. But we'll find out what's happening. I have cards in my bag."

Opening her beach bag, my confidant withdrew a deck of cards. Slowly, deliberately, she cut them into three piles. Taking her time, she turned the cards face up, one by one.

"I don't know if I should tell you this." She shifted her position on the sand. "But, well, Pat, the cards never lie."

"What? Tell me." Tears seeped from my eyes.

"Well," she tapped the black queen with a pink fingernail. "The cards say that Al will never come back to you."

"No, no, no!"

"You'll not get any money, either."

"No!"

"And . . . well . . . Sean. Al will take him, too."

"No! I don't believe you!"

"That can't be right. I'll do it again." Three times she dealt, and three times she gave me the same message.

"You're crazy!" I stood up. "I don't care what the cards say! Do you think I'm an idiot? Al would never take Sean away from me." I kicked sand at her.

She slowly wiped the sand from her face and chest. "Don't kill the messenger, Pat. Don't get mad at me. I'm your friend. I'm the one who loves you."

I put my head down and wept. Dede encircled me in her arms, rocking me back and forth, soothing me. Totally distraught, I had no clue Dede had inside knowledge about my marriage or that for three years she had schemed to catapult herself up the marital food chain by taking my husband.

Back home from Mexico, I began to hemorrhage. My gynecologist said I was going through The Change and to take it easy. I was weak, shaky, tired all the time. I wanted to die.

Val Arnold, a well-known interior designer and the man who had decorated our penthouse when we were first married, called. "Pat, I can't tell you how sorry I am about you and Al. You seemed like the happiest couple in town. But I suspected something was amiss at your River Meadow house blessing party."

"Why? We were so happy then. Benny Goodman's orchestra, our gorgeous new home, friends gathered around us. It was perfect."

"Do you know what Dede said to me that night? I'll never forget it. She was sitting beside me on the lawn during the concert. With both hands spread out, she pointed at the beautiful estate, the gardens, the house, and whispered, 'This will all be mine someday.' "

"No! You can't be serious. That was three years ago."

"She said it honey, she really did. Maybe you had better find out what's going on." I called Al at the Broklebank apartments where he was staying.

"You bastard! You lied to me. You are having an affair. It's with Dede, isn't it? You two planned the whole thing!" I was sobbing so hard I could hardly talk.

"Get hold of yourself, Pat. Stop crying or I won't talk to you."

"You should be the one crying for me to forgive you, Al," I said. "Now I know that you and Dede have been screwing each other and laughing at me all along! I should have known, you bastards!"

"Listen. I am not, I repeat—not having an affair with Dede." His voice was soft, wheedling. "I would never do such a thing to you."

I couldn't imagine Al lying to me. I called Dede, who said people were trying to break up our friendship. She would never do such a thing to me. I decided that the story Val told me could not be true. No one could be that calculating. Besides, Dede was my friend and she was married.

A few weeks later, in an effort to get support, I invited women friends to a Roundtable luncheon, and still thinking Dede was a friend, I included her. By 12:30 everyone had arrived except Dede, among them Merla Zellerbach, a writer friend I had known since I first came to San Francisco. I decided that Dede wasn't going to make it when she blew in, out of breath, seemingly on a high, and immediately walked up to Merla.

"There's a rumor that you and Al are having an affair, Merla. How about that?"she said.

"Sure Dede, and my mother is a nun," my friend said, dismissing her.

"Maybe you're the one having an affair with Al," I said.

"Oh, Pat, don't be silly," she laughed. But it was obvious, even to me, that she had tried to muddy the waters by dragging Merla's name through the mud.

I called Al. "Stop lying to me, Al! You and Dede have used me, set me up, and made me into a real patsy. You've been laughing at me, playing a game, making fun of my misery. You are both despicable!"

"Pat, listen to me . . ."

"Stop ordering me around! In Mexico, Dede even tried to convince me she could tell the future by reading cards. She thought I would fall for anything. And I did. I was in so much pain that I couldn't think straight. You two planned it all, you deceitful evil bastards!" I said, slamming down the receiver. When I got off the phone I was shivering. What terrifying people they were.

A few months later, the judge granted Al a bifurcated divorce. That meant we were divorced before our financial settlement was made, which would take three more years. When I protested to my attorney, he shrugged, saying there was nothing he could do about it. I had been given the apartment and enough money to live on but, I was coasting, waiting for our financial settlement hearing, not knowing or caring about anything else.

We had been divorced a year when Al called with unsettling news.

"Patsy, I'm taking Sean to visit Ruth and Wiley Buchanan, in Washington, D.C.," he said. Dede's parents were acquaintances of ours.

"Sean's in school." My voice was sub-zero.

"I've arranged to get him out of school. As you know, the Buchanans are a socially prominent family in Washington. Her father was an ambassador . . ."

"I gave a luncheon for Ruth and Wiley, remember? What does this have to do with Sean?"

"Dede and I are getting married."

My heart skipped beats.

"The ceremony will be at her parents' home in Washington. Sean wants to attend." I tried to put the receiver back in its cradle, but everything went black. My housekeeper found me on the floor, revived me, and helped me to bed. I lay staring out the windows seeing nothing. The shakes, as I called them when my father died, began to rack my body.

Two days later an item in Pat Steger's column said that Dede had quietly divorced John and married Al. Soon afterward John married my friend Danielle Steel. I was odd woman out.

# 8.

# ILLUSIONS
# OF LOVE

Before we could get the legal end of our parting underway, I was summoned to family court. Al's face seemed made of granite as he denounced me before a female judge. "You're not a qualified mother," he said.

The mahogany-paneled walls of the hearing chamber seemed to contract against my chest. "You know I'm a good mother," I angrily responded, reeling from his recrimination.

"Sean prefers to be with us, which pretty much explains it."

"He wants to be with Dede because she made him her pal before you were married," I said. "But I'm the woman who gave birth to him and nurtured him, taught him to read, and played games with him, entertained his friends, and took care of him when he was sick."

"Come on, Pat, with your feminist ideas, your writing, your column in the *San Francisco Examiner*, you can't devote enough time to be a mother to Sean. That boy needs discipline." A ribbed sweater over beige corduroy slacks revealed a small roll of fat around Al's waist. "You're lucky that Dede opened my eyes and cares enough to straighten him out."

"Sean doesn't need straightening out! Dede's a traitor, she . . ."

"You manipulated me!"

Al leaned against a bookcase in the hearing chamber, seemingly relaxed, in charge. But I knew he was probably craving a cigarette.

"Dede opened your eyes? I manipulated you? I manipulated you?"

My ex-husband, whose muscled arms had once embraced me with love put a heavy hand on my shoulder. "Wouldn't use my name . . . remember? Dede is proud to be Mrs. Alfred Spalding Wilsey."

"So is her dog," I wanted to shout. I couldn't believe Al was saying this. He had encouraged me to use my own name from early on in our marriage. I had loved Al with all my heart but now I couldn't reconcile the stranger, a bullying prosecutor, with the warm and devoted man I had loved for a decade.

Having been put on the defensive I responded in kind. "You said you wanted me to use my own name, that married women shouldn't become 'Mrs. Him,' that a man who insisted on a woman using his name was insecure, that . . ."

"Cool it." The judge called a halt to our row.

Al continued speaking softly now, seemingly calm. "I'm sending Sean to a boarding school back east next year, or maybe to reform school. He needs strong discipline."

"Are you crazy? What are you talking about?" I said, with a mounting sense of dread. What could Al be thinking? I wondered. Did he truly believe that Sean needed more discipline or was this his way of punishing Sean and me? And for what? He was the one who had abandoned us. After many sleepless nights I came to the conclusion that Al needed to make both Sean and me look bad in whatever way he could to justify what he had done to us. He was trying to remain a saint figure in the eyes of his world by demeaning us.

Al kept talking as if I had said nothing. "This morning I told Clifford to take Sean up north to Redding tomorrow, to a boot camp. They're leaving as soon as you get Sean to the Napa house tomorrow. Be there at two." Al's lips were in a tight line, his face a mask. He leaned toward me. "You won't be seeing Sean for a while, Ms. Montandon."

"You can't do that!" My shout caused pigeons roosting on the window ledge to flutter away. "Stop him!" I addressed the judge.

"It's in the best interest of the child." The woman was dispassionate.

"No, no, no!"

"Ms. Montandon, I suggest you calm down. Mr. Wilsey reared two boys. He knows what's best for his son." The judge stood up. A golden medallion dangling from a golden chain glinted against the tailored neckline of her black suit. She threw Al a half-smile and left the chamber.

"No," my voice was a cry. "No. You're monsters. Both of you!"

In a low growl through tight lips, my husband made a declaration. "I can buy and sell anyone in this town. Dede and I are the power couple in San Francisco. Better give up any ideas you have of Sean living with you. He is my son and I will see to it that he is disciplined appropriately or he'll become a fag like your designer friend Richard Tam."

Al's jaw squared, eyes flinty, he snapped open his briefcase, placed a sheaf of papers inside, closed it back up and then, in an aside, dropped a bomb. "My first wife Doris tried to buck me and you know where that got her. Mike and Lad hate her." In dry hands he took my arm and forced me to look directly into his eyes. "Sean will hate you, too. I guarantee it."

"You cold-hearted bastard!" I twisted away from his hold on my arm, and ran past him, out of the room, down the dirty grey steps of city hall and onto the street. I ran and ran, crying, hysterical, as pedestrians dodged and an unseasonable rain began to fall.

I had gotten lost in the parking garage but finally found my car and headed home, sobbing all the way. Sean would be there so I tried to pull myself together. Sporadic drops of rain splashed on the Olds as I drove through once familiar streets. I was a stranger in a foreign land. Everything appeared shrouded in mystery. Even the buildings seemed threatening. The city itself had turned against me, I thought.

At home the rooms spun around me. My skin burned. My eyes stung. Slowly I made my way up the stairs to Sean's room. He was lying on his bed reading. I said hello. He looked up at me, nodded, and then went back to his book.

"I'll cook dinner as soon as I change." My voice was a whisper.

"What?" Sean glanced up at me again.

Was the floor shaking? "I'll cook something." I leaned against the wall for balance.

"I ate a sandwich at Dad's," he said. "Dede made me stand over the sink so I wouldn't get crumbs anywhere."

"That woman," I mumbled.

"It's not her fault. I'm messy." I wondered why Sean always defended her.

I got to my bedroom. I changed into a white granny gown and then cautiously wandered back into the hallway. Sean was still reading.

"Do you want some ice cream?" I asked.

"Mom, you eat too much ice cream. Dede says you're fat." Sean did not look at me when he spoke.

I sat down on the top step of the circular staircase, next to Sean's room, cushioned by my fat. Reproachful black clouds pressed against the two-story tall windows.

The room seemed to be swirling around me. I tried to stand up but could not. Suddenly a searing pain exploded in my chest and radiated across my back. I dug my fingernails into my skin trying to get at the pain.

Hard rain pelted the windows.

"Mom?" Sean stood beside me. "Are you okay?"

"Ohhhh," I said as I kneaded my chest. My voice trembled. Sweat ran down my face. "Sean, do . . . you . . . hate me?"

Sean sat down beside me. He did not answer my question. I reached over to rub his back through his thin t-shirt but it was impossible to concentrate. I couldn't focus. Everything was blurry.

Rain poured down. Maybe the two-story windows would break. Maybe the penthouse would fill like a swimming pool and drown us. Maybe we would be washed out to sea. Death was inviting. Sean did not want to be here either, I thought.

"Sean," I said, my voice in slow motion, my breath ragged, "I'm going to kill myself." Wind driven rain beat furiously against the skylight. "Do you want to go with me?"

Sean stood up.

"That's not a good idea, Mom," he said.

My body was an anchor. I couldn't move. "Okay."

Finally, I managed to get to my feet. On unsteady legs I made it to my bedroom where I lay down on the bed, gasping for breath, scratching, trying to pull the pain out of my chest. Struggling to the bathroom, I got a bottle of aspirin and downed five. I lay down again. I fell into a fitful sleep.

I woke up throughout the night and prayed for help. "God, please help me." I prayed over and over, a mantra. Eventually I fell asleep.

Awakening to a clear dawn I felt as if I had endured a debilitating bout of flu. I was weak. Scratches on my chest gave testimony to my night of agony.

Sean was in his room. "Hi," I said. He mumbled something and looked away from me. "Are you okay, Sean?"

"Yeah. Can we go to Napa now?" His backpack was near the door and was already stuffed with his books and clothes. He wanted to be with his dad and stepmother.

"As soon as I have a glass of orange juice for energy we'll go," I said.

"You're always talking about your energy as if you were a car that needed gas."

He stood with his backpack ready, a cap on his head, waiting for me to gas up. Vaguely, I remembered saying something to Sean about killing myself. Had I actually said those words to him? It was unfathomable.

"Sean, I don't know what's wrong with me. I did a terrible thing last night when I talked about killing myself. I'm so, so sorry. Please forgive me."

"Can we go now? Sean said, edging toward the door.

I took the familiar road from San Francisco to California's Silverado Trail in my Oldsmobile through acres of ripening grapes in the Napa Valley. Sleep-deprived because of constant chest pain, it was hard to focus. The August sun reflected off the hood of my car in ripples of heat, blinding me to everything except the two-lane road, and my child.

"Mom, I don't want to live with you!" Sean said. "I want to live at River Meadow Farm with Dad and Dede, not you!"

"Don't say such things to me, Sean." I glared at my ten-year-old son, noting the sweat on his fair skin, the dampness of his brown hair. Wearing beige shorts, a Star Wars t-shirt, and dirty sneakers, he crossed his lanky arms defiantly. His eyes, hazel like his father's, looked sullen. His lower lip was thrust out. Thumping rhythmically against the seat he swung his slender legs back and forth, back and forth.

"Mom, I want to stay with Dede!" Sean whined.

"Sean, stop it!" I tried to control the shrill tone of my voice to stay calm, but unbidden, pent-up words came tumbling out in staccato bursts. "That woman . . . wanted money . . . jewelry . . . courted you to get your father . . . stabbed me in the back . . . betrayed . . ."

At the top of his little-boy soprano voice, my son screamed, "No, no, no! Dede has money, she's a Dow!"

"She had very little money of her own," I said. "She told me so when I thought we were friends. Your dad had to pay her debts after they got married. You told me that yourself, remember? You said your dad was upset about it. That woman plots and plans. She's using you just the way she used me."

"Don't say that! I love her!"

Oblivious to the honking horns of oncoming traffic, I veered off the road. As the car skidded onto the shoulder of the highway, my foot hit the brake. The tires, spewing gravel, permeated the air with the stench of burning rubber and a cloud of dust. In a frenzy of anguish I let go of the wheel and slapped Sean hard on his exposed thigh.

We stared at each other, blue eyes meeting hazel, stunned. I had never hit him before in his entire life. I sagged against the steering wheel and began to cry. My sobs echoed in the claustrophobic space. They seemed a proper metaphor for life without my family and the only man I had trusted since my father died.

Sean leaned against the door, as far from me as he could get, rubbing his eyes, trying to stop the tears mingled with little boy dirt running in tracks down his face. My heart contracted with a mixture of love and concern that recognized his pain and confusion as my own.

"I'm sorry . . ." I reached across the seat, longing to take him into my arms, to feel him nestled against my neck. Dark hair plastered to his head, my child covered his ears and turned away from me to gaze out the window. White California oleander whipped back and forth in the sweltering summer wind. Farther on were views of the Valley vineyards, and in the distance our beautiful country home, a house I had designed down to the last nail, now occupied by Sean's dad and the woman who had pretended to be my friend.

Sean broke the silence. "Will you take me to Dad's now?" he said.

"Yes," I replied with resignation. I paused. "I love you, Sean. Always remember that."

My son continued to stare out the car window, giving no indication he heard me, or cared if he had. I started the engine, drove him to the whitewashed entry gates of River Meadow, and stopped the car. "I love you," I repeated.

"Love you, too," he replied. He opened the car door and slammed it shut before running up the long cobbled driveway toward the house.

I don't remember driving back to San Francisco, but as I crossed the Golden Gate Bridge I knew that I no longer wanted to live. My husband had left me. My son had rejected me. I was being jeered at in the papers. I was fifty-one years old. I felt worthless.

At home I assembled keepsakes of Sean's childhood: a drawing of his smile, a plaster handprint from kindergarten, a crayon heart with "I love Mommy" at its center, and the ceramic cross Sean had given me on that long-ago birthday. After arranging those sentimental riches on the bed, I donned pajamas and got a bottle of Nembutal, a medication I had been on since my heart surgery, from the medicine cabinet. Forty yellow capsules were packed into the tall brown vial. I counted them out, one by one, onto my bedside table. I decided to take the pills gradually, a few at a time, in order to avoid throwing them up.

Choosing the recorded noise of a thunderstorm, I inserted it into my tape deck. Immediately the sound of torrential rain, rolling thunder and strikes of lightning filled the room, reminding me of my Texas girlhood.

Locating a Bible, I crawled into bed, turned up the electric blanket, and prepared to die. It did not occur to me that I was giving those who had harmed me the precious gift of my life. Nor, in my irrational, depressed state, did I think of the long-term tragedy I would be inflicting on my son.

Opening the Good Book to the Twenty-third Psalm, I swallowed four sleeping pills, and began to read: "The Lord is my shepherd . . . he leadeth me beside the still waters . . ." Two more pills . . . "Yea, though I walk through the valley of the shadow of death, I will fear no evil . . ."

Two more Nembutals. ". . . thou art with me . . ." Limp tears fell as I took more capsules. "Thou preparest a table . . . in the presence of mine enemies . . ." I was groggy. "Surely goodness and mercy . . ."

Tenderly, above the violence of crackling thunderbolts, as if from a vast distance, I heard the voice of my father. Loving energy surrounded me. "There's a reason for you to live, Chik-a-lik. Be patient. You will be shown." A luminescence filled the room as I began to fall asleep.

The insistent ring of the phone roused me from the seductive whirlpool of death. I had no idea of how much time had passed. By reflex, voice slurring, I answered. "Hell . . . oo."

"Pat, this is Jean Bolen. Sorry to just now be getting back to you, but I've been away."

Jean was a psychiatrist friend. I didn't remember calling her. "Jean . . ." my mouth seemed to be filled with peanut butter. "Does . . . n't matter."

"It does matter, Pat. Please listen to me." I tried to focus. "You're going through a hard time, but I know a terrific therapist, Dr. Sheila Krystal. She can help you." Jean paused. "I'll call her for you, okay?" She was insistent. "Okay?"

"Ok . . . ay."

"Promise you won't do anything drastic. Okay?"

"Ok . . . ay." Her offer gave me a glimmer of hope. Hanging up, I stumbled into the bathroom, put my finger down my throat and vomited repeatedly.

Collapsing there, a towel for a pillow, I moved in and out of consciousness. I thought I was a young girl back in Texas, and my mother was beating me with a switch she had made me select from the salt cedar tree growing in back of my father's Church of the Nazarene. Her judgmental voice cut through time.

"You're a sinner, Patsy Lou, a vile sinner." My legs stung from cuts made by the switch. "It's your fault your family has abandoned you."

Later that afternoon, when I finally awoke, I called Dr. Sheila Krystal.

# 9.

# THE VISION

Fog covered the windshield like a curtain of gauze as I drove across the Bay Bridge to Dr. Sheila Krystal's Berkeley office. Shivering, I turned the wipers to high and cut my speed, as the mist became a downpour. The angry slap of tires against slick pavement and the bitter gray day suited my mood. I felt hopeless, angry, and nauseous. I was also menopausal. My gynecologist discovered indications of cervical cancer and performed a freeze procedure to kill the lethal cells.

When I had finally seen a cardiologist about the pain in my chest, he said that my heart showed signs of a minor heart attack. He put me on medication and told me to stop worrying. But how could I stop worrying when Al had terminated my health insurance and I didn't know how I was going to pay my medical bills, including these sessions with Dr. Krystal. How ironic. I lived in a multimillion-dollar penthouse, but couldn't pay my medical bills. The money Al had to give me was quickly eaten up by maintenance of the penthouse and my routine bills.

Clutching the steering wheel as if I could change history with the pressure, I drove across the Bay Bridge. Red taillights reflected off rain-soaked asphalt like Satan's fire. I thought of hell. Perhaps I should give up, let the Devil take me. But quickly reversing myself, I prayed. "Oh God, let Dr. Krystal have an answer for me."

Exiting onto a quiet tree-lined street, I found her office. Greeting me with warmth, the casually dressed and youthful Dr. Krystal ("Call me Sheila") seemed nice. Thin, with long, brown hair and no makeup, her manner was unpretentious.

"Dr. Bolen thinks you can help me," I said, although it was difficult for me to admit that I needed help.

"Jean is a fine psychiatrist and a talented writer as well. Have you read *Synchronicity and the Self*?" Sheila spoke in soft tones.

"Synchronicity?" The word meant nothing to me.

"That's when, say, you need a plumber, and a truck with a plumber's sign and a phone number parks in front of your house. That's synchronicity." The doctor's gentle laughter put me at ease. "I'll explain more later, but now I need to learn about you." She drew me out, asking questions, probing. I told her about Sean, my husband's betrayal, my loss of River Meadow Farm, personal attacks in the press.

Explaining that she was a Jungian analyst and often used guided visualization techniques and meditations, Sheila asked if that was okay.

"Guided visualizations?" This was Never-Neverland.

"It's easy to do," she said with a smile. "Honest. With your eyes closed, you do deep breathing exercises to help you relax. Then I talk you through a routine that can help tap into your unconscious, see with your mind's eye. That way, we often get to the problem beneath the surface. Does that sound okay?"

"It's worth a try," I said, agreeing to take a crack at anything that might ease my pain.

"We'll do a mini version today. Just to give you a taste of how visualizations work."

"All right," I said, making myself comfortable.

"Now close your eyes," Sheila instructed. "I want you to take several deep breaths. Inhale, exhale, inhale, exhale." She continued the deep breathing exercise for several minutes. "Now, Pat, in your mind I want you to find a beautiful sandy beach you love. Stretch out on the warm sand and soak up the rays of the sun. Breathe deeply, taking the warmth of the sun into every cell in your body."

In my mind I was lying on a white sand beach in Hawaii, the hot sun penetrating every muscle in my tense body. I began to relax.

"Now, put a circle around yourself, a circle of gold like a giant bracelet. This is your private space," the doctor spoke slowly in order to give me time to "see" the things she asked me to imagine. "Now, with your mind's eye, pull a bullet-proof shield up from the base of your golden circle. Let it cover you completely." Sheila paused. "Are you able to do that?"

"Yes," I said.

"That shield will protect you from the slings and arrows of gossip. Notice how when cruel things are said about you, they are deflected back onto the person saying them."

"Okay, I can see that," I said, as Al sent snakes of words toward me that were instantly deflected back onto him.

"Whenever you feel others are trying to take your energy by angry words, dishonesty, or betrayal, remember to consciously put your shield up and you will be protected." When I opened my eyes Dr. Krystal said that was a short example of how visualizations work.

"I like it," I said. We decided on two meetings a week for now. Our goal was to restore my self-esteem and relieve my depression.

"You should go back to work at the *Examiner*," Shelia advised. "That's the best thing you can do for yourself while going through therapy. And start keeping a journal. If you stick with this, you'll feel better."

My editor said she would be glad to have me back. Writing a column forced me to pay attention to my appearance, socialize, and to cover a variety of events even though I wanted to stay in bed. The *Examiner* kept me busy. I covered Ronald Reagan's 1981 inauguration, the wedding of Prince Charles and Princess Diana, as well as two Super Bowls, both of which got page-one coverage along with multiple photographs; a feather in my literary cap. I was always glad to get out of town. Even so, distress trailed me like the churning wake of an ocean liner.

Six months after their wedding I saw my ex and Dede at a social event, acting as though they met a week before they married. I wrote an inane item about them in my column: "How about that older man and his twenty-plus years younger wife pretending they just met and fell in love. There's an ugly history there. Beware of 'friends' in lambs' clothing, I say."

Al immediately asked the court to issue a gag order so I could not write about them. The *Examiner* said they would back me up, but I was too exhausted to pursue yet another legal battle even though I did have to make another court appearance.

The next night, I was awakened by the sound of breaking glass. A split-second later I heard the door from the upper floor leading to the interior fire escape click shut. I called the police. When they arrived, they insisted I stay put. With drawn guns and strong flashlight beams they crept down the stairs. I stood on the landing in an old terry bathrobe, shivering. "Don't shoot the mirrors," I whispered, knowing the illusion created by huge mirrored walls could trigger a shoot-out.

They didn't find anything but they were glad I had warned them about the mirrors.

The next morning I discovered the remains of a champagne flute scattered in shards beneath my photograph. The names Al and Pat were decipherable between etched hearts that were once intertwined on the crystal. Did Al or someone else familiar with our lives and this apartment do this? I wondered. And why?

The phone rang. My editor was calling to tell me there had been a death threat made against me. They were taking it seriously. Pam played the tape for me. The male caller's hard-edged voice was scary. "Pat Montandon is not to write about her current problems or something will happen to her: a fire, a car accident. Believe it!"

"Pat," my boss said when the tape ended, "keep your column bland for a while and be careful. We don't want you to end up dead."

Fearful of what Al could do, I never again wrote about him or Dede.

An anxious six months had passed since the break-in, but I could not get over my husband's infidelity or his threats. I was, however, looking forward to picking Sean up from summer camp. Reform school, which Al had once suggested, had not materialized after all.

Driving my son home from Orme, a summer camp in Arizona, I sensed a wavering in his devotion to his stepmother. "Dede makes me sit separate from everyone else at the dinner table," he said, counting bug spatters on the windshield, distracting himself from his admission.

"What does your dad say?"

"Dad says I should be sent away to boarding school."

"Never. I'll never let you go."

"It's okay, I don't mind." He closed the subject. I knew better than to discuss it further. His loyalty was with them.

These conversations always depressed me. The lack of stability in my son's life, torn between his dad's house and mine, worried me.

"Divorced parents should be the ones to move in and out of the house, not kids," I said to Sheila.

When my lawyer said we were finally going to court to resolve the money issue, I was glad. Perhaps after that I could get on with my life. Thinking it would be a simple matter, I was in for a shock. The process dragged on, intermittently, through the winter of 1981, the spring of 1982, into 1983, and finally ended in the summer of 1984.

The interminable process was made longer by the constant gossip and rumor mongering. Gossip columnist Herb Caen lambasted me almost every week. "Who says athletes are overpaid? That blonde dumbshell is demanding Big Bucks from Mr. Nizeguy for the few years they were married." In the same column he lauded the other woman: "Dimpled Dede Traina not only left John to marry Multibags Al Wilsey, she is collecting $675,000 from John's new wife, best-selling author Danielle Steel. That represents Dede's half of the Traina mansion, wherein John and Danielle will dwell starting in November."

I was often asked if Al had paid Herb off. I didn't know. But I did know that when we were married, Al would send case after case of French champagne to the columnist, assuring favorable items about his generosity.

"Before they ask for it, always give money to important charities, like the opera and the right museums," Al had advised. "That way you get more credit for the give. I'm a Republican but I donate to candidates of both parties. Money equals power and you can get people to do anything to hold onto power."

In the courtroom of Judge Anthony Klein (new to the bench and presiding over his first divorce trial), there was no doubt about the center of power. Listening to my ex-husband's cold assessment of our marriage, I wondered once again what had happened to the man I had loved so passionately and who every day for eleven years told me how much he loved me.

I wondered when the "saint" I married had turned into the terrifying inquisitor who now strutted across the floor like a bantam rooster. I couldn't believe it when the judge allowed Al to take over the cross examination from his lawyer. "Do you keep a diary, Ms. Montandon? Answer yes or no," Al said.

"Yes," I replied.

"Is this your diary?" he asked, holding the cloth-bound book I had kept in a drawer of my dressing table at River Meadow over his head as if it were an Oscar.

"Yes," I replied, realizing that this was a game to Al. He enjoyed hammering at me and seemed to swell with power as he tried to diminish me.

"Read page ten," he said as if he were entitled to order me about.

Fumbling with the pages, I began to read aloud. "We made love twice last night. Alfred doesn't like it when I laugh during sex, so . . ."

"No! Stop." Al snatched the diary from me. "That wasn't page ten," he said. He looked at the judge. "Admonish the witness to follow directions, your honor." Expressionless, Al indicated the correct passage and thrust the book back in my hands. "Read only the parts indicated, Ms. Montandon."

With a quavering voice, I read about a time when I was angry with Al because he insisted I fly with him in his helicopter to Lake Tahoe. When I said I didn't want to, Al took it as a personal affront, an insult to his masculinity and his ability as a pilot.

"So, you didn't love your husband enough to fly with him?" Al's third person reference threw me.

"It was after our crash," I said, trying to remain calm.

"Just answer the question. Did you refuse to fly to Tahoe with your husband?"

"Yes," I answered, hoping that my attorney or the judge would stop Al from badgering me before I fell apart on the witness stand.

"But you knew there was nothing to be afraid of, didn't you? I put that chopper into auto rotations and brought us down safe and sound, right?"

"Yes," I admitted, demoralized by the exchange. Every day at the end of court, I would flee to the restroom with a violent roiling in my bowels and sit on the toilet crying and vomiting into a paper towel. My husband's unrelenting assault was making me sick.

Sheila had said that during court appearances I should continually envision a scale of justice held over the head of the judge. Through it all, I kept visualizing the scale, large bronze pans held by a blindfolded female, weighing truth.

But when two of Al's employees carted in blue metal footlockers filled with printouts purportedly showing we had consumed our community property, all I could see was the look of triumph on Al's face.

Jerry Solari, Al's company accountant, opened the footlockers and pulled out reams of paper. As if in a choreographed ballet, he strung the printouts across the courtroom and recited numbers. With chalk, he wrote out figure after figure on a blackboard. Both my attorney and the judge seemed overwhelmed.

Still, in spite of evidence to the contrary, I assumed I would be treated fairly. Even when Al slammed down a piece of paper, and declared that it was an anti-nuptial agreement, I could not grasp the significance of what he was trying to do to me.

"It's usually called a pre-nuptial agreement, not an anti-nuptial," Charles Morgan whispered to me. "That fact alone raises a red flag. If that document was authentic, it would mean you signed away all rights to your property."

"I never signed anything," I protested.

"It can't be valid," Charles said. "I was your attorney before you married and I would have counseled you before you signed it."

Although both Charles and I knew that I had never signed the agreement, Pegi Brandly, Al's longtime secretary, said that I had. In fact, she testified that on the date in question I had left Al's office stating, "I've given up everything for love." Her fabrication was backed up by a former part-time employee, a person I had never met.

Helen Zurcher, my former housekeeper, came to see me. She had read in the paper about the so-called anti-nuptial agreement.

"Pat, on the date they say you signed that agreement, you were doing a TV show in Los Angeles," Helen said. "I waited up for you although you didn't get home until after midnight." I nodded my head. "I'll testify if you want me to, but it has to be soon. I have cancer and I don't have very long to live."

"Oh, Helen, I'm so sorry," I said, hugging her. I was deeply touched by Helen's unselfishness. How could she be thinking of me when she was dying? I wondered.

Because of the severity of Helen's illness, Charles asked Judge Klein to take her testimony out of order, but the judge refused. Helen died three weeks later.

For me, the trial was a series of unfathomable setbacks. In spite of the fact that Pegi Brandley had testified under oath that Al's office—in which I had allegedly signed the anti-nuptial agreement—was located in a building that he hadn't yet moved into, and that the log book in which the anti-nuptial document was supposedly notarized had conveniently disappeared, Judge Kline accepted this testimony and ultimately ruled that I was not entitled to my share of our estate. When Al was given River Meadow Farm, I felt like a fish gutted for my eggs so Al and Dede could eat caviar.

"I've lost my home," I sobbed to Sheila. "I love that place more than I can tell you. It meant family and security and beauty and, oh, everything to me."

"You must let go of River Meadow, Pat. Are you ready to do that?"

I did not want to let go. After a long discussion, I agreed to try. Sheila told me to close my eyes, to breathe deeply, and then in my mind's eye "see" my former home. "Go inside the house Pat, and into each room. Look at the space. Absorb what you're seeing. Thank each room, and then say good-bye."

With a sob, I brought the picture of River Meadow Farm into my mind. Starting with the living room, I recalled its beauty: the stone and timber fireplace, the sunflower yellow fabrics, the hand-woven carpets. But the place was more to me than a piece of real estate; it was where I had taught Sean to read, we had picked wild blackberries to make jam, and I had taken family movies of Sean skimming down our creek on a raft.

Eventually I was able to say thank you and good-bye to the house and then, following Sheila's instructions, I placed River Meadow Farm on an ice floe. As the water carried it around a bend in a river and it disappeared from view, I sobbed, grief-stricken.

"Pat, take a deep breath, relax. That's it, breathe deeply," Dr. Krystal's voice was soft, sympathetic.

"Now, allow yourself to see your new home, a home that will always be yours, a home that can never be taken away from you. A home anchored in your heart."

"I see a teepee. An Indian teepee, of all things," I said. It took me an hour to describe the teepee to Sheila and as I talked I felt that what I was seeing was real.

When I opened my eyes, Sheila explained. "The teepee represents a home that can never be taken from you. I think there's an important meaning to that image that's not apparent to you now. Someday you may understand what it means."

"But what about the ruling of the judge? I kept seeing the justice scale balanced with equal amounts of money, but it didn't happen."

"Justice isn't necessarily equated with money." Sheila took my hands in hers. "If you're lucky, you'll discover that."

I did not believe her.

My attorney was trying to work out a settlement. He said I was entitled to something, in spite of the ruling. He told me it would take months more to resolve and that I should remain patient and stay put. Easy to say, hard to do. I knew I would have to give up the penthouse, but I would delay it as long as possible. It was, after all, my home.

"Pride goeth before a fall," my mother would have said. Without my husband and son, I no longer knew who I was. It felt like I had fallen into a bottomless dark hole, spiraling forever downward.

As our legal proceedings dragged on, Sean was with me off and on and I wanted new memories with him, good memories. So I took him, my niece Linda, and her twelve-year-old son Patrick on a weeklong rafting trip down Utah's Green River to the confluence of the Colorado River. Not knowing how to swim, I was fearful of the rapids but we had a great time together.

Returning from our trip late at night, tired and sleepy, Sean crawled into his lower bunk bed, his cousin on the top. Before I could undress, a loud knock on my door and a scream from Sean frightened me half to death. My heart was thumping wildly as I ran to the door, yelling for Linda at the same time, expecting a bloody accident. Sean was babbling.

In his hands he held two ruby and emerald bracelets and two diamond rings, all mine.

"Mom, Mom look! These were under my mattress! I was reading and my flashlight fell between the bed frame and the mattress and when I got it, these were sticking out from under there."

His cousin joined in, "Yeah, sorta under the mattress."

I had not changed the locks since my split with Al. He was the only person, so far as I knew, with a key. He also knew the combination to my safe. But why would he do such a thing?

"Someone wants me to look like a thief," Sean said. He was pale and his lips quivered. "Dad says I steal things and Dede says so, too. But honest, Mom, I didn't do this, honest, cross my heart."

"I know you didn't, Sean," I reassured him. We sat in the kitchen drinking hot chocolate and discussing the incident into the early hours of the morning.

Al called a few days later, his voice a rough complaint, telling me our son should be sent away to school. "Sean is a thief and he needs discipline," Al said.

Refusing to give permission, I choked back the tears that were always near the surface, especially when I talked to Al. I was afraid to stand up to Al for fear that he would manage to cut me off without a cent. Irrationally, I could imagine myself huddled under cardboard on the cold street near their opulent mansion while Dede and Al dined by candlelight and chortled at my plight.

"It's going to happen whether you give permission or not," Al said.

"Screw you, you cheating cold-hearted jerk," I said, banging down the receiver.


Parties and socializing, both part of my newspaper job, no longer interested me. Some of those whom I once thought to be friends now seemed full of self-importance and swagger. I didn't want to be around them. I marked each day off the calendar as if I were a prisoner waiting for release. Dr. Krystal was my one source of hope.

Usually I enjoyed meditating with her, but on a day in October of 1982, I did not want to; I was decidedly out of sorts. At Sheila's insistence, however, I closed my eyes and began to follow her instructions. "Breathe deeply," she said, "and imagine that you can fill your body with sunlight."

My breathing deepened. It took awhile but eventually I was able to see the sunlight and almost at once a circular image formed that took me aback. "It's the earth, Sheila, I'm seeing the earth as if I'm looking at it from the moon." Then, as the picture continued to unfold, the perimeter of the circle exploded in enormous bursts of orange and red flames like those we see in photographs of sun flares.

My heart raced and sweat beaded my forehead. "Oh no!" I cried. "Oh, my God, Sheila," I moaned, "I'm seeing the earth. But not our beautiful blue planet. I'm seeing an inferno."

"Take a deep breath, Pat. What you're seeing isn't real, you know. It's symbolic. You can open your eyes anytime."

The illusion held me in its grip. "Oh my God, there's been a huge nuclear explosion!" I gasped. "I'm seeing the destruction of the earth . . . the seas are lava, boiling oceans, buildings are rubble . . . there's nothing left, people, animals, plants, trees, have evaporated. Oh, my God," I wailed.

"Open your eyes, Pat. It's okay."

But the horrific vision continued to unfold. "No, it isn't okay. Children are standing in the debris, in gray ashes amid melted bridges and crumbled buildings. They're terrified. The kids are sobbing, crying out that no one cared enough to stop this holocaust. They've lost everything, everyone. They are the only survivors. They're wailing, 'Why didn't you help us?' "

"Open your eyes Pat," Sheila instructed.

"No. There's more." The projector in my brain continued unreeling images. "A white-winged horse is coming into my vision. It's Pegasus," I said, "flying out of the ash-filled sky, gliding inside a bright light. The horse has a rider who's dressed like a magician," I paused. "The magician is reaching down with rays of light and he lifts the children onto the horse. He's carrying them to safety, away from our annihilated planet."

My distress was profound, my grief piercing.

"Concentrate on your breath, Pat," Sheila said. "Relax . . . let go of the pictures in your mind and open your eyes."

An hour after the vision had begun, I reluctantly opened my eyes and blinked. Sunshine was streaming through the windows. Still in the thrall of my vision, tears coursed down my face. "Sheila, that was frightening, terrifying really."

"Did you recognize the children you saw?"

"No. They were strangers. Black, Asian, Caucasian, they represented all races. Why would I see such a thing? I never think about nuclear war."

"Maybe your subconscious is giving you a message," my therapist suggested. "Do you feel your life is a holocaust?"

"No. That's not it."

The session was over, but the horror of my vision lingered. The next day, I cancelled all appointments. I did not feel like dealing with people who wanted a mention in my column. I needed time to digest my feelings and to meditate. Still in my pink wool bathrobe, I had just fixed myself a cup of hot tea when the doorbell rang. Startled, I spilled my beverage.

Looking through the viewer on my door, I saw Dr. Jerry Jampolsky (a man whose appointment I had canceled) with two people. A well-known psychiatrist and author, he had once given me a copy of his book, *Love Is Letting Go of Fear*.

Smoothing my hair, blotting the tea stains on my robe, I opened the door. "Jerry, hi, I'm sorry but I canceled our appointment for today."

For an embarrassing moment, we faced each other in the doorway. "Oh, I'm sorry, Pat, we'll come back later . . ."

Regretting my bad manners, I tried to make amends, "Well, since you're here, come on in." I opened the door and led them into the living room.

"Pat, this is Carol Howe and Tom Green," Jerry said.

"Hi," I said. "Would you like a cup of tea?"

"No, thanks. We won't take much of your time." Jerry seemed ill at ease. "Pat, some people in Denver put together a little book I edited. It's written by children and concerns their fear of nuclear war, the number-one fear of kids today, you know."

I did not know.

"The book is also about their hope for peace," Tom explained, sitting on the edge of my white sofa. "Madame Jehan Sadat, the wife of the assassinated president of Egypt, Anwar Sadat, is coming here in two weeks to launch it. We need to publicize the event but we don't know how. We thought you might give us publicity in your column."

Jerry handed me a glossy, rainbow-colored paperback, *Children as Teachers of Peace*. Trying to be polite, but wanting to get them on their way, I casually leafed through the little book. Sipping my tea, I studied the colorful drawings and poems.

"I think these kids show rare insight," Jerry said.

Turning a page, my interest picked up. What was this? I began reading the messages, paying attention to the drawings. There were letters and poems from kids expressing their fear of nuclear war and their thoughts about peace. A chill went up my spine. Jerry had brought the book the day after I had had a vision about nuclear war.

"We would really appreciate your help in getting the word out about this event, Pat. Madame Sadat should be a big draw." Jerry gave me a penetrating look. "Will you help us with this project?"

"Yes," I answered with unexpected conviction. "I'll do more than a mention in the paper," I said. "I'll help with the whole event." Jerry and his friends were thrilled. Four hours later, I had telephone commitments from thirty-five people to be in my home the following Monday. My former TV station agreed to do a half-hour special and the *Examiner* said they would initiate a peace essay contest for young readers. Diane Feinstein, our mayor, said she would participate. The event was soon sold out.

"Jerry," I said, as we talked together one day, "this is a worldwide movement for peace." I didn't know where such a notion came from.

His hand on my arm, Jerry interrupted me. "Pat, we sincerely appreciate your wonderful cooperative spirit, but I hate organizations."

Sean, with me for the week, raced in from school with an over-the-shoulder "Hi," and headed for the kitchen. "Sean," I said, following him. "Do you ever think about nuclear war?" He looked at me as if I had just emerged from the Ice Age.

"Get serious, Mom," he said. "Yeah, I'm scared of nuclear war." He was making a sandwich. "When the Russians push the button, we'll all be blown away. Or even if we push the button . . . wham-oh! All my friends are scared, too. We have no future."

His matter-of-fact approach to what he considered the inevitable stunned me. In the 1950s, we thought we could hide from a nuclear attack by crouching under a school desk. But now kids did not think there was any hope at all.

That night I was jolted awake as the holocaust vision replayed in a dream. Had I truly had a vision? Did I have a part to play in this?

When I once again mentioned to Jerry the international aspects of kids and peace, he said, "Pat, if you feel so strongly about it, then you do it."

"Okay," I said. "I will."

# 10.

# IT CAN BE DONE

Now I had a purpose. I wanted to devote every waking moment to this new passion, not knowing where it would lead. I called Pam Scott, my boss at the *Examiner*, and told her I wanted to resign so I could work on getting kids involved in writing letters about their fears of nuclear war to Reagan in the U.S. and Andropov in the USSR. She suggested a leave of absence and I agreed. I was committed. It was not a sacrifice.

Al still had to support me until we reached a financial settlement, so I would use that money for my work. Volunteers tumbled out of nowhere to help organize. Many were friends and acquaintances from my Roundtable luncheons. They, too, feared a nuclear war. Barbara Ross became a stellar volunteer after seeing me interviewed on television. The appearance was worth the effort, even though I had to respond to the Herb Caen accusations and questions about my divorce before the hosts let me talk about my project. I invited kids to write letters about their concerns of nuclear war and send them to me. A slide showed my address and phone number.

The phone never stopped ringing. We had touched a nerve. Now we had to plan ways to get more children involved, to give them a voice in their future. Deciding on outdoor concerts where kids could bring mail for President Reagan and Soviet leader Andropov, expressing their fear of nuclear war and their hopes for peace, we got to work.

Calling friends of friends, getting a network started, we enlisted the help of famed artist Ruth Asawa. Ruth got her students involved in designing a billboard for the events. Soon, coffee cups and remnants of sandwiches littered my apartment, accompanied by the hum of well-placed energy. Sean, with me for two weeks, joined in with a joy and eagerness I had not seen in a long time.

After two weeks of nonstop calling, requesting schools to bring their students to our Union Square event, officials at fifteen schools finally said they would participate. Mayor Dianne Feinstein declared the two weeks before Christmas a celebration of Children as Teachers of Peace, the name we chose to use for these events.

In early December 1982, it all started to come together, with bands, clowns, Christmas fairies, and Santa Claus entertaining at the open-air happenings. The largest celebration, a concert in downtown Union Square, was scheduled for December 10, when kids would be bussed in from towns throughout the Bay Area. But we awoke to a huge storm that morning. Thunder roared, lightning flashed, and torrents of rain flooded our state. Television reports showed cars washed off roads, houses buried in mud.

Rain obscured the view as Sean and I tried to look out our windows. "I'm afraid there won't be a concert today," I said.

"Mom, we should go anyway," Sean said. "If even one kid shows up, we need to be there."

"You're right, Sean." I was proud of him. "Get your slicker. Let's take the peace bags too, just in case." The peace bags were blue, green, yellow, red, and purple nylon sacks, each painted with a letter in the word "peace," and they were to be used to collect letters from the children.

Turning the windshield wipers to high, I eased onto the street. The wind had quieted a bit, only blowing in gusts now, but rain flooded the streets.

"We're late, but no one will be there anyway so can we go to The Good Guys?" Sean loved to shop.

"Maybe later," I said pulling up to a curb near the plaza, "but for now, go on up there while I park."

After parking in the underground garage, I ran up the steps to the square. Just as I arrived above ground, a brilliant flash of lightning illuminated the scene. I was amazed by the number of wet, bedraggled children gathered in the square. Hundreds sheltered by brightly colored umbrellas were trying to stay dry in the deluge. Another lightning flash, thunder rumbled, and yet above the noise, the song "We Shall Overcome" could be heard. The children's voices, high and sweet, rose and fell on the rain-soaked wind blowing across Union Square. Huddled together, clutching plastic-wrapped mail, they sang, "We shall live in peace some day."

Volunteer Anne Thomson, her blonde hair soaked, and her nine-year-old son Angus, along with Sean, held the peace bags open so kids could stuff in their messages. We exchanged quick looks. Youngsters crowded around, eager to find out what we were going to do with their offerings.

"I saw you on TV," a kid said, "and you said you'd be here at ten. It's eleven now."

"I'm so sorry, I didn't think anyone would come out in this weather," I said.

"This is real, real important." The child's red jacket was bunched around his ears. He was chewing gum.

Droplets fell from a girl's eyelashes. "We've been waiting a long, long, long, long time for you," she said, wiping her nose on the sleeve of her jacket. I dug a Kleenex out of my purse and handed it to her.

"We're scared," a boy said, stuffing his mail into the green bag with the letter "P" that Sean held open. "We want our letters to get to those guys who can blow us up, you know, the guys in Russia. Are you going to get our letters to Russia?"

They were determined.

"We're really really scared. Will you help us?" The requests came from an African-American, a Caucasian, and a Hispanic child. "Will you get our letters to those guys in Russia to stop nuclear war stuff?"

With startling clarity, I saw that these were the children in my vision.

"Yes," I was barely able to speak. "I'll mail your letters, even to Russia."

"Mail them?" Sean pulled at my slicker. "Mom, they'll end up in a shredder! We've got to go there. We've got to take them there ourselves!"

"Are you going to go there?" The children were incredulous. "To Russia?"

My fate was sealed. "Yes," I said, "somehow or other we'll go there. We'll take kids with us, too."

Sean hugged me. Others pushed forward in youthful exuberance, wrapping themselves around my legs, pulling on my raincoat.

"Thank you," I whispered, looking up at the blustering sky. "Thank you." That day I did not know it, but above the zigzag lightning and the rolling peals of thunder, a far greater sound was directed toward me. That reverberation, like the ocean roar, fierce winds, birdsong, and all the natural sounds of earth, was a whisper from God.

It took Sean four trips to drag the heavy bags of mail we collected in Union Square from the car to our apartment. He did it willingly, pulling the nylon sacks by thick rope handles, wiping off the rain, stacking them neatly in a hall closet, his feeling of responsibility to the letter writers was obvious. A transformation had occurred in my child and in me. I hoped it would last.

"You deserve a treat, Sean. How about hot cocoa and Famous Amos cookies?"

"Mom, please, just cocoa, no cookies, ugh!" During Jehan Sadat's visit to my home, the famous cookie maker Famous Amos had brought us four large cartons of his cookies. We had gorged ourselves to the point of pain and didn't want to see another of his goodies for a long time.

"Okay, just hot chocolate then, but get out of those wet duds. We've got lots to do."

"Yeah, going to Russia. That's awesome." He took down the world atlas from a shelf and began flipping though the pages.

"No reading until you put on dry clothes. If you get sick, we won't be going anywhere." My words were motivation. Returning from his room, Sean slid down the banister wearing dry clothes and the tweed-billed cap he was seldom without, ready to tackle the USSR. Noticing that his pants were too short, I became acutely aware that he would be twelve in May.

We sat at the kitchen table sipping chocolate, conscious of the furious rain beating against the windows, and began planning our trip. The soothing scent of chocolate, along with gingerbread I had popped in the oven, was the aroma of home and family. It had been two years since Al dismantled our family and I sorely missed times like this.

"It's not just the Russians threatening war, it's both countries." Sean drained his cup and continued talking. "We've gotta go see President Reagan, too."

"You're right. We should see the heads of both countries. I'll call David Myers at Montgomery Street Travel. He'll know how to get us to Moscow by way of Washington."

"We've gotta have all kinds of kids on the trip, too, Mom, you know, not just a bunch of rich kids." He was on the right track. I waited for him to think it through. "Why don't we ask for essays, you know, so kids who want to go can tell us why?"

"That's a fine idea. I'll call Melba Beals, ask her to get out a press release. She's in public relations, so she'll know what to do."

"Way to go, Mom." He gave me a high five.

"Sean, I'm thinking the kids should be eight to twelve. Children that age speak the truth. They don't pretend to be something they're not. Airfares are cheaper, too," I said, getting to the bottom line. "We've got to go while school's out, you know."

"Let's leave on Christmas Day. Wouldn't that be awesome?" He was drawing pictures on the fogged windowpane with an index finger. "I'm with you this Christmas, too. So Dad can't object."

"That's right." I said, relieved that Sean finally wanted to be with me.

I also liked the way my son's mind worked, that he knew the importance of having children from different ethnic and economic backgrounds along. His idea of using essays was a good way to recruit candidates, too. But there wouldn't be time for that. Anyway, how could we leave for a country so far away, one that was our expressed enemy, in ten days? "Sean, I don't think it's possible to make all this happen so quickly."

Abandoning window art, he stood up and pushed his cap back. "Mom, remember what your dad always said. 'It can be done.' "

It Can Be Done. When Daddy was raising money to help a sick child, for instance, he stood behind the pulpit and held up that sign. "It can be done," he said. "Brothers and Sisters, I know you don't have a lot of money and neither do I, but we are our brother's keepers. It can be done," he intoned. Waving the blue lettered sign over his head, he said, "I'll give the first five dollars." Mama muttered "Lord help us" when Daddy put five crumpled-up dollar bills into the collection plate. Other creased bills as well as shiny quarters soon ensured help for a poor young boy.

Once again, my father's motto pushed me over the edge of indecision. Dad not only used that adage to inspire his family and parishioners, he believed every word of it.

"Okay, we'll do it. But we'll need lots of help."

Giving me a second hug that day, my once-again affectionate child agreed to do whatever I asked to make the trip happen.

I knew practically nothing about the Soviet Union. How would I arrange everything? After several phone calls to people involved in world affairs, I discovered that my lack of knowledge was shared by almost everyone.

"Your life will be in jeopardy if you attempt to talk peace in the Soviet Union," I was warned.

"The U.S. government will never condone such a trip."

"It can't be done, you're wasting your time, and anyway, what do kids know?" "Are you nuts, trying to take kids' letters to the Soviet Union?"

Melba Beals was an exception, which was why I knew she was the right person to handle our campaign. Melba was one of the first to integrate Little Rock High School in the 1960s, and a former news reporter for the NBC television affiliate in San Francisco, so she understood the issues. "Patsy," she said, giving me a speech, "you're tackling a very serious problem. The Cold War is scary to everyone, not just kids. When Reagan called the Soviet Union "the Evil Empire" and Congress increased money for nuclear weapons, it was like a kid thumbing his nose at Russia. It could get us all blown to kingdom come. Don't forget, one of our Senators, Joseph McCarthy, said, 'Better dead than Red.' It's a scary scenario."

Nevertheless, she liked our cause and our commitment. She would start a publicity blitz at once. I would only have to pay her costs, not a fee.

The next call was to travel agent David Myers. When I told him we wanted to go to Moscow, he thought I was joking. Realizing I was sincere, he discussed various airline schedules and began planning an itinerary. The least costly route was from San Francisco to Washington through Houston. From there we could go to New York, make connections for Rome, then fly on the Soviet airline, Aeroflot, into Moscow.

"If you want to leave on Christmas day, you'll have plenty of room. No one flies on December twenty-fifth. But you're fooling yourself, Pat. You'll never get a visa," he said with a laugh, "You can't just decide to go to the Soviet Union. It's not that simple. The Soviet travel agency, Intourist, has to approve. And they never okay anything, at least not for months. Your trip will never happen."

"Where would I go to get a visa and permission?"

"The Soviet Consulate on Green Street. But forget it. You aren't important enough to get an appointment."

I had enough church going as a kid to last a lifetime. But those old hymns still kept running around in my head. Like a jingle you can't forget, a tune burst through, I know the Lord will make a way for me. If I live a holy life, shun the wrong and do the right, I know the Lord will make a way for me.

From the moment of my vision in Sheila Krystal's office, it was as if a higher force directed my actions, removing fear and manifesting faith. I did not have an explanation for it. It was a fact.

A soon as I got off the phone with David, I drove to the Soviet Consulate. Two San Francisco police officers parked across the street in case of a demonstration against the treatment of Jews in the totalitarian state, recognized me and waved. Pulling up to the curb in front of the three-story brick structure, seeing the red Soviet flag with its gold hammer and sickle snapping in the wind, I felt as if I was already on foreign soil. I bounced out of the car and tried to open the iron entry gates, but they were firmly locked.

I pushed an intercom button below a surveillance camera.

"What you want?"

"I want to see the Consul General, please." Silence. I buzzed again. Nothing. Once again. No reply. One of the policemen got out of the patrol car and sauntered over, "Chikvaidze. Ask for Chikvaidze," he said. "The Consul General."

As soon as I said the magic words, the release buzzer sounded. I was permitted inside, but not very far.

"What you want?" The sour young man, trying to look grown-up in a brown and red military uniform and billed cap, was sitting behind a thick glass barrier. "Appointment? You have appointment?"

"Yes, with Mr. Chikvaidze," I bluffed.

"Name, you?"

"Montandon." I hoped that somehow my name would miraculously appear in the book he was studying. After a quick perusal, he banged the red-bound tome closed and glared at me. "No appointment!"

Stuttering, trying to fake it, I was saved by the appearance in the hallway of a tall robust man with a full head of black hair touched by gray, bushy eyebrows, wearing an ill-fitting suit. "I am Consul General Chikvaidze, and you are . . . ?"

I introduced myself, admitted I didn't have an appointment, and plunged in. "I've got to talk to you. I'm taking a bunch of kids to Moscow on a peace trip and I need your help."

"It's better to talk sitting down, out of the hallway. Come."

The sentry, unhappy with this turn of events, gave me a killer look.

Following the Consul General through a large, sparsely furnished reception room, I noticed Russian artifacts in glass cases and two large picture windows embracing a spectacular view of San Francisco Bay. My host beckoned me on, past a second cabinet displaying black lacquer boxes, into a small room dominated by an enormous portrait. Pointing toward the painting, the Consul General said in tones worthy of a benediction, "Portrait is of our great leader, Vladimir Ilyich Lenin, addressing workers during 'The Great October Revolution.' "

The insignificant room in which we stood had no windows or decoration save the towering picture. "Sit, please, tell me about this plan of yours." The Consul General was genial, relaxed.

"Mr. Chikvaidze, I want to take American children to Moscow to talk to your Mr. Andropov. He needs to hear how scared our kids are of a

nuclear attack from your country." The gentleman raised bristly eyebrows, questioning, not relaxed now, a frown replacing his smile.

Before he could respond, a woman wearing a kerchief on her head,
muttering, I supposed, in Russian, entered with a tray of refreshments.

"Would you like coffee?" The man handed me a cup without waiting
for an answer. Pouring spoonfuls of sugar into his drink, he stirred it,
took a sip, scrutinized Comrade Lenin, and finally said, "Ms. Montandon, when exactly are you proposing such a trip?"

"December twenty-fifth."

"Next year, 1983?"

"Oh no, this year, 1982."

The career diplomat chuckled. "You want to go in ten days? You
aren't serious?"

"I'm serious."

"Well now, Ms. Montandon, I'm afraid such a trip is not possible. It's
extremely cold in Moscow this time of year. It would be far too hard for
the children. Go later, in the spring. May is a beautiful time to visit our
country."

"The weather doesn't matter to us. Our kids are scared to death of the
possibility of nuclear war. They want to talk to your leaders and the children of Russia, to let them know how they feel, to get us talking to each
other. We are also going to Washington, D.C., to talk to President Reagan. We can't afford to wait."

He sipped his drink, nibbled a sweet, lit a cigarette, inhaled, then exhaled. I waited anxiously for his comment. Another long puff on the
Marlboro and he spoke. "Our children also are frightened. We are terrified of each other, your country and mine."

"We have bags and bags of messages from school children for your
president and ours," I rushed on. "Please give us visas. Help with Intourist." I felt an overpowering urgency, as if a clock was ticking a countdown to destruction.

A pause, a thoughtful look. "No one has ever before done such a thing
as you propose, taking kids to talk to presidents. You really believe such a
trip can make a difference?"

"Yes, I do. We adults must do everything we can to try to stop what could be the most horrible war the world has ever known."

The Consul General looked at me for a long moment, sighed, and then excused himself. "I'll only be gone a few moments. Please, coffee, cookies."

Sipping the strong beverage from delicate blue-and-white china, nervous, waiting, gazing at Comrade Lenin's beard, I wondered what Mr. Chikvaidze was doing. Half an hour passed then forty-five minutes. I wondered if I should ask the guard if he was coming back.

A few minutes later, a smiling Consul General Chikvaidze returned. "I was calling Moscow," he apologized. "Sometimes it's hard to get through, even for me."

Pulling his chair closer to mine, he continued. "What you are doing is a very important thing. Moscow thinks so, too." A big grin. "You will get your visas and without charge. That's my gift for your project." He sighed. "You need to let me know the makeup of your group right away, as I must now deal with Intourist. They can be very difficult. Red tape, you know." He grinned at his little joke.

My smile matched his. I was elated.

"Also, I will get an appointment for you with the Soviet Peace Committee."

That was the first I had heard of such an organization. Ushering me out, Mr. Chikvaidze said it was unusual to receive an okay from Moscow so quickly. "This is a first."

And then, standing in the entry hall, ready to open the iron gates, and under the hostile gaze of two Soviet guards, he hugged me. "God bless you," he said, "and that's coming from a communist!"

## II.

# DOING GOD'S WORK

The trip began to come together. We put ads in local newspapers to attract children for our journey. The generous volunteers, who had helped with the outdoor events, continued their assistance. Barbara Ross sorted the mail, answered the phones, wrote letters, and became a highly valued logistics expert.

The day Melba's press release went out, the phone rang and rang. Requests for interviews poured in. My divorce was still the "hook" because of a pending court action regarding my settlement. The story was always the same: my marital problems, money, uncomplimentary quotes from Herb Caen, and even the ancient history of my nonmarriage to Mel Belli. It was disturbing that my personal life was still considered "newsworthy" but it was a small price to pay to get this more important message into public awareness.

The media relished the idea of me, a "socialite," taking kids to Russia to talk to the "Reds." Sarcastic reports followed. Al was quoted as saying this was just another social fling, without merit, and wouldn't last. I knew that he was not alone in his feelings, just the only one to say them for attribution.

Al called, his breathing ragged. "If you think I'm going to let Sean take part in your crazy scheme, think again." He coughed.

"Are you sick?" I asked. My ex-husband had always enjoyed extraordinary good health, but I was told he hadn't been looking well lately.

He coughed again. "You're avoiding the subject. Sean is not to go on a wild goose chase with you."

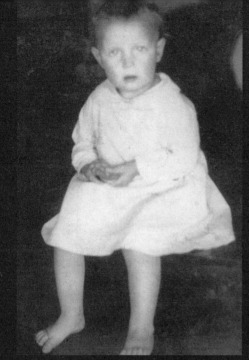

At age 2

Granddad Taylor and Grandmother Taylor.
Granddad carried his Bible wherever he went.

Mama and Daddy on their wedding day, 1909

I accidentally burned down the house I'm
posing next to when I was fifteen.

My marriage to Howard Groves in 1947. Howard's sister Edith and his friend Jack were attendants.

A week after our wedding, Howard and I had our picture taken.

Modeling a Dior suit dress for I. Magnin in 1962

My sweet fan club kids on the opening night of *Doctor Dolittle*, 1967

My friend Mary Lou Ward helps me with an Indian-themed party in 1965. She died in a mysterious fire in my apartment in 1969.

Mel Belli watches as I drink sake during our Shinto marriage ceremony.

With Mel Belli during our brief courtship and before an even briefer "marriage"

I'm smiling even though I knew my "marriage" to Mel Belli was virtually over before it began. Note the grains of rice in my hair.

Al and I on a President Line cruise to Hawaii, 1972

On safari with Al in Mozambique. I was two months pregnant with Sean.

Al and I make our entrance to opening night at the opera, 1974. I later sold that dress at my auction to benefit Children as Teachers of Peace.

I threw a surprise fiftieth birthday party for Al in one of his warehouses four months after we were married.

Clint Eastwood was a charming guest at our Sentimental Journey bash in 1971.

Gone with the Wind, indeed, 1979. Al as Rhett Butler and I'm, well, Patsy Lou.

My yellow sunshine living room at River Meadow Farm, 1978

The house-blessing ceremony, River Meadow Farm, in 1976 with Benny Goodman

I'm a happy and proud mom with my four-month-old baby Sean.

Our happy family, complete with our dog Ping-Pong. Sean was three.

Before Al bought a helicopter of his own, I gave him a Christmas gift of a helicopter tour of the San Francisco Bay with Sean and his grandson Trent.

Andy Warhol posed on my bed with me in 1982.

One of my legendary Roundtable Luncheons

Lounging on a sofa in the penthouse

A view of the penthouse living room. The eighteenth-century chandelier burned real candles.

View from the pool during the house blessing of River Meadow Farm

A happy couple, I thought, shortly before Al

Dede shows off her diamonds to Al.

Pope John Paul II blesses me and our peace trip, 1982.

Mother Teresa gives me a lesson in forgiveness at her Missionaries of Charity in Calcutta, India.

Prime Minister Indira Gandhi greets us and signs the Children's Declaration of Dependence, 1983.

A friend gave me this sack dress when I
announced my auction to benefit Children as
Teachers of Peace. I sold the furs in the picture
but not the sack.

Our second Children's International Peace Prize
Ceremony in San Francisco's City Hall Rotunda,
1984

An afternoon in the sun with James Borton, 1981

Sean, Jonathan, and Matt wear Arab bedouin headdresses while meeting with Madame Jehan Sadat at her home in Cairo, Egypt.

President Mikhail Gorbachev opens the International Women's Congress in 1987. Seated on the tier behind him, I sweat, knowing I will speak next.

Raisa Gorbacheva during the Gorbachevs' visit to San Francisco in 1990. We had tea together in spite of the "Friends of Raisa."

Katya Lycheva was a media magnet. Here we appear with Jane Pauley and Katya's translator Demitri Agratchev on the *Today* show, 1986.

President Ronald Reagan embraces Katya. Star is on the left. Although we had confirmed the appointment, the official press release said Reagan had accidentally run into the child while she was touring the White House.

Katya helps Star try out her ballet shoes while I smile encouragement.

My Enchanted Cottage

Sean visits me at the Enchanted Cottage, 1990.

The Banner of Hope

Nathaneal and I pose in Russian military coats we bought off the street in Moscow before going into hiding from the mafia.

I found the food donated by Americans for Russian children on a paratrooper base outside Moscow. My life was threatened by the Russian mafia and I had to go into hiding after discovering it.

Giving a hug to an Ethiopian child after presenting him with a new shirt

Sean and Daphne were married under a bower of sunflowers in 1999.

Visiting with Sean and my grandson, Owen, 2005

"He's with me this Christmas. It's my right to take him."

"I can get a court order forbidding you to take him out of the country," Al said, his voice hard-edged. The phone went dead.

Taking a slow breath, I tried to stay calm. I couldn't understand why Al continued to torment me. He knew that Sean's safety and well-being would always be my top concern. I wondered what his real motivations were—aside from trying to control me and undermine my work.

In a cluttered junk shop on McAlister Street I found a small Thai altar painted in vibrant reds and yellows. I imagined monks in saffron robes hitting the small brass gong that accompanied my find. The altar fit perfectly in a niche on the west wall of my bedroom. On it I placed a drawing of the face of Christ, a photograph of the Indian guru Sai Baba, an image of the Buddha, and a Menorah. My life became a meditation. I burned candles there twenty-four hours a day. I prayed for guidance. Every morning, I walked down the steep hills from where I lived, to pray at Saints Peter and Paul Church on Washington Square. I wasn't a Catholic, but I enjoyed the atmosphere of the church.

Three days later, Al called. His tone was flat. "We've decided you can have Sean for the holiday. But don't think this means I agree with your crazy plans. You won't get anywhere."

"Al, I might not get anywhere, but wherever I get will be better than where I've been."

"Pat, I give money to all the politicians. I can stop anything you try to do."

"Not in the Soviet Union. You have no clout there."

I wondered what kind of game Al was playing with me. It sure felt like harassment. At least, I thought, Sean would be with me.

This trip would be expensive. So far I had paid for everything, but with each phone call, the bills got bigger. I could not afford to do much more. We needed sponsors, as well as youngsters who felt strongly about the issue and wanted to go. Martha Lyddon, a member of the Dough-Nuts, a group of young adults with inherited money, said she would pay for two children and accompany them on the journey.

At first it seemed an impossible task to find kids with the passion for what we were doing and who wanted to go on such a focused trip. But, as word got out, I realized that I did not have to worry; the right kids would come together. I was correct. Friends told friends about our trip, my niece wanted to go and take her son. Soon six youngsters, along with Sean and a TV crew that wanted to go with us, were committed to the journey. We would meet as a group five days before departure.

A believer now, travel agent David Myers worked hard to get us inexpensive hotel rooms and cheap airfares, even convincing Pan American Airlines to donate two roundtrip tickets from San Francisco to Rome. But Aeroflot, the official Soviet airline, was the only way to fly from Rome to Moscow, and they were not about to give anything away.

Following David's suggested itinerary, we would have a thirty-minute first stop in Houston. From there we would fly to Washington, D.C., stay two days, then fly to New York and catch our flight for Rome. Two days in Italy and we'd be off to Moscow where we would arrive on New Year's Eve, 1982.

Sean said he hoped we would be seeing his Aunt Glendora in Houston. "Maybe she'll give me another chicken," he grinned. "A Rhode Island Red, as our mascot."

"Don't mention it, or she will."

"Mom, I've got a great idea, really. Let's go see the pope when we're in Rome." It surprised me that Sean had suggested we try to see the pope. I had just learned that Al had gotten an annulment from his first wife, Doris, the mother of his four adult children; and his second wife, Laurie, although she had died; and me. And he and Dede were remarried in the Catholic Church. Apparently even the Holy Catholic Church jumped to the tune Al's money played.

"If Dad annulled you, does that make me a bastard? " Sean had pretended to be joking.

"No, son, it's your father who's the bastard," I said.

My boy closed his eyes in a futile attempt to stop the moisture that was leaking out from under his lids. "What about Mike and Lad and Sue and Wendy? Did Dad annul them, too?"

I hugged my child. "You aren't annulled, Sean. Neither are the others. Your dad doesn't know what he's doing. He loves Mike and Lad and Sue and Wendy, but especially you. I know that for a fact."

"Really, Mom?"

"Really," I said, wondering how a father could do such a thing to his child.

But if he wanted to attend a Catholic Mass, I would try to make it happen.

"That is a great idea, Sean, but it might be too late to get tickets." Sean looked disappointed. "But we'll never know unless we try."

I called Father Miles Riley, a longtime friend, and asked for his help. He graciously wired a letter to Monsignor Tom Powers in the Vatican, appealing for seats for a general audience mass. The monsignor said yes. Tickets would be waiting for us at a convent near our hotel in Rome but we should not expect good seats. There would be thousands of people there. Most had planned their trip years in advance.

When I called Karna Small, President Reagan's appointee to the National Security Council and a longtime acquaintance from my television days, she said she would set up an appointment for us with the president. Everything was falling into place. In three days, we had our visas, adults to help care for the kids, a television crew, and seven children. We had the right mix, too; African-American and Caucasian kids, those who could pay their way, and those who could not. We would get together on December 19. And at my Christmas Roundtable celebration, I would introduce my peace group.

Meeting the children and their parents for the first time in my penthouse home, I was touched by their trust and belief in what we were trying to do. We sat on beige silk pillows in a circle on the living room floor, eager to get acquainted.

"You kids were selected for this trip by the universe," I said.

"Mom, that sounds hokey," Sean said, embarrassed.

"Hokey or not, that's the way I feel," I laughed. "Each one of you wants to make the world a safer place, that's what counts."

The youngest, eight-year-old Rachel Skiffer, an African-American girl, was soon nicknamed Nefertiti because of her long neck and clean jaw. Rachel was wearing overalls with her hair in ponytails on each side of her head. She had a huge smile and almond-shaped eyes fringed by super-thick lashes. She spoke in a barely audible whisper. "I just want to, um, well, grow up, you know, not have to think about nuclear war stuff. Someday I want to be a lawyer. But I'm kinda afraid, to go on this trip. What if the Russians won't let us out?"

"I don't think they would want us for long, Rachel." I tried to reassure her. "Somehow, I think we're protected, held in the hands of God. But, Rachel, if you don't learn to speak up, the Russians won't even know you're there. You've gotta let your light shine like a beacon, honey, never mumble. Be proud, stand up and shout."

Shifting on his pillow, restless, nine-year old Matthew Nolan was a Norman Rockwell picture of the typical American boy. Freckled, with blue eyes, his straw-colored hair on end, he said he thought it his duty to try to stop nuclear war. "If we don't do it, who will?"

Raquel Bennett, an articulate eleven-year-old, would be accompanied by her parents, Ralph and Shelly. She knew a lot about the Soviet Union and knew how we should talk to the "enemy." "They're people, just like everyone else. They'll listen to us. They don't want to die in a nuclear war, either." Her remarks, made in a strong voice and with a toss of long brown hair, got everyone's attention.

Jonathan Dearman, who was over my arbitrary age limit, was fifteen and tall enough to be thought of as an adult. He was so convincing in his argument that I allowed him to come along. African-American and a rock musician, he wanted to see what the "dark side of the forest" looked like and talk face-to-face with kids there. "If we just look at each other, see there aren't any differences between us, we can, well, have peace." Like a big brother, Jonathan was rubbing Matt's feet, which he had unceremoniously plunked in the older boy's lap.

My great-nephew, Patrick Morris, twelve, studious, showing a hint of a smile, was concerned nuclear war would happen soon unless people acted to stop it. "I want to be a teacher, not killed for no reason while I'm still a kid." He craved the opportunity to say that to the Soviets. His mom, Linda, would also be on the trip.

I was so glad to have Sean along. The trip wouldn't have been the same without him. With his cap pulled down so far he had to tilt his head back to see, Sean made a wise statement. "This year in the space program we have enough technology to send man into space, maybe even someday live out there. But, we're still building weapons that can destroy where we are now. Our leaders should be putting that money into helping the poor, not killing people."

Martha Lyddon, our Dough-Nut angel, was a fey cherub. Generous and willing to do whatever it took to make our journey successful, she was an instant hit.

Answering questions about our itinerary as best I could, I handed out a list of instructions. I was winging it all the way, learning on the job. "And," I said, "you are never to chew gum, except on airplanes." The vigorous chomping and popping sounds I had been hearing stopped at once. "Have you seen cows chew their cud?" I pretended to chew, slack-jawed, dumb. "I don't want you guys to look like that." They giggled when I passed around a wastebasket to collect their gum.

Each youngster was assigned to an adult who would be responsible for the child's safety, getting him or her to bed, bathed, dressed appropriately, and on time for appointments.

As would later become our routine, I chose a child, this time Rachel, to light a candle for peace. Then Dr. Krystal, who was at the meeting at my invitation, led us in a meditation, a visualization regarding what we hoped to accomplish on our journey. The children took to visualizations the way a thirsty plant absorbs water. The kids thought the pictures they "saw" in their minds' eye assured us success. That's when I decided that meditations and the lighting of candles would become an integral part of our trip.

On December 21, 1982, at my tenth holiday Roundtable luncheon, to which those who had attended the lunches throughout the year were invited, two hundred friends gathered. Among them were Danielle Steel and John Traina, Dr. Rollo May, Jessica Mitford, and Joan Baez. Laughter rang out as we greeted each other. Blue helium-filled balloons with the word Peace written on them decorated forty tables.

After I told my friends about our peace trip, Joan Baez got up from her table and sang a tender rendition of "Silent Night." I was touched by her thoughtfulness.

At the end of the party, our modest circle of crusaders gathered the balloons and released them from an outdoor balcony. Watching them bob into the cool air, play tag across the city skyline, catch updrafts, bounce off buildings, I identified with their unpredictable flight.

I, too, followed the pull of an uncharted course, inspired by a vision.

The volunteers had arranged a grand send-off for us on the morning of our departure. All the kids' parents were there, a choir sang, dancers performed, and Pan American Airlines personnel held up signs wishing us God Speed. The hullabaloo was fun and energizing.

In Washington D.C., I expected a message confirming our appointment with President Reagan, but it wasn't there even though Karna Small had told me it was a slam-dunk. Secretary of Defense Casper Weinberger had also written letters on our behalf, but nothing materialized. I was barely able to scare up an appointment with Mr. Wingate Lloyd, an official in charge of Egyptian affairs. He met with us in the unheated lobby of a government building. Still, we were not discouraged and the kids proved their dedication when they dumped two bags of mail for President Reagan on a State Department sofa. Uncomfortable, as we all were, Jonathan made the first remarks.

"We just hope, um, that President Reagan gets this mail and reads it, because he needs to, you know, know what the children are thinking. We're really scared and he has the power to make change. Besides, we're going on to Russia to see everyone else."

Scooping the missives back into a bag, Jonathan was adamant. "The kids who wrote these letters expect us to deliver them to the president, not leave them on a sofa."

"I promise to deliver the mail to President Reagan," Mr. Lloyd promised, flummoxed by our insistence on respect for the letter writers.

Disappointed about not being able to give the mail directly to the president, we went to the White House and tried to get a guard to deliver it, and we got our first taste of bureaucracy. The sentinel kept saying over and over that he could not accept anything, that it was not his job to do so. Which of course it wasn't.

Postal duties were forgotten, however, at the sound of Matthew's excited, high-pitched cry. "Hey, look guys, look," he was pointing to an upstairs window in the White House. "It's the president. He's waving."

They all ran to the fence, shielding their eyes, trying to penetrate opaque windows.

"Oh, my goodness, oh, my goodness, look, Pat, it's him. It's really him." Rachel was jumping up and down.

Laughing, I said they might be right, and told them to wave back. They kept waving until I told them it was time to go, that the president was probably tired of returning their greeting.

"Maybe we weren't supposed to be received by Reagan," I said during a sharing session that evening. "Think about it. Our meeting would probably have been construed as being endorsed by our politicians. The Soviets would then think we were representing the U.S. government, making chances of a breakthrough zilch." A rationalization perhaps, but one with a ring of truth.

After a moving visit to the Vietnam Memorial, which dampened even Sean's irrepressible humor, we flew to New York to make our connection for Rome. I was happily surprised that Melba's public relations efforts had paid off. Several reporters from major news agencies were waiting for us at JFK Airport. In our stumbling effort to answer questions from seasoned journalists, our vulnerability and naiveté were obvious. But so was our belief in what we were doing.

During the long flight to Rome, where we were to spend two nights before going on to Moscow, we continued to get to know one another. The kids opened up, showing wisdom beyond their years. They were concerned that even if people survived a nuclear war, they would be sick from radiation poisoning.

"Babies born today will be affected by what happens. It's not fair because they haven't had a chance to live, they'll be mutated," Matt said. "It will just destroy our future."

By the time we landed in Italy, we felt like a family. After checking into our hotel and getting settled (the older boys bunked two to a room, the younger kids shared a room with an adult), everyone came to my room for a meditation. The kids loved seeing the pictures in their inner vision, recognizing the power in doing so. We would visualize the way we wanted things to go, making it a fact in our minds and feeling it was true.

Later that night, alone, the responsibility of taking so many kids to the USSR hit me hard. What if something happened to even one child? What would I do? How could I cope? And what about the people behind the Iron Curtain? Could we trust them? Would we be kidnapped, used as a bargaining tool?

My palms were sweaty at the thought. I needed to meditate the way Sheila had taught me to do. Perhaps I would be given an insight to help me through the days ahead. Settling myself on the bed, I closed my eyes and began to relax with deep breaths. I became calm. Before long I was given a message:

Love is the motive.

Peace is the message.

Compassion is the emotion.

Hope is the outcome.

I was comforted.

En route to a nunnery the next morning to pick up our tickets for the Vatican Mass, my footsteps echoed hollowly on the ancient cobblestone streets of Rome. As I walked along, I thought about the "good Christians" in the towns of my youth and their attitude toward Catholics. There was only one Catholic family I could remember during all those years. They were referred to by almost everyone as "those ole Catholics" and we were not allowed to associate with them.

And now here I was knocking on the door of a Catholic cloister in the heart of Rome.

A smiling nun answered my knock. She spoke in English. "You've come to collect your tickets, right?" She explained that it was her job to dispense reserved tickets. After giving her the information she needed, the woman pulled a large square envelope from a file. The Papal seal was on the flap, my name on the front. "May I open it? To see where your seats are?" she asked. "Oh my," she smiled, "you have five front-row seats."

"That's wonderful, but there are twelve of us, plus a two-person television crew. I can't leave anyone out."

"Oh, all of you have seats, but the rest are several rows back. Put the children there, and you sit up front." I thanked her, having immediately decided the youngest would sit where they could see best, up front.

It was early Thursday morning, December 30, when we pulled away from the Spanish Steps aboard a pink-and-white American Express bus bound for St. Peter's Square. I gazed around at the ancient architecture, the grand fountain in the center of the square. Policemen in red-lined capes on horseback, a young woman playing Vivaldi on her violin, and the melodious peal of church bells calling all to worship echoed over a huge throng waiting to enter the audience hall.

After standing in front of a metal barrier for an hour, fearful of being crushed by an eager crowd, we were allowed to enter the hall. Immediately, I was swept up in the excitement and pageantry, awed by the joy and enthusiasm of the faithful.

Hundreds were singing the Ave Maria. French, Italian, English, Hindi, Spanish overlapped in a babble of languages, interspersed with "Hail Mary, Full of Grace. . . ." People waved flowers, statues of Mary, medallions. The smell of incense added a heady fragrance. Nuns, black habits defining them as brides of Jesus, flocked together chattering like birds on a glorious spring day, secure in the knowledge that there were no heathen cats in this congregation.

Seating the five youngest children in the front row, I made sure they were okay and aware of how special this occasion was. Matthew, Raquel, Patrick, and Sean were gawking, but Rachel was taking the pageantry in stride. "Oh well," she yawned, "I know the pope and he knows me, too." No one challenged her statement.

As the hall filled, solid gray barriers were locked in place along both sides of the aisle and small platforms were spaced along the route. We moved against the barrier next to the path Il Papa would tread. The singing grew ever louder, each group vying to outdo the other, having fun. Overpowering odes of joy filled the chamber.

Abruptly the room became quiet. Everyone turned toward the entrance. There Pope John Paul II appeared wearing white robes, a white cap on his silver hair. His face radiated light.

Pushing into the barrier, I watched as his measured steps took him on an unhurried journey toward the high altar. Periodically mounting the small platforms in the aisle, he turned to each side of the hall, waving, smiling, and giving those seated in the furthermost corner the opportunity to see him.

Shouts of Viva Il Papa, Viva Il Papa, accompanied his appearance. In his wake, an array of bishops, cardinals, and priests carried wicker baskets to collect gifts. Flowers, statues, books, teddy bears, and dolls soon filled basket after basket.

Standing on their seats, straining for a glimpse over the heads of others, many seemed in danger of falling on those of us standing below. When the pope paused to bless someone, hold a baby, touch a rosary, the roar from the crowd was deafening.

"Awesome man," Jonathan murmured. Squeezed next to me against the aisle boundary, we had a terrific view.

As the pope advanced closer, I somehow knew he would come to me. Walking toward us, waving to the crowd, Pope John Paul first reached out to Jonathan. Taking his hand, he covered it with both of his. "God bless you, my son." He placed his hand on Jonathan's head. Then he turned to me.

Taking both my hands in his, giving me his full attention, he said. "Where are you from?" His English was clear, his eyes green.

"The United States, San Francisco."

Reading the words on a pin I was wearing, his voice was soft. "Children as Teachers of Peace, beautiful, that's very beautiful." He looked directly into my eyes, as if we were alone. "Why are you in Rome?"

"I'm taking a group of children to Moscow to talk to the Soviets about peace. Our kids are so scared there will be a nuclear war, we've got to try to stop it."

"You are doing God's work," he said, and then, making the sign of the cross on my forehead, he repeated his pronouncement. "You are doing God's work." My eyes grew misty.

As he began to move away, I reached out and tugged his sleeve. "Please go to the children, they're in the front row." He smiled and continued on his way to the high altar and his gilded chair. I was disappointed. But after the long service in several languages, Pope John Paul walked slowly down the marble steps from his throne, waving to the right and then to the left as shouts of "Holy Father pray for us" filled the hall. And then, just when I thought he was leaving, he went to the children and, taking his time, blessed each one.

# PART TWO

# STUMBLING TOWARD REDEMPTION

# 12.

# THE EVIL EMPIRE

We were nervous but excited when we boarded Aeroflot, the Soviet airliner, for Moscow. We had heard horrific stories about the Evil Empire, midnight searches and bugged rooms. We had also heard scary anecdotes about the Soviet airline, which were proving to be true. As we took off, the blue-and-white plane shook as if it would fall apart. Bundles and suitcases, stowed wherever they would fit, tumbled into the aisle as the police-like flight attendants scowled. When Sean asked for a Coke, I thought he might be thrown off the plane.

"Nyet, nyet!" The flight attendant acted as if the request was for cocaine. "No Coca-Cola. Nyet."

It was New Year's Eve by the time we landed at Sheremetievo Airport. We were in Moscow, the home of our avowed enemy, five years before the advent of President Gorbachev and perestroika, armed only with tourist visas. As Jonathan said, "we're now in the dark side of the forest."

"Listen, all of you, stay close to me," I implored, feeling the enormity of caring for so many kids. But I did not need to warn them. They clung to me as if I were the old lady in *The Nutcracker* ballet.

I had expected a hassle going through customs and passport control, and I was not disappointed. Hours after our arrival, we were finally allowed to collect our luggage, but were told to leave our reading material behind, even the kids' comic books. Finding the guide assigned by Intourist was also daunting, but we finally found him and boarded a bus for the Soviet capital.

Our guide, a tall, trim, handsome man with a fur hat instead of hair, seemed indifferent. He curled his full lips in contempt when we told him why we were there, and recited facts about Moscow with all the enthusiasm of a funeral director talking to a family contemplating the cheapest casket.

My attempt at introductions was cut short. "I'm Pat, this is Rachel, Sean, and . . ."

"I know your names."

"Well, we don't know yours."

"You won't be able to pronounce it, so why should you know?" Brightening a bit when Robert Weiner gave him a Marlboro, he said, "Call me Val."

As our bus groaned along the highway into Moscow, we peered into the dimness. It was only three o'clock in the afternoon, but the gloom made it seem like evening. In the Soviet capital, the winter light begins to fail at noon, Val grudgingly told us. There was no traffic except for caravans of military vehicles. There were no light standards along the road and certainly no billboards.

The gloomy feeling persisted as we entered the city. "I don't like it here. Why is it so dark?" Rachel complained.

"They don't have any neon signs, dummy, that's why," Matthew replied. He was right. In our ad-saturated culture, we had learned to expect blinking cola signs and in San Francisco giant depictions of topless dancers lit up Broadway.

As we were driven across the city, we saw long lines of women standing in ankle-deep snow, holding string bags, waiting. When we asked why there were lines at every shop and kiosk, Val shrugged. "They're waiting because they saw a line."

"That doesn't make sense, man," Jonathan said, "They look like they're freezing."

"Yeah, there are lots of old people, too. They look like my grandma," Rachel chimed in.

"That can't be true. They're white and you're black," Raquel Bennett spoke with authority.

"Well, some of them do too look like my grandma." Rachel had the last word.

"Well, man, if you were Soviet, you would know why there are lines, man," our leader Val said sarcastically.

The kids giggled, whispering to each other, "Man, man, man," until I told them to stop.

Later we learned that because of severe shortages of almost everything, whenever shoppers saw a line they would join it, hoping that something they needed would still be available by the time they got to the front. The string bags, we learned, were called "perhaps" bags; perhaps today we will find something we need. Standing in line was a full-time job, and a necessary one just to keep the household alive. It was the mothers and grandmothers of Russia who took on this duty. We were told that men stood in lines only for tobacco and vodka.

The Cosmos Hotel, a monstrosity with curved hallways that made it hard to remember where your room was located, was in the midst of a New Year's Eve celebration. Decorations of what we considered Christmas ornaments, as well as fir trees, dotted the lobby. On our floor of the hotel, a rotund woman (the "floor lady") sat at a battered desk guarding the dark hallway. With gold teeth flashing and a frown on her face, she indicated through gestures that we were to leave our keys with her whenever we left our rooms. In return, we would get a piece of paper, which could be redeemed for our keys.

Our jaded guide added to our knowledge of hotel protocol in the USSR. "If you lose that paper you will have to wait hours to get into your room. Better not lose it," he said. "Well, good night. I'll see you tomorrow for your appointment with the Soviet Peace Committee."

"Before you go," Shelly said, "tell us where we can eat dinner."

"This is New Year's Eve, all the tables are taken," Val said.

"You can't do that to us!" Shelly was adamant. "We paid for all our meals as well as our rooms and transportation. We're hungry and we expect to be served a decent meal, New Year's or not."

Reluctantly, Val escorted us to a large dining room where the light fixtures hung so low we bumped our heads against them every time we stood up. The place was filled with noisy revelers celebrating the New Year, 1983. Confetti and red paper hats decorated the tables. After filling out the paper work for our meal, Val left. Forty minutes later, a surly waiter finally arrived with plates of boiled chicken.

"I don't like this food," Rachel whined as she tried to eat a piece of pasty-looking chicken. The others chimed in with the same complaint.

"Yeah, Mom, this tough ole' bird must have lived a hard life." Sean's contribution to our dinner conversation got a laugh.

"Okay, if you guys want to be ugly Americans, go right ahead," I said, wishing for a piece of Kentucky Fried myself. "Otherwise, eat and keep quiet about it. We're on a peace mission, not a gourmet food tour." They ate. So did I.

"Remember to drink lots of water," I said at the end of our sorry repast. "We need to stay hydrated in this cold weather." Setting an example I lifted my glass and took a big sip of what I thought was water. "Don't drink the water!" I sputtered, "It's vodka!"

Too late, Sean, Matt, and Jonathan had already sampled the alcohol. Reaching across the table I dumped what was left of their beverages into a bowl. "Come on guys, let's get to bed," I said, "and no more drinks of unknown content." The kids were giddy as they led the way to the cranky elevators. "Lordy," I whispered to Shelly, "I'll be accused of letting kids drink alcohol."

"They didn't drink much," my stalwart friend reassured me, "they're just pretending to be drunk. Anyway, vodka looks like water. How could we possibly know that the waiter would serve liquor to children?"

I said good night to everyone and after they calmed down I reminded them of our morning meeting with the Soviet Peace Committee. "We want to be alert for our first official appointment. So, sleep tight," I said.

In my room, with Sean already asleep in the other bed, I had started to drift off when there was a knock on the door. Now what? I thought, as it had taken some doing to get everyone settled. I pulled the door open and was confronted by a stranger, a very large stranger.

"My name is Joseph Golden," he whispered, pointing to the dozing floor lady. "Must talk to you. Special human rights agents told me you were here." Joseph Golden fit the description "a bear of a man." Overweight, medium height, with a round, rough-hewn face, thick dark eyebrows, wearing a black coat and fur hat, he was the stereotypical Russian.

"Is important we talk," he repeated, his voice low. "Your trip to USSR is break for all Russians. So, you have meeting with Soviet Peace Committee. Is very important I speak with you. Yuri Zhukov, President of Peace Committee, hard-liner, has power, can get you in Kremlin."

Without further ado, Joseph propelled himself into my room. And then, a finger at his lips, he turned on the ancient television set, static issued forth. "You are watched. Bugs everywhere." He pointed at the light fixture overhead. "Must cover words with static," he whispered.

Glancing into the bedroom I noted that Sean was still snoozing away.

Without bothering to take off his coat, the man proceeded with a preprogrammed monologue. "So, Russians respect force, Pat. So, must be forceful. Is very important." Fascinated by the man's intensity, I stared at him.

"Who are you? How do you know my name? Who are these special human rights agents?" If I were a smoker, this would be the time to light up.

The small sitting room was dim, sinister. Green horsehair furniture cast elongated shadows against the gray walls.

"Pat," Joseph lit up a gross-smelling cigarette, "is no problem who am I. Problem is tomorrow. Tell Soviet Peace Committee that our own Mr. Andropov has said is time to stop slogans and get to work. Insist going to Kremlin. Get foreign newspapers to cover visit. Is very important, Soviet people and world know you are here, that you allowed to be in country that refuses to let own citizens travel." Joseph appeared to be pacing while sitting perfectly still.

"Must go now, might be arrested. Put in mental hospital. So Pat, is necessary you act as I have said." Departing, trailed by cigarette smoke, he walked away in the opposite direction from our still-sleeping floor lady guard. Was he a crazy person, I wondered? Instinctively, I felt that he could be trusted.

The next day we went to meet the Soviet Peace Committee which was located in a four-story cement building on Mir Prospekt. A large coat-check room, where we were asked to also leave our snow boots, dominated the first floor. A young girl, attempting to speak English, took us up a curving stairway to the second floor and then into a large room.

Tables, with red upholstered chairs arranged in a U-shape, were decorated with microphones and bottles of a fermented drink called Kvas.

Eight people were seated there: six adults and two young girls. A Mr. Kudnetsov greeted us with a warm smile, shaking our hands. Seated at the top of the U, we were told how to use the simultaneous translation equipment at each place.

The Committee was especially curious about who had paid for our travel. When I told them we had paid for ourselves, they were confused. "You paid for yourselves? Did we understand correctly?" I assured them we had indeed paid our own way and initiated this trip ourselves. They had trouble comprehending such an action, referring to it time and again.

After several lengthy speeches, it was our turn. I told the children to think about what they wanted to say, but I did not tell them what to say.

Joseph Golden had said the Soviet Peace Committee was an important arm of the government. If they wanted something done, it could be accomplished. With that in mind, I quoted my night visitor as if his words were my own.

"Your own Mr. Andropov has said it's time to stop slogans and get to work," I said. Although I was nervous, I tried not to let it show. "We are here as private citizens because our children in the United States are extremely fearful that there will be a nuclear war between our countries. We want to tell General Secretary Andropov, in person, how we feel, and get a commitment from him not to deploy nuclear weapons."

"But, that's not possible. You see, Mr. Andropov is in Prague," Mr. Kudnetsov said. While still smiling, obviously he had not expected such a request.

"We'll go to Prague," I responded.

The six people in the cold building on Mir Prospeckt maintained pleasant expressions, but seemed taken aback by my declaration. They leaned toward each other, whispering. I heard the name Yuri Zhukov, the man Joseph Golden had told me about.

"You can't go to Prague," Mr. Kudnetsov said, "but we will see what we can do to help in your most noble efforts toward peace."

"We have bags of mail from American school children for

Mr. Andropov," I said, as Jonathan, Raquel, and Sean emptied bag after bag of letters onto the tables. Messages, drawings, and small gifts tumbled out, spilling onto the floor. Surrounded by mail, the children spoke up, one by one, as I called on them.

"Well, you know, we're not just mail carriers," Jonathan said. "Hey, man, we're afraid we won't have a future because of how we hate each other. You know, the Soviet Union and the United States. I don't see any reason for it."

"I agree with you," Mr. Kudnetsov replied.

"Yeah," Sean spoke up. "We promised a bunch of kids we would deliver this mail to people who can stop a nuclear war. We've already delivered mail to President Reagan."

Raquel had a way of summing everything up. "We think if everyone would just get together and talk about peace, well, we could have it. It's that simple."

Matthew, his hair uncombed, his blue eyes sleepy, had something to say. "You know we've come all this way because we want to live, you know, like we don't want to be afraid all the time. I'll bet your kids feel the same way."

"And peace to the animals, too," Rachel said. "Sometimes I worry about dogs and cats being beaten and stuff like that. I saw a man hit a dog with a stick once. That's not peaceful."

Rachel's love for animals and her wish to include them in our plea for peace was endearing. But would the Soviets think we were ridiculous? A quick look was exchanged between members of our group. Was Rachel too far off target?

"Your name is Rachel? Yes, well, you are right. Cruelty often begins by the way we treat animals," Mr. Kudnetsov said, glancing at his comrades. He cleared his throat and went on. "We think what you are doing is very important. We, too, want to live in peace as do our children and grandchildren." The man seemed sincere. "You are good mail carriers." Once again he conferred with his colleagues. "We will see what we can do to get you an appointment in the Kremlin."

"Way to go, man." The kids were giving high-fives under the table.

Before leaving, we told our hosts we would like to sing our peace

song, "Children as Teachers of Peace." Since most of us had trouble carrying a tune, I had brought a shoe-box-size recorder and a tape of the San
Francisco Girl's Chorus singing a beautiful rendition of our theme.

Standing in front of our colorful banner, four hands, fingers touching,
wrapped in the flags of the USSR, USA, China, and Japan, smiling, ready
to impress our Soviet hosts, I turned on the recorder. We began to sing
along with the tape. But something was wrong. The recording was out of
whack, sped up, going faster and faster. The Girls' Chorus sounded like
Alvin and the Chipmunks. The kids began laughing, holding their sides,
giggling, all but rolling on the floor, as the maverick tape continued to
play. Our communist friends joined us in laughter, sealing our friendship.

Trudging through deep snow from our bus to the warmth of the hotel
lobby, we were startled when a man wearing a fur hat called out to us.

"Where have you been? We need you now, right now." It was a man
from the Peace Committee. Extremely nervous, smoking the inevitable
cigarette, sweat ran from under his hat down his face.

"My name is Valrey Zhikharev from Peace Committee. We must have
names of everyone, passport numbers, ages. This has never happened before. Hurry please. Tomorrow morning at ten o'clock you are being received in Kremlin!"

"The Kremlin?" I wasn't sure I had heard correctly.

"Yes, the Kremlin, now hurry."

The kids yelled. Joyous, we hugged each other.

"I thought you already knew all about us. I thought you had our fin-
gerprints by now," I laughed.

"You Americans," Valrey said. "You think there's a spy behind every
birch tree."

At nine the next morning, we gathered in an excited knot to board the
bus taking us to the Kremlin. As Joseph Golden had told me, the Soviet
Peace Committee, although not an official part of the government, obviously had strong ties. Being received in the Kremlin was like being ushered into the White House. Kremlin: I kept turning the word over in my
mind. We were going to the Kremlin, which housed the highest execu-
tive body of power in the Union of Soviet Socialist Republics.

Soon we were being driven through snow-blanketed Moscow to the red-brick-walled Kremlin. Val was subdued. The day before he had made a rude sound and laughed at us for thinking we would get inside the Kremlin.

Now, Val recited facts as if in a daze. When I asked him about a bizarre structure on Red Square that was a conglomeration of color, form, and texture, he said it was Saint Basil's, the Cathedral of the Intersession of the Virgin. "Ivan the Terrible had the architect blinded after the cathedral was built so it could never be duplicated," Val said.

We entered Kremlin grounds and our bus pulled up to a stately old building, our destination, Val said. Once inside we were led down a wide corridor toward the office of Vitaly Petrovich Ruben, Chairman of the Union of Nationalities. Luxurious red carpet bordered in green, spread like the red menace we had heard so much about, up the stairs and over all the floors. Several doors down the long hall, past rows of glass display cases, stood a group of men apparently waiting for us.

Bathed in the glow of television lights, startled by camera flashes, we realized we had become news in Moscow. Skeptical Val was stupefied. I asked if he was the same person who told us we were crazy to think we would ever be received in the Kremlin. He could only nod his head and mutter, "I don't believe it." His hands were shaking. I felt shaky myself, although I did not feel awe. No, I felt right. This was exactly where we were supposed to be.

We were greeted by a receiving line of men, one of whom was Yuri Zhukov. We were made to feel welcome in what Ruben said was his office study. Paneled in mahogany, it featured a long table where red Kremlin-shaped plastic boxes filled with candies rested in front of each chair. Huge windows looking out over the grounds, a sofa, a large desk, and a grandfather clock completed the room.

Sean sidled up to me, "Way to go, Mom." I winked at him.

"Look, Pat, look." Rachel pointed to the gifts and candies.

"Shush, Rachel. We have to be on our best behavior." I hugged her to give myself courage. All the others were silent, wide-eyed, drinking in the scene.

"Please sit. Anywhere you wish." Ruben indicated the table as a translator made rapid notes of our conversation.

The highly polished, twenty-foot-long mahogany table where we were seated was impressive, as were the chandeliers and the lush red carpet. I glanced at the children. They were trying not to squirm. "Think about why we are here and what you really want to say," I had told the kids, "but remember, whatever you say is the right thing to say."

God, I prayed, let us create a breakthrough. For the most part, the children listened intently to the silver-haired orator, Chairman Ruben, whose words were being translated to us with such robot-like clarity they did not seem to belong to the dark-suited man whose arms cut the air as he talked. He wore silver-rimmed tinted glasses, his face was florid, his voice filled with emotion and fire though his hands shook.

A melodious chime rang from the grandfather clock. How appropriate, I thought. We haven't much time before we blow each other to pieces. I looked past the clock, the reporters, and camera crews, to the large window framing a Christmas-card view of snow falling on golden onion domes. The full impact of where we were and the meaning of the vision that led us here struck me afresh. Even the ubiquitous portrait of Lenin, staring down at us, could not shake my composure.

We fourteen were the first American peace group ever to be officially received within the Supreme Soviet. We carried with us the multicolored nylon bags spelling out P-E-A-C-E, each heavy with thousands of letters from children in the United States. We were good mail carriers, as Jonathan had said, but we were also ambassadors, and when it was their turn, I knew the kids would speak up with intelligence, innocence, and truth.

Robert and Eli, our two-man television crew, were taping the proceedings, although the day before they had been rudely denied access even to tourist areas. At the far end of the table the other adults sat taking it all in.

"Comrade Yuri Petrovich Andropov has requested I tell you how important your mission is to us," the interpreter relayed the words of the chairman. "In fact, Comrade Andropov would have received you personally if he were not in Prague," he continued, "because we in the USSR consider your noble actions for peace extremely vital to the future of our country and to the future of the world."

He then launched into an hour-long monologue peppered with anti-American propaganda and charts showing the number of American missiles aimed at the USSR.

Finally, it was our turn. Remaining seated, I seized the moment. My television experience stood me in good stead.

"While you were speaking, I heard the chime of a clock. I think that's appropriate because time is running out for both our countries. We have precious little time left in which to work before we blow each other to bits, so please remember that, whenever you see a clock." I paused and waited for the translator to catch up.

"These children represent thousands of others like your children and grandchildren, who want to grow up in peace. The Soviet Union and the United States hold the key for stopping the threat of nuclear war. We hope to create a ripple of change in the Cold War mentality. Please listen to these brave children and act on their behalf," I said.

"Rachel, what would you like to say to Chairman Ruben?"

Wearing a red dress with a frilly white collar, her eyes huge, Rachel stood up and held out her own chart, a drawing of the Soviet flag on half of the paper and the United States flag on the other. She had selected it from a mailbag. Clearing her throat, she read the caption: "Dear Mr. Andropov and Mr. Reagan, Kiss and make up."

There was silence. I wondered if we had lost our point, but the translation caught up with the reading, evoking laughter throughout the room.

"You tell Mr. Reagan that Mr. Andropov is ready to do that," Chairman Ruben said, shaking his finger at Rachel, smiling with pleasure, "and that he should also get ready."

As the others spoke, they each conveyed innocent sincerity and their deep conviction, that we, Soviets and Americans, had to talk to each other. "Especially the children," said Sean, "because we are the leaders of tomorrow."

"Chairman Ruben," I had an idea, "we want to see an exchange of children (dettya, the Russian word for children I had just learned) between our two countries. We do not want this visit by these children to be the anomaly it now is." I paused for interpretation. "We have come

here to build a bridge, to be a pipeline, between the Soviet Union and the
United States. We come in innocence without a hidden agenda."

Ruben smiled and nodded, but looked in the direction of Yuri
Zhukov, an abrupt, dour man who, Joseph Golden had told me, was a
hard-liner within the hierarchy of the communist system. His ill-fitting
gray suit stretched over a big belly. Over six-feet-seven, he was obviously
monitoring this meeting.

Raquel spoke up, "May I say something?"

"Da, da," said Ruben.

"We've been to the Pioneer Palace (a government recreation center
for children) where your kids meet for activities here in Moscow, and I
made friends with a girl named Natasha. She's my own age, and like me,
she doesn't want a war or stuff like that. Soviet kids aren't any different
from us, so please let your kids come to see us so we can all be friends,"
she pleaded.

Yuri Zhukov nodded to Chairman Ruben, apparently giving him a
green light, "We will put your request to Mr. Andropov and give it the
most serious thought. I have grandchildren your age and I want them to
live to see, I don't know, a thousand sunrises. We have a children's group
in the Crimea, and we invite you to be our guest there."

Was this the breakthrough we had been hoping for?

"If we may, Chairman Ruben," I said, "Jonathan would like to light a
candle for peace. We carry them with us for this purpose." This was a
routine we had established at our first meeting.

"I will be grateful to you. It is noble to cast light into the world."

Jonathan placed a white votive candle in an ashtray, which had been
quickly provided. "I'm lighting this candle to unite the leaders and adults
of our countries, hoping they can see with our eyes. The children are already united." Jonathan's innate dignity gave his message serious weight.

The Soviets looked at the candle flame, at the children, each other,
and then at me. "Speciba. Thank you for coming," Chairman Ruben
said. "Your visit gives us hope." Standing, we reached out to form a circle.
We began to sing, "We Shall Overcome," substituting the words, "We
shall live in peace someday." To our surprise, the Soviets joined in, humming the melody, recognizing the tune.

The hard-line bureaucrat, Yuri Zhukov, did not sing. He did take the small hand of an American girl (though somewhat reluctantly) as we sang out, without our errant tape machine, in that room deep within the Kremlin: "Oh, deep in my heart, I do believe, we shall live in peace, someday."

Outside, in the bitter cold of a Russian winter, the blasts of frigid wind awakened me from the control into which I had willed myself. I experienced a sense of elation and freedom as if a burden had been lifted. We had achieved what we had set out to do and in the doing of it, I sensed we had set a process in motion that would continue to unfold.

Just across the threshold of the building, still on Kremlin territory, we yelled, "We did it . . . we did it!" Our words echoed across the frozen ground, circling the golden onion domes, attracting the attention of guards. They stood watching us, not knowing what to do when we began throwing snowballs at each other and at Val. We were acting like crazy people.

And then half laughing, half crying, we came together within the walls of the Kremlin, under the Soviet flag, and near an enormous mural of Lenin, we howled with joy.

We had lit a candle for peace in the Supreme Soviet. We had talked about the similarities between our children and theirs. We had asked for an end to the Cold War and an exchange of children. We had done all the things we had set out to do only a few days before.

As we stood there, under the perplexed gaze of Russian soldiers, not feeling the cold, for a brief moment even Val allowed a flicker of emotion to cross his face as we included him in our warm embrace.

## 13.

# AND A LITTLE CHILD
# SHALL LEAD THEM

During the long trip back to San Francisco, we were elated, laughing, happy to be going home. The Pan Am flight from Rome was virtually empty. No longer concerned about meetings and grooming, the kids chewed gum, relaxed. The flight crew had seen television reports about our Kremlin visit and wanted to know how we had done it.

"We vibed it through," Jonathan said, laughing.

Our television twosome set up a battery-powered viewer so we could see pictures of ourselves with the pope and our reception in the Kremlin. The kids spilled across the seats laughing and teasing. It was great to have documentation of our pilgrimage. Otherwise, I wondered if people would believe us. We could hardly believe it ourselves.

Jonathan, his pal Matthew asleep on the seat beside him, had a question.

"Hey, Pat, what's next?"

"There is no 'next,' Jonathan." My next was yet another exhausting court battle. Al was saying that we had consumed all our community property and that I wasn't entitled to any money at all. I had to fight for what was mine.

"Mom, there's gotta be a next." As usual, Sean was wearing his tweed cap with the brim pulled low over his eyes, not chewing gum because of his braces, but playing an electronic game that was driving me nuts with its incessant beeps. "We've just started."

"Well, if we are really, really 'Peace Children,' we have to keep working at it. Isn't that right, Pat?" Rachel's hair stuck out every which way, her supply of pretty ribbons lost somewhere in Moscow.

Raquel scowled, puffing out chubby cheeks. "I don't like it when people call us 'peaceniks.' We're peacemakers, not peaceniks." Her mom, Shelly, a great help in keeping order in our ranks, nodded agreement.

"Yeah," Sean concurred. "I don't understand, you know, how people who believe the Bible can put us down. Doesn't it say, 'Blessed are the Peacemakers?' "

"For they shall be called the children of God," Rachel said with an expression of triumph.

"And a little child shall lead them," Patrick supplied. "Except we're youths, right Aunt Pat?" The older kids did not like being called children.

"If we should continue, what do you think about having some kind of peace contest for kids?" I asked.

"Awesome!" they said in unison. Thrilled to have played an acknowledged role in international relations, they did not want to stop.

"Well, I think it should be a contest, you know, like having kids say why peace is important to them," Rachel said, while she was drawing. She had sketched a circle of the earth and was coloring the Soviet Union red, the United States green. "Maybe the winners can go on the next trip, and . . ." she made sure she had my attention, "and I can, too."

"Mom," Sean said, "I don't like the word 'contest,' that makes one person better than the others. I think we should give everyone a certificate or something."

"But shouldn't a kid who puts forth the best effort be acknowledged?" I asked. "How would you feel if you did the best drawing, but were lumped in with those who put no thought into their work?"

"Well, okay, but all of them should get a letter or something," Sean responded. It was unusual for Sean to change his mind. He was stubborn like his mom.

After a spirited discussion, we decided we would award seven California children a Peace Prize during a ceremony in June. To receive the honor, they would have to answer, in any art form, the question: If you were a world leader, how would you create peace? Details of how to proceed would be worked out the same way the trip had been: get volunteers involved, work hard, and let it happen. June 1, 1983 was a good date to aim for. We thought six months would give us plenty of time.

A sense of urgency became my companion, as if that clock in Chairman Ruben's office was lodged in my head. "Hurry, hurry," I kept hearing. "You haven't much time." This unmitigated desire to press forward was underscored a few days after our return from the Soviet capital. A letter from *Go*, a magazine for young girls, arrived. "Your actions on behalf of children have given many of us hope. We are interested in hearing about your plans for the future so we can inform our readers."

There had been numerous stories about our quest for peace in the national press. Teachers and students from across the country were contacting us wanting to know how they could become involved, making the Peace Prize idea all the more viable.

I was eager to get started, but could not do anything until major problems on the home front were resolved. Sean was back with his dad and I sorely missed him. Soon I would be back in court battling for my monetary future. Frustrated with my San Francisco lawyer, Charles Morgan, I asked one of his assistants, with whom I had become friendly, if she thought I should change lawyers. "That wouldn't be a bad idea," she said. I decided to take her advice.

The only divorce specialist I knew of was Marvin Mitchelson in Los Angles. The man had made headlines when he filed the first palimony case and his high-profile divorce cases were often in the news. I called his office, made an appointment for the following week, and sent him the relevant court documents to analyze. Raquel's mom Shelly, who had been on the trip to Moscow and had become a friend, said she would go to "Tinsel Town" with me.

Movie-star-like women glided about Marvin Mitchelson's office in impossibly high heels and tight clothing. After a nervous half-hour wait, Shelly and I were ushered into the celebrated attorney's office.

"This is so Sunset Boulevard," I whispered to my friend. Red velvet couches and gold satin pillows were scattered about the large room. An enormous mural of Botticelli's *Birth of Venus* was the perfect backdrop for the man sitting at the huge oak desk. Tanned, wearing a superbly tailored suit, a cigar in his mouth, Marvin Mitchelson did not rise to greet us. Indicating we were to be seated, he blew thin tendrils of smoke in the air and without fanfare proceeded to tell me how he could rescue my settlement.

His convincing words fell on receptive ears. I was persuaded he could reverse the ruling of San Francisco's Judge Klein. Like Morgan, Mitchelson also thought the anti-nuptial agreement was a fraud and would not stand up in the long run. After a discussion of the details and strategy, I agreed to let him handle my case. Before he could proceed, however, he said he would need fifty thousand dollars.

"I don't have that kind of money," I was shocked. "Can't I pay you later?"

No, I could not. He suggested I think it over and picked up the phone and made lunch reservations for my friend and me at Spago, the new "in" restaurant in Los Angeles. "I don't take many new clients, so let me know your decision soon," he said.

At Spago, we gawked at the movie stars: Joan Collins (petite, fragile, not at all like her *Dynasty* persona) and Clint Eastwood, who along with his wife Maggie had come to one of my parties in 1974. Mostly, however, we talked about Mitchelson and how I could come up with the money. Judge Klein had said during one of our hearings that I should get a television show and start over. Not such an easy thing to do at my age, or any age, for that matter. Besides, no one was asking Al to start over. I figured there had to be someone who cared about fairness. Motivated by the words of my lawyer's assistant, I borrowed money from family members so I could hire Mitchelson.

The famous attorney made a couple of flamboyant court appearances, put me in the hands of his young associate, and a financial consultant, Larry Biehl, and left before earning the money I had paid him. Eventually we began to work out a settlement of sorts. It was obvious that contrary to California law, I would not be awarded anything close to a fair split of our community property, even though I learned that during our marriage we had accumulated over $250 million in assets.

My San Francisco lawyer, Charles Morgan, back on the scene,

suggested I should not settle. "With a different judge you'll win," he said. But I did not want to continue the fight. I had begun to believe my own bad press and the negative attitudes of those I once thought of as friends. On a subconscious level, I felt I didn't deserve to be treated as an equal to my husband, who was regarded as a saint. Giving up the battle, I agreed to discuss a trust of two million dollars, small in view of the assets we had acquired, but large enough to make me feel comfortable (or so I thought at the time).

Al and I met with our lawyers in a room at the courthouse. The industrial paneling, austere chairs, and beat-up table lent the right atmosphere for the cold ending to our marriage. Al, in a tailored gray suit, crisp white shirt, and blue tie hid his eyes behind aviator-style sunglasses. He did not speak to me or look directly at me.

Larry Stoddard, Al's lawyer, sat beside him and across the table from Larry Biehl, the financial consultant Mitchelson said could handle the financial aspects of this painful ending.

"I'll agree to a two-million-dollar trust," Al said, "but only if Pat names Lad and Mike and Sue and Wendy as the Remaindermen."

"What are Remaindermen?" I asked.

"Remaindermen are the heirs to any money left in the trust," Larry said.

"In other words, if there's any money left when I die, they will inherit it?" I said.

"That's right," Al said.

"Sean should be named and no one else."

Al took his sunglasses off. His eyes were bloodshot. He leaned toward me. "Pat, I think you should at least name Sue and Wendy, too." His voice was soft. "I know how much you value women. The girls love you, too. How about it?"

I agreed. Sue, Wendy, and Sean would inherit the money when I died. Al's son, Mike, would be the trustee.

A week after signing the document, I learned through officials in the Bank of America trust department that the Remaindermen shared equally in my money and along with Al would determine how much I was to receive each month.

I called Charles Morgan. Nothing could be done about it, he said. I was angry at him because I felt that he didn't handle the matter properly. "You should have referred me to a divorce specialist at the beginning." He danced around the issue and tried to placate me. But I was still angry with him and with myself, too. I had been such a pushover.

At least Al had agreed to donate fifty thousand dollars a year for eight years to my peace efforts. He made it clear that he was certain my work with kids was a passing fancy and he did not think he'd have to pay more than once. While it seemed like a generous gesture to outsiders, I knew Al's real motivation. We were now a nonprofit organization and his donations were tax deductible.

I was also given the high-maintenance and heavily mortgaged penthouse, which I would have to sell when the divorce dust settled. Larry Biehl assured me I would have plenty of money. He showed me chart after chart of figures, saying he would get donations from his clients for my peace work—a promise that never materialized.

Was I only a figure to be mocked? Not only was I a target for Herb Caen but Armistead Maupin (author of a serialized quasi-soap opera called *Tales of the City* that had blazed a trail through popular culture—from a groundbreaking newspaper serial to a novel to a television event) had taken me on, savaging me week after week in the form of a character named Prue Giroux: There was even a rumor that the main character, named Mary Ann Singleton, was also based on me.

"People said the meanest things about Prue Giroux . . . She was a simple country girl from Grass Valley: a tractor salesman's daughter. They said her looks had gotten her everything. Her social aspirations—they said—were tainted by a kind of girlish desperation, which rendered her utterly impotent as a beautiful person . . . Furthermore, her husband, Reg Giroux, had always been the nice one. He was also the one with $40 million. It didn't matter, Prue had discovered, if your blood wasn't blue and your wealth was solid alimony. So what if you slipped up and pronounced Thais "Thayz" or applauded after the first movement, or held a black-tie function in mid-afternoon?"

"[When she had a column], it was important for the social lionesses to be nice to Prue . . . they invited her to lunch. Not to dinner usually, just lunch. When, for instance, Ann Getty threw her February soiree for Baryshnikov at Bali's. It wasn't really necessary to include Prue in the proceedings; the guests simply phoned her the juicy particulars the morning after."

Like hyenas circling wounded prey, I was fair game. Attacking me had become a blood sport. Caen, Maupin, KABL radio reporter Bill Moen (who at every break read from the routine declaration of expenses my lawyer had filed with the court: "Five hundred dollars a month for flowers! Sowee!") and all the others knew they had nothing to fear. They were free to entertain the public by treating me as if I had no worth except as fodder for titillated readers.

Friends told me I should sue for slander, but I was so numb and so tired of court and lawyers that I could not even entertain such a thought. It would have killed me to go through another libel suit. I called Dr. Krystal.

"Sheila," I said, "there must be something missing in me, some key ingredient. Why do I allow myself to be taken advantage of so often and not react with anger? I feel sad instead of angry."

"I think the pattern for the way we are is set when we are very young," Sheila said. "Think back, Pat. Perhaps your father set the pattern for your behavior. You said that he gave everything away and saw the good in everyone. You told me about that man who repaired your dad's car and then stole it. Your father said the man must have needed that car more than he did. Are you like that?"

"Yes," I said. "Glendora says I trust everyone just like our father did. But I would rather be that way than suspicious of people. That would be a horrible way to live."

"Your dad died young as a result of his beliefs. From what you've told me, he forgave his enemies. He never fought back. Could that be what you are doing?" she asked.

I realized that forgiveness was what I was taught in our Christian home. And even though I'm not particularly religious, that message must be ingrained in me.

The day after that session with Dr. Krystal, Al called. He wanted to see me that afternoon. He was so friendly and warm, it was almost as if he were asking for a date.

"Well, okay, I guess." I was so taken aback by his friendliness that I hardly knew what to say. "We can meet at the Washington Square Grill."

"No, that's too public. We need to go where we won't be noticed," he said.

"Why? We aren't exactly illicit lovers."

"Dede wouldn't like it," he volunteered. "Let's meet in Washington Square Park."

It was a beautiful sunny day so I walked to the park. Dressed in an outfit I knew Al liked, a blue skirt with a matching sweater, I sat on a bench waiting for him to arrive. Why did I care what he thought of my appearance? I asked myself. Could I possibly still love him?

I remembered how Al had once chastised me for wearing a lavender tweed skirt and pale violet panty hose to the school Sean had attended along with Dede's sons Todd and Trevor. "Bad taste! You are dressed in bad taste. Go home and change your clothes," his voice was a command. Standing nearby, Dede smiled while my ex-husband, but not yet her husband, laid down his fashion law to me.

No, I did not love him. I only loved the illusion of the man I had once thought he was. How could I have been so easily fooled? I berated myself for allowing Al to manulipate me so thoroughly and for not standing up to him.

"Hi," Al said as he snuck up on me.

He was wearing a white dress shirt open at the neck and khaki pants. Freshly shaven, his skin looked sallow and he had lost weight.

"Hi," I replied.

"You look good," he said, softly. At one time Al had thought of becoming a Jesuit priest and he enjoyed acting the part. His soothing voice was a musical instrument that he used while slipping a knife into my back.

I smoothed my skirt and said nothing.

Al reached for my hand, but I pulled away.

"Clifford told me you have a new car, a convertible," he said.

"What does that have to do with this meeting, Al?" I wanted to hit him.

"Well, I needed to see you. You know, away from lawyers." He seemed nervous.

"Why?"

"I love you," he said.

"Ha!" I replied, noticing that sweat had stained the underarms of his shirt. "I don't want your kind of love."

"I . . . lost perspective. You understand?"

"No, I do not understand." My voice was frosty.

"An innocent . . . flirtation . . . you know . . ." His glance swept the park. ". . . got in deeper . . ."

"Al, cut the crap!"

My once-upon-a-time husband stood up. He blew his nose. "I take Communion now . . . important Catholic . . ." He tried to smile. His voice trailed away.

"Al, who are you? You've become a person I never knew. You're acting crazy. What's wrong with you?"

"There's nothing wrong with me." Suddenly his face became the stone mask I had seen in court. He had reverted to his old conning self. "Patsy you will always belong to me. I'll bet you would fuck me right here on the grass if I wanted you to. Wouldn't mind getting your panties pulled off so all the little boys in the park could see."

"You're a pervert!" I tried to slap him, but he grabbed my hand, laughed, and kissed me. Before I could react further, he took off. A short-cut across the grass and he disappeared into the shadows by Saints Peter and Paul Church. A black limo with Clifford at the wheel pulled up. Clifford, a former Marine, idolized Al. Al got into the car. They drove away. Al was nuts; otherwise I couldn't imagine his motivation for subjecting me to such an astonishing attack.

I stood there numb, trying to understand what had happened. My stomach rumbled. I had to get to a bathroom. Dashing across the grass, I made it to the public facility just in time. I sat on the filthy floor and retched into the toilet. My bowels had also let go and I soiled myself. Finally, I crept to the sink, rinsed my mouth, and splashed water on my ashen face. I rinsed out my underwear and scrubbed at the stains on my skirt with paper towels as best I could. When I felt steady enough I climbed the steep hills and went home, my shoes squishing with every step.

My degrading encounter with Al had taken my energy as surely as if he had put a tube in my veins and drained my blood. I fell into a well of loneliness. My incentive to work on the proposed Children's Peace Prize evaporated. I was back at square one, catatonic.

Feeling dizzy one afternoon, I crawled into bed and fell asleep. Immediately a vibration and a tingling sensation shook me. It felt as if my soul was departing my body. I was on the ellipse of a golden funnel, which was dotted with black holes. "Time tunnels," a voice said. At the far end of the funnel was a circular image of the face of Christ. A drawing of that expression, emanating love, had graced our family homes throughout my childhood. It was totally familiar. A band of barbed wire surrounded the image of Jesus.

A message materialized across my inner landscape. "You have a choice to continue on or to return to earth." The pull forward was a magnet. I wanted to go on. Another communication came to me. "Sean needs you. Your work isn't finished. But you must hurry."

Reluctantly, I allowed transparent cords to pull me back to Earth. Enveloped in a supporting cocoon of light, the final message was reiterated. "You must hurry. You haven't much time." A ring of barbed wire was placed on my wrist.

The intense tingling began again and my soul re-entered my body. I awoke feeling sluggish and heavy, as if I had gained weight. The dream seemed so real, I checked to see if the circle of barbed wire was on my arm.

Picking up the phone to call my niece Linda, I was startled into full wakefulness when she answered before I dialed.

"Linda?" I stammered, "Is that you?"

"Pat, are you all right? I had a feeling you had died." She laughed. "I'm sorry. That was a stupid thing to say."

"God, Linda, something weird just happened to me."

When I told her about my death dream, we began to laugh. "Be glad you didn't see the devil," she said.

Was it possible that I had inherited my visions and dreams from my faher? I wondered. The dream and the message to hurry were engraved in my consciousness. But I pushed the image of the barbed wire into the recesses of my mind.

My work wasn't finished. I didn't have much time. A bit of adrenalin began to pump through my body. And then my depression lifted. I was motivated again and began to put plans for the Children's Peace Prize into action.

I sallied forth into the nonprofit world and CATP (Children as Teachers of Peace) soon received classification as a 501(c)(3) non-profit organization. Now all donations to our foundation would be tax deductible.

Soon press releases were sent out announcing a contest for California children, ages seven to ten, asking for their answer to the question: "If you were a world leader how would you create peace?" Seven partici-pants would be chosen from throughout the state. The judges would be the Moscow trip kids including Sean, who would be with me for two weeks by then.

Usually Sean still spent every other week with his Dad, Dede, and her two sons, Todd and Trevor, both of whom were near his age. I was keenly aware that Sean needed to respect his father, but there were times when I could not stop myself from lashing out, venting my frustration at the be-trayal that had cut so deeply, and Al's actions since our divorce.

I heard that Al was making suggestive phone calls to prominent women we both knew, even identifying himself to them. I continued to wonder about his mental health, especially after his strange actions in Washington Square Park.

In spite of Al's behavior, the intensity of my work allowed me to begin feeling good about myself again. It also enabled me to dissipate the disap-pointment I felt when I thought about Sean's choice to live with Al and Dede rather than me. Rarely did Sean allow me to glimpse his struggle to survive in his dad's household. One evening for supper, during one of his court-mandated weeks with me, I had cooked Sean's favorite fried chicken meal. We were sitting in the kitchen eating the crisp chicken when my twelve-year-old son opened up to me.

"Mom, I like sitting here and having you talk to me. They only talk to Todd and Trevor."

"What do you mean?" From past experience, I knew that if I seemed too interested in what Sean was saying he would shut down, so I acted as if I were paying more attention to my potatoes than his answer.

"Well . . ." he said, playing with his fork. "Well . . . at dinner Todd and Trevor sit next to Dad and Dede and I have empty chairs on either side of me. Like I'm different from them. I'm left out."

He had told me that once before. Oh, my poor baby, what could I do to help him? "Hasn't it changed, Sean? What does your dad say?"

"He's right there, Mom. I make jokes and pretend I don't notice."

"That's awful! Do they include you in their conversation?"

"Only if I, like, use the wrong fork or something, then Dede yells at me."

"That's plain mean! Your dad should not let you be treated that way. Does he say anything to Dede about it?"

"No, nothing," Sean replied. "Dad says Todd and Trevor are better and smarter than I am." He hung his head. "I guess he's right."

"That's outrageous!" I reached over and took his hand in both of mine. "You are very smart. Your teacher told me you have a college vocabulary."

"Dede says I'm spoiled and that I shouldn't have a nice room like Trevor and Todd until I learn not to . . . ," he reconsidered his words. "But I have a little room near the roof and Geri gave me a pretty chair to use."

Geri Crumpler, our cook, an African-American woman with a sweet face and a personality to match, had defected to the other camp. "Ms. Montandon, I've got to go look after Sean," she had said. "You know I've been with him since he was a baby."

"I'm glad Geri gave you a chair, but what is it you have to learn?"

Sean fidgeted. "Nothing, Mom, really. Nothing."

"You can tell me. I'm your mom."

"Well," his posture was rigid, "Well, Mom I . . ." He made a brave effort not to cry.

"I must be really bad. They say I should be sent away to reform school because I'm a fraud." His eyes were misty.

"That's ridiculous! You are not a fraud. You're a good person and smart, too. Your dad shouldn't allow such things to be said to you. I'm going to call him."

"No, Mom, no! If you do, I'll never forgive you. Dede loves me. She tells me so over and over and over. She's my best friend in the whole world and I love her, I really do. It's only when Dad's there that she yells at me." Tears ran down his face. "Dede loves me lots more than you do. She said so."

I was stunned by Sean's admission. "That's not true. You just told me she treats you like an outcast!"

"I knew I couldn't trust you!"

Pushing away from the table, my son ran sobbing up the stairs to his room.

"Sean, please come back and have dinner with me. I promise I won't call your father, okay? I promise." No matter how much I tried to protect Sean, he wouldn't let me.

He returned and tried to finish his dinner, but the tension between us was palpable. We were both relieved when it was bedtime.

Only the memory of the vision that led me to create a peace foundation kept me sane.

# 14.

# SELLING OUT

And then I met Star. It was the spring of 1983. One afternoon, as I was leaving the Celeste Ballet School after talking to the director about their participation in our Peace Prize Ceremony, a fragile little girl ran down the cracked sidewalk toward me.

"Will you give me a ride to Fisherman's Wharf?" she implored, wiping her nose on the sleeve of her green sweater.

"You shouldn't ask strangers for a ride," I said, startled that such a young child had approached me.

"Well, you're not a stranger. You're Pat Montandon," she said.

"How do you know who I am?" Fine blonde hair hung over her pale face. Her dress was too large for such a slender child and her socks were hanging down over worn shoes. She reminded me a little of myself at her age, when I might have had holes in my shoes and straggly locks.

"I know you because my ballet class is going to dance for your Peace Prize Ceremony." Green eyes looked up at me.

"You're one of the ballet dancers?"

"Yep, and I'm good, too, and I'm seven years old, and my name is Star," she announced all in one breath. "Starling Rowe."

"Well hello, Star. Why do you want to go to Fisherman's Wharf?"

"Because my mother, Mari Ellen, works there. She makes really beautiful earrings and pins and stuff out of feathers and sells them at Fisherman's Wharf."

Star was a stream-of-consciousness talker. "You work for peace and I know what peace is. It's a man who says he's your father not hitting you, and not putting his fist through the wall and pulling your mother's hair. That's what peace is."

Compassion welled up in me. "Okay, Starling Rowe, come on, I'll give you a ride to the Wharf."

Jumping into the car, she fastened the seat belt while continuing her monologue at a nonstop pace. "You know, Pat, Mari Ellen says peace is being kind to people who don't have a home, and not complaining if you're hungry, and . . ." My new friend pointed out aspects of peace I had not considered.

"I would like to meet your mom. Do you think that would be all right?"

"Sure! Mari Ellen is fun. We buy hamburgers together and on Saturday I get to help her sell stuff."

Double-parking on a street crowded with tourists, I held the child's hand and at a lull in traffic we sprinted across. I was led past card tables where vendors were selling everything from sketches of cable cars and the Golden Gate Bridge to belt buckles and the ubiquitous t-shirts. Each seller called out a greeting to the delicate Star.

It was easy to recognize Mari Ellen. Feathers of every color spilled across her table in a profusion of artistic interpretation.

"Mari Ellen!" Star yelled at the rounded woman wearing a floppy straw hat adorned with peacock feathers. Star's mother was a delight to behold. Her selection of a brilliant red-and-orange dress worn with black lace stockings and gold shoes made a definite fashion statement. She greeted her daughter with a hug, and plopped a plumed hat on Star's head.

"You're Pat Montandon," she said, all the while keeping an eye out for customers.

"How do you know who I am?" I asked.

"Because I read the papers and Star told me about the Peace Prize Ceremony."

"She gave me a ride," Star told her mom.

"That's good, Pat, because Star has to take four buses to get here and sometimes she's real late." I smelled alcohol on the woman's breath and immediately felt concern for little Star.

"You have a terrific little girl, Mari Ellen. We had quite a conversation driving over here."

"Yeah, she's smart and a good dancer, too. Someday she'll be a star in every way. That's why I named her Star."

"I have a friend named Angel," Star contributed. "Can I come see you sometime and bring her? You live in that penthouse up there, don't you?" she asked, pointing up to my building that from this vantage point dominated the skyline.

"Sure, if it's okay with your mom."

"Actually, Pat, it would help me out a lot," Mari Ellen, said. "We're having a little trouble right now making ends meet, and you know the tourist business is off . . ." Her voice trailed away on a vague note of melancholy.

Impulsively I made a proposal that to some could seem outrageous. But Star had touched my heart. It was obvious that she could use a bit of tender loving care.

"Would you let Star come stay with me for a while? Say, a month? She's good company and I could take her to school so she wouldn't have to ride so many buses."

"Oh, Mari Ellen, can I?" Star fidgeted in anticipation, the feathers in her improbable chapeau bouncing up and down.

"Sure you can. We know all about Pat. It isn't as if she's a stranger," Mari Ellen said. "I'm looking for a good place for us to live and this will give me a chance not to worry about her." Star's mom spied a customer and got busy trying to sell a pair of earrings. Later, I learned that Mari Ellen and Star had moved twenty times in less than two years.

It was that chance meeting that brought Starling Rowe into my life. At the tender age of seven she had already seen a side of life that would disillusion most, but she was cheerful, clear-sighted, and fun. Buying pretty clothes for her, getting her hair cut by a professional, and helping her with schoolwork was very satisfying for me. She was responsive to my care and thanked me for anything I did for her. I remembered back to my own childhood of being taken in by family friends when times were tough and only hoped that this would be a positive experience for Star.

Even Sean seemed to enjoy having her around. Star gave us back our sense of family that had been so brutally smashed. She was unspoiled and comfortable in any situation. I was astonished that a child raised in such difficult circumstances could possess so much dignity.

When her friend Angel visited, the two girls played dress-up, preening in front of a mirror wearing my old silk and velvet dresses and high heels, lipstick smeared on their tiny mouths, just as I had done as a little girl. It was great to hear the sounds of children's laughter—to cook—to care for a child again.

Two weeks after Melba's press release went out, Peace Prize entries came flooding in. It wasn't long before five thousand submissions were stacked in my library. It took four weekends for the Moscow trip kids to weed out the submissions. Putting the poems, essays, books, and drawings in piles, they categorized them by region and then by how convincing they were. After spirited discussion, the children chose winners from seven regions in California.

And in the midst of all this, we were also planning another trip. Two weeks after the awards ceremony we would leave for West Germany, East Berlin, and Israel. This journey, too, had been inspired by another of my nightmares.

In the dream the sky was overcast, threatening, heralding a cyclone, a huge storm. A young man, the wind and rain whipping his dark clothing, tried to find shelter. I warned him that there was danger, but he paid no attention. The man ran across a field laced with land mines. Panting, out of breath, he finally reached an opening in a cement wall. I screamed, "No, no, it's the Berlin Wall." The young man continued on. A rain of bullets pierced his skin. His blood seeped across the land, covered the wall, and threatened to drown me.

I awoke with my heart pounding. The next day, in the morning paper there was a story about a young man gunned down in East Berlin as he tried to escape across "No Man's Land" at the Berlin Wall. Dreams that seemed prophetic were extremely unsettling to me. I wished I could shut them off. But I knew I had to go to East Berlin.

Expenses were growing. We had bills for phones, stationery, telegrams, a salary for my assistant Barbara Ross, the award sculptures, the Peace Prize Ceremony. Working on a world scale was expensive and peace wasn't "social" enough to gain much support from my old crowd.

"Please, Pat, try something else—not peace," people would say. Or, "You're not becoming a 'Red' are you? Why don't you work for the Opera or the Symphony? They could use your energy and you wouldn't have any trouble getting donations."

Danielle Steel, a longtime friend, said she would donate when I did something for local kids, like those who were abused. "But, Danielle," I said, "the worst abuse possible is suffered by innocent victims of war." She was not impressed.

I began to realize that by working for peace I had to be prepared for ridicule. Few could understand the importance of what I was doing, or my all-consuming commitment to the world's children. But then, I no longer understood them or the social world I had so recently inhabited. Having gone from childhood poverty to making a good salary in television and becoming super-rich (I was often called "San Francisco's Golden Girl"), it was sometimes difficult to adjust to the new realities of my life.

When I read newspaper and magazine accounts about the doings of my ex and his wife, the focus was always on her jewelry: her emeralds, rubies, diamonds, necklaces, rings, and brooches filled column inches. A cartoon in *The New Yorker* popped into my head. Nine people in formal attire are seated at an elegant dining table set for ten. At the empty place, a plate overflows with jewelry. The caption reads: "Sylvia couldn't come but she sent her jewelry."

That caricature triggered a thought. My jewels were worth a lot of money and that's just what I needed. What a perfect solution: I would have an auction and sell it all. I might as well throw in my furs and designer clothes, too.

"I'm going to have a public sale of my couture gowns, furs, and jewelry to support CATP," I announced to my board on an afternoon in 1983. I could tell by their startled expressions that nobody thought this was a good idea.

"Your clothes?" Melba exclaimed. "Does that mean, Patsy, that you are now going to expose that lily white body of yours to the public?" She enjoyed teasing me.

"Seriously, Melba, I have some pretty expensive designer clothes. I have jewels. I have fur coats and jackets. We can make money from all this stuff."

My vague plan for an auction quickly took form and became the focus of attention in certain Bay Area circles. Most people thought I was crazy. On a radio call-in show, a woman screamed at me, "You had it all: social position, money, a beautiful home, jewels. How dare you give it up!" It bothered her that I was turning my back on her version of the American dream.

Fashion designer Richard Tam helped coordinate a professional, chic fashion show with my clothing. Even so, he was upset over what I was doing. "Glamour has always been Pat's entree to the world," he told people. "Now she'll be nothing."

Glamorous or not, everyone I asked was helpful, renewing my faith in friends. Professional models contributed their time, the Fairmont Hotel donated the Gold Ballroom for the evening event, and San Francisco's famed Walt Tolleson's orchestra agreed to play without charge. I also called in chips from the Napa Valley since it was my idea that had launched the very first Napa Valley Wine Auction. Everything was falling into place.

When reporters asked for interviews, I took full advantage of their interest to talk about the work we were doing and to tout the auction. Half-page photographs of me at past social events wearing the gowns that were to be auctioned appeared in newspapers and emerging plans kept columnists busy. However, some of my former acquaintances dropped me; I was no longer socially acceptable. "Pat's become a peacenik" was a refrain I heard several times. I did not mind at all. I knew that what I was doing was much more important than premieres and black-tie dinner parties.

"I'm having fun," I declared to Barbara Ross. My chic assistant's short blonde hair went well with her high energy level. "All those clothes and baubles don't mean anything to me now," I said.

"Okay, Lucy, just be sure." Barbara had dubbed me Lucy to her Ethel.

My sister Glendora called, pleading, "Patsy, don't you remember how poor we were as kids? How can you sell everything? Are you crazy? Have you lost your mind?"

"No one thought I was crazy when I bought these things. Besides, I'm not giving anything up, I'm just letting go." I hung up, dismayed by her attitude, and headed for my closet.

Inside my thirty-five-foot-long walk-in closet, the fragrance of Joy perfume permeating the air, I looked past the dresses, ball gowns, coats, sweaters, pants, rows of shoes, and handbags to a tall window at the far end of the space. The view was spectacular. In the city air-conditioned by God, the usual fog was spilling over the top of the Golden Gate Bridge, fingering into the bay, forming a halo over Alcatraz Island. Beyond the former prison site, I could see Angel Island and knew there would be sailboats and yachts anchored in the harbor that always seemed to have sunshine.

Star wanted to help my housekeeper, Cecelia Avila, and I sort through the clothing.

"Star," I said, "you can gather all the accessories like scarves and hats and handbags, and put them on the bed, okay?" She was happy to be able to help and to play dress-up at the same time.

"Cecilia," I said. "I'll need your help to catalogue everything."

"You're not really going to sell your jewels, are you?" Cecelia asked.

"Yes, those too. I can use the money for my work."

As we sorted through the clothes, designer labels flashed past: Yves St. Laurent, Christian Dior, Galanos, Halston, Oscar de la Renta, Bill Blass, Coco Chanel. I stopped at a gorgeous Valentino evening gown I had bought in France. The voluminous red silk-taffeta skirt, topped by a strapless bodice encrusted with hand-sewn ruby beads, was a knockout. I wore it only once, to a Christmas party. I felt a special affection for the Italian designer because of his graciousness when he came to a "Sentimental Journey" theme party Al and I had thrown. It was great fun. The music of Les Brown and his Band of Renown played while Ethel Kennedy, Clint Eastwood, and Valentino joined other guests in a lively conga line.

Valentino had selected this gown especially for me. Oh well, it's just a dress, I thought, putting it on the sell rack. It was time to move on.

Al and I had shopped together for most of this finery, on many of our whirlwind buying expeditions. Money had been no object then, and Al had enjoyed seeing me in expensive clothes, relishing the effect my attire had on others. I was a great arm piece, he had said.

By the time we finished, our inventory listed one hundred and twenty evening gowns, thirty suits, fifty dresses, two mink coats, a lynx coat, a sable coat, a Norwegian fox cape, and several fur jackets. Most were sizes eight and ten.

There is nothing intrinsically wrong with having expensive clothing, jewels, or furs, but it is the importance we attach to owning them that is wrong.

I was beginning to understand that there is a reason for everything. If we could look at our lives as we view a map, we could see the purpose for bridges, boulders, curves, and even the wrecks. We would say, "Oh, now I realize why that happened. It was to get me on this road where I belong, instead of staying stuck over there on that dead end." I was sure I had been given these clothes and jewels so I could do exactly what I was now doing with them.

I wanted to confront my bejeweled past alone, so I asked Cecilia to take Star and work downstairs. I opened the safe. Spread out before me on black velvet sat a glittering jumble of memories. Sparkling from a gray velvet box was a diamond-encircled, five-carat emerald ring Al had given to me after our marriage.

This was the ring my husband bought me after the death of my dearest friend Mary Lou Ward. Now, as I held the jeweled symbol of love, I wept. I wept for Mary Lou, for Sean, for myself, and especially for Al.

Each expensive bauble was painful to contemplate. I tried to work quickly, but was overwhelmed by memories. A magnificent snowflake pin of cabochon rubies, sapphires, and emeralds brought back memories of a giddy fifth wedding anniversary. We had bought three rings—a pavé diamond cluster, a ten-carat sapphire, and a lapis lazuli—in one fell swoop during a trip to Florence. Ruby bracelets from India, golden hoops from Greece, and Tiffany pearls interspersed with diamonds were all displayed before me. How dazzled I had become.

I wondered when I had allowed myself to become seduced by material possessions. And when had Al stopped holding hands with me, working in the garden with me, going on picnics? Looking back I realized there had been plenty of signs.

Our marriage had begun to change in the place I loved most and where I thought we were the happiest, at River Meadow Farm in the Napa Valley. The turning point had been at an al fresco lunch at Fred and Ann Lyon's vineyard. Charlie Crocker moved Al from his place next to me to sit next to Dede. "Your place is over here Al," he had said, smiling. This wasn't the first dig I'd felt, but it hit close to home. I knew for sure that I didn't fit in with this group. I was outspoken, I didn't play their social games, and I didn't pretend to have a Mummy and Daddy who had sent me to finishing school. They didn't like that a man as rich as Al was married to a woman who didn't care about climbing the ladder, a "shop girl" who had risen in the ranks all on her own. They wanted to keep Al's money in their upper-crust gene pool.

Al had laughed and told me I was acting like a jealous housewife when I complained about how I was treated, so I stifled my objections. But Al's lack of support hurt me more than the worst treatment by any of these people ever could.

In retrospect I realized that not long after that, my husband and I stopped talking to each other. We were polite, we made love, we were affectionate, but we did not talk to each other about our deepest feelings the way we once had. He didn't want to know what I thought.

Now the precious stones Al had given me, along with ropes of pearls, golden bangles, and even an emerald and diamond tiara I had worn to an opera opening, held no value for me. What they had once represented was as shattered as a glass house in a hurricane. Would I awaken from the excitement of the auction and be filled with remorse? My friends thought so. My sisters, Faye and Glendora, thought so, too. I had to look deep inside myself to find the answer.

I left my closet and went into my bedroom, locked the door, pulled the curtains to shut out the view, settled into the middle of my bed, and closed my eyes. It took a few minutes to calm myself, but soon I was able to relax into a meditative state.

An image of the gems I once saw in a museum in Istanbul, Turkey, flashed across my mind. Reflecting the exotic excesses of the Ottoman Empire, the cabochon emeralds, rubies, sapphires, and diamonds were weighed in pounds, not carats. They were heavily guarded and encased behind bulletproof glass. In spite of the legends surrounding these precious stones, I felt a stifling sense of mold and dust as I gazed at them. I recalled a cemetery we had passed on our way to the museum, the final resting place of the owner of the jewels. It was clear to me: we own nothing. Our actions, our integrity, and our compassion are all that matter.

There was no longer a single doubt in my mind that I had made the right decision. On a beautiful evening in May, one hundred twenty glamorous pieces of clothing were in the dressing room of the Fairmont Hotel's Gold Ballroom. My emeralds, rubies, pearls, and diamonds glittered in glass cases in a side room. Champagne was served to a hoard of people who arrived for the unusual event. Some were curious, some supportive, some were there to scoff, but most were there to get a bargain. My sisters looked as though I had died.

With Sean, Star, and Raquel beside me, I walked on stage wearing a simple, Grecian-style ivory dress with gardenias in my hair and no jewelry.

"I've enjoyed wearing the beautiful clothes and jewels, furs and accessories you're going to see, and I hope you enjoy them too. All of the proceeds from this auction will go to our peace foundation. Thank you for coming and bid high. Please remember everything you buy is tax deductible!"

The rousing soundtrack from *Guys and Dolls* filled the room as I mimed, "Take back your mink . . ." My early and brief experience as a model was now coming in handy as I swept down the runway modeling the first item for sale, a mink and sable coat. Friendly laughter and applause lifted my spirits as I took my seat, the kids beside me, to watch my former life go on the auction block.

As music set the tempo, gorgeous models strode down the runway under glittering crystal chandeliers, wearing my clothes. They looked spectacular. I was having more fun than I had had when I wore those gowns myself. Even my nemesis, gossip columnist Herb Caen, was there. He bought my golden brocade cape, lined with blue silk made from fabric that had previously been part of the San Francisco Opera curtain (now replaced). He, too, was looking for a bargain and a bit of history.

The bidding was spirited but low, making me glad I had kept my more expensive pieces of jewelry in reserve and sold them privately. Even so, when we tallied the score everyone had gotten a bargain and we made three hundred fifty thousand dollars!

"Brilliant," my friend Merla Zellerbach said. "I was shocked when I heard what you were doing, but now I applaud you. It's not everyone who can make money from her old clothes!" We laughed together as old friends will, enjoying the delicious moment.

Everyone wasn't as excited as we were. One news reporter said I must have sold my clothes because, "While still handsome, Patricia Montandon is thicker in the middle, and therefore her clothes probably don't fit anymore." Stung by his remarks, I wondered why God had not taken away my vanity. I was ten pounds overweight.

Al called. "How dare you sell the jewelry I bought you?" He sounded far away, disembodied.

"Knock it off, Al. I have the right to do whatever I wish with my property."

"Dede has enormous emeralds. She appreciates the jewelry I buy her."

"I don't give a damn about Dede or her jewelry, " I said, placing the phone back onto the receiver. And it was true. I did not care about Dede or her ill-gotten gains, or Al either, for that matter.

While busy with travel plans, my top priority was the Peace Prize Ceremony. But we needed a star to bring attention to the event. I had stayed in touch with Jehan Sadat since that initial event with Jerry Jampolsky in 1982. I called her at her home in Egypt to ask if she would be our presenter. Only a year had passed since her husband, President Anwar Sadat, had been slain. Across the continents, her lovely calm voice with her distinctive accent greeted me.

"My dear," she replied to my request, "it would be a pleasure to once again see you in San Francisco. Of course I will come. Giving children a voice is very important."

On June 1, 1983, the day of our ceremony, the sun came out,

warming the cold air, melting my apprehension. The stately marble staircase under the dome of San Francisco's City Hall was covered with a wide red carpet. Ribbons of white paper bearing the names of all entrants hung from balconies, making an appropriate backdrop for the ballet dancers. That morning I had helped Star into her white tutu and pink ballet slippers, delighted at how pretty she looked. I was sorry her mom wasn't there, but Mari Ellen had seemingly dropped out of sight. I wasn't worried as she had disappeared before and always resurfaced.

A fanfare from a marching band, and then Madame Sadat and the seven award winners were escorted down the stairs to a podium on the lower landing. The audience of five hundred children bused in from various schools seemed delighted to be there.

The Soviet Consulate had, indeed, sent four young children, progeny of consulate employees, who sang a child's song in Russian. "May there always be sunshine, May there always be blue skies, May there always be Mommy, May there always be me." A tape of their performance was shown repeatedly on the evening news. Those lovely children underscored how much alike we are and how important it is to give children everywhere a chance to grow up in peace.

Jehan Sadat, ever beautiful, was a magnet. It seemed like every television and radio station in the State of California was represented.

"There are two subjects very close to my heart," Jehan said, "children and peace." She spoke of her wish that all people could learn to love one another in a "oneness of spirit, regardless of color or creed or conviction." Evoking the strength of her late husband's faith in peace, she cited "that force which can move mountains." After her remarks, with her usual graciousness, Jehan turned the focus of attention to the children as she presented their awards, hugging and kissing each recipient.

Toward the end of the event, I was handed a telegram. It was from the President of the United States. Standing beside the former First Lady of Egypt, looking into the sweet faces of the future, I read the message:

> There is no more important goal for our country than peace. And these
> children, at a very early age, are making a difference.
> —Ronald Reagan, President, United States of America

An Associated Press report said, "The tiny snowflake that appeared last December in the form of a twelve-member peace pilgrimage may be growing into an avalanche whose momentum might indeed turn peace into an idea whose time has, at last, arrived."

But the best message I got came from Star. It was written in pencil on lined notepaper with rabbit stickers. "Dear Pat. You have made me not afraid anymore. You are my mother. Love, Star."

Mari Ellen showed up the next day and took her daughter home, but I tucked Star's sweet note into my wallet so I could read it when my spirits were low.

# 15.

# PLEASE DON'T
# SHOOT MY MOTHER

The prophetic dream I had about a man being killed while trying to scale the Berlin Wall propelled me toward Germany. But a few days before our departure on June 15, 1983, Al called to tell me that in the fall, he was sending Sean to St. Mark's, a school on the East Coast.

"Are you also sending Todd and Trevor away?" I angrily asked.

"They're doing fine right here in San Francisco. Sean needs the discipline of a boarding school," he said, in his Jesuit-like mode.

"Are you telling me that Dede's boys are living at home while you send your own son away? How can you do that? What kind of father are you?"

"Sean wants to go, Pat. And I'm paying the bills," he said, as usual. "If you hadn't thrown money away on this peace thing, you might have some say. But you've mortgaged the penthouse and sold your jewelry, the jewelry I gave you, to finance your folly. Now you have to live with it."

"My peace work has nothing to do with our son. I want him at home with me."

"He doesn't want to be with you. He wants to go east to St. Mark's School."

When I asked Sean how he felt about going away, he hung his head and said he wanted to go. "It's what Dad wants me to do. Dede knows a lot about East Coast schools."

"Sean, I love you and wish you wanted to stay home with me. If we worked at it maybe we could begin to heal."

"Dad says the divorce was your fault, that you manipulated him. He didn't want to go to all those parties or buy you jewelry or anything."

Against all I knew about not putting your child into the middle, I pressed on. "Is that why they have their picture in the paper all the time, showing off her jewelry?"

I turned away, not wanting to continue a conversation that was going downhill fast. How could I head a peace foundation when I was so lacking in personal peace?

"Sean, I love you. Never forget it, okay? I'm sorry I yelled, but . . . I'll miss you, okay?" I mussed his hair. "Okay?"

"Okay," he muttered, not looking at me, but getting in a final jab. "You hardly even went to school. Dad said you picked cotton when you were a kid."

My child could not know the pain his words caused. They triggered memories of another time, another era, when I was younger than he was now. I could still remember the stinging stickers on the bolls and see the long rows of cotton plants struggling to grow in the hard-packed Oklahoma soil.

"Growing up poor made me a better person, Sean, gave me insights I wouldn't otherwise have," I said with a sigh. It seemed a less daunting task to bring East and West Berlin together than to heal the wounds between Sean and me.

During a phone conversation with my brother Charles, he said, "You're carrying on our father's ministry, you know." There was a parallel, but unlike my father, my most intense prayers at this moment were not for others. They were for my son and myself. I was worried about Sean. He seemed to cover up his feelings with horseplay and laughter, never revealing the pain I knew he must feel about being edged out of his dad's life in favor of Todd and Trevor.

As we prepared to board a Pan Am jet for West Germany, East Berlin, and Israel on a warm day in June 1983, Sean was with me as reporters crowded around shouting questions. We hoped to have those countries send children for our Peace Prize Ceremony the next year. Curious about a slender, dark-haired reporter who hung back a bit, smiling, taking notes, not pushing or asking questions, I asked Melba (who was handling the press) who he was.

"He's the new editor of the *Nob Hill Gazette*, James Borton. Cute, isn't he?" Before I could answer, she motioned him over. "Pat, this is Mr. Borton. Don't be shy, James, you know you only came out here to meet Pat. The *Gazette* never covers events like this."

"Hi," he said. A quick flush made him look even younger than he was—about thirty, I guessed. "Could we, would you have time for a quick cup of coffee?"

"I would if Melba keeps an eye on my charges," I said. Melba's wink assured me everything was under control. "The coffee shop is right there."

We found a small round table near a window.

"Melba's right, I did want to meet you," James said.

He was cute.

"I've been following your work for a year, ever since I got here from Boston. I went to your auction, too. I think you're fantastic." James's full lips were appealing. So were his long-lashed hazel eyes. "May I call you when you get back?"

"You're an editor?" I asked, delaying my answer. He was far too young for me.

"May I call you?" he persisted. "I'm thirty-two and I know you're fifty, so if that's what's bothering you, well, don't let it." Laughter bubbled up as I looked at the sincere young man scribbling his phone number on a card. "Here, call me when you get back." He tucked the paper into my coat pocket. I had not a whit of interest in a possible romance, but it was fun to know I could still attract male attention.

I heard Sean before I saw him. "Mom," he said, as he pushed straight brown hair off his high forehead, "it's almost time to go, everyone's looking for you and . . ." Seeing James, he came to an abrupt stop.

"Sean?" James said.

My son nodded.

"My name is James. I'm a writer just like your mom. Maybe when you get back, you can come to my waterfront office and help with my magazine."

"Yeah," Sean's eyes were shining, "I'm going to be a writer someday, too." That was the first I had heard of his ambition.

"Hey, we've gotta get out of here!" I said. "It's time to board. Thanks for the coffee. Take care." James whispered a soft good-bye, making me feel that maybe someone besides Star would be happy when I returned.

Surrounded by luggage, kids, parents, relatives, and other travelers, I checked to see if everyone was present. "Okay, kids, I'm counting. Sound off." I needed a whistle like Captain von Trapp from *The Sound of Music*.

In Bonn, Germany, we were excited because we had a confirmed appointment with Chancellor Helmut Kohl. At the Bundestag, the German house of parliament, a man ushered us into an Oriental-carpeted room packed with reporters, and then departed. No one greeted us or explained what we were to do. Flustered, trying to regain my composure, I introduced myself to the reporters and explained why we were there.

"Would you kids like to say anything?" I asked. No, they had nothing to say. An awkward fifteen minutes passed. Then Chancellor Kohl arrived and immediately all the oxygen evaporated from the room. He shook hands with us in a perfunctory manner and headed for the door.

"Chancellor Kohl," I had to get his attention, "these children represent thousands of kids who want to grow up and live in peace. They are serious about their quest, and they have letters from other kids for you . . ." I talked fast. "Kei, present the mail to Chancellor Kohl."

Sean and his friend Kei lugged the bag of letters over to Kohl, whose eyebrows had become question marks, and then unceremoniously dumped the letters out at his feet. Letters, drawings, trinkets, bubble gum wrappers, cards, tumbled onto the Oriental rug. A coin, which had somehow gotten mixed up with the mail, rolled across the floor. I was mortified. But then I noticed a smile tugging at the corners of Kohl's mouth.

"The mail might be a little mixed up," I pressed what I hoped was an advantage. "You may find mail for President Reagan or President Andropov, but there's mail for you also." Chancellor Kohl could not suppress his amusement. "We think perhaps all the world leaders should read each other's mail," I said.

We had broken the ice. Chancellor Kohl and his translator joined in the laughter. I was certain they had never experienced a meeting like this one.

Getting down on one knee to be closer to his audience, Chancellor Kohl spoke directly to the kids. "I know how you feel about seeking peace in a nuclear world. I know what war is. My uncle was killed during the First World War, my brother in the Second World War. I know what it's like to hear air raid sirens. I know what it's like to be in a bomb shelter, to be afraid you're going to be killed." He seemed surprised at himself. "What you are doing is very worthwhile." He blew his nose. "More people should speak up about such matters."

At the end of our brief meeting Kohl agreed to send a child from Germany to the United States for our next Peace Prize Ceremony and to take the money out of the defense budget.

During our wait for our East Berlin visas, we made a grim pilgrimage to the Berlin Wall. Alongside the road bordering the forbidding Wall were crosses with the names written of those murdered while trying to escape to freedom.

From a wooden viewing platform, we looked at East Berlin from across a space known as "No Man's Land." Laced with barriers, barbed wire, and landmines, it was a forbidding sight. Cement watchtowers with guards and machine guns were visible a few hundred feet away.

Shaken, we descended wooden steps and walked across a curb to get close to the Wall. "Let's meditate on this Wall coming down," I said.

Placing our hands against the battlement, we closed our eyes, thinking of a time when the people behind the Wall would no longer be closed off, when the two Berlins would be reunited.

"I'll light the candle today," I said, taking a white votive from my purse. When I struck the match, the kids cupped their small hands around it to shield the flame from the wind. In the twilight of West

Berlin on June 24, 1983, the warm glow of our offering cast iridescent patterns of light against the sinister structure. That gleam was a beacon of hope from eight American children.

In East Berlin we met with Gerhal Goetting, head of the Christian Democratic Party. As was true in the Soviet Union, before being allowed to speak, we were subjected to a long speech about the benefits of Communism.

"Sir," Rachel said, asking a question. "When we were in West Berlin we went to the Wall and we put our hands on it. My hands got all tingly. I didn't like it. Why do you have a Wall around your country?"

Clearing his throat, Mr. Goetting smiled and explained that their best and brightest people were leaving the East and flooding to the West, the "brain drain" he called it. The people in the East had to do something, he said, or they would no longer be a country.

Sean said, "Today we went to the Tomb of the Unknown Soldier and we felt sad that so many people died in World War II and that your country got divided. Do you think you will ever join the West? That you'll ever tear the Wall down?"

Again, the answer was respectful. "We are talking to President Richard von Weizsaker in West Germany and we are trying to be friendly." At that time, 1983, no one I knew expected the Berlin Wall to come down, except Rachel.

"Well," Rachel said, "can we be here when the Wall comes down?"

"By all means. We would want you here," Mr. Goetting said, continuing to smile politely. In the end, he agreed to send a child and an adult from East Berlin for our Peace Prize Ceremony if we could get them visas.

"We'll get visas," I said, not knowing how to get them but assured that I would. "Don't worry!"

Back in West Germany we flew to Israel where we had a confirmed appointment with Prime Minister Menachem Begin, and at the Arlozorov School where Arab and Israeli children studied together. We were up early the next morning so we would have time to sightsee and go to the Holocaust memorial before our appointments.

The males donned black yarmulkes before entering the cool vaulted space, housing yet another eternal flame. This one was in memory of the millions of people who were tortured and murdered because they weren't Aryan, the "Master race," as decreed by Aldolf Hitler, but were simply, fatally, Jews. Kneeling at a railing built above and overlooking the flame, I read the names of the death camps inscribed on the floor below— Auschwitz, Treblinka, Belzen, Sobibor—places where Jews were starved, beaten, and marched naked into gas showers to their deaths.

Overwhelmed with grief for the suffering of those subjected to the madness of the Nazi regime, I walked outside into the hot sun. Sitting on a bench under the shade of an olive tree, I tried to regain control of my emotions but began to weep. Suddenly, like a sweet vision, the children engulfed me with words of concern. Hugging me, kissing me, they bestowed compassion.

In the Children's Holocaust Museum, looking at pictures drawn by children who had been in the concentration camps, I was impressed by "my" children's rapt attention and the connections they made.

The next day we met with Prime Minister Begin. After clearing intense security in the Knesset, a man led us through a marble foyer, down a flight of stairs, and into what seemed to be a bunker. One small window overlooked a dune where armed soldiers stood guard. A round, doughnut-shaped table surrounded by chairs, and a black piano, were the only furniture in the room.

We were told that we had only two minutes with the Prime Minister. Without any kind of announcement, Prime Minister Begin entered the room, frail, his gray suit looking too large, and his tie loose around his neck. Walking around the table, smiling, patting the children on the head, he greeted each one of us. Keeping in mind our two-minute time limit, I hurried everyone along. The Prime Minister of Israel sang "Hava Nagilah" along with us and was visibly touched when Raquel spoke in Hebrew. He helped her strike the match and guided her hand to our candle. When Kei presented him with a stack of mail, he muttered, "Beautiful, very beautiful indeed, kids for peace." And then he rose to leave.

Without thinking, I reached up and put my hand on his arm, "But Mr. Begin," I said, "we aren't through yet." Later I wondered where I had gotten the nerve to do such a thing.

The Prime Minister sat back down. His associate glared. More relaxed now, Mr. Begin joined our discussion about war and peace. Sean asked about the Arab–Israeli conflict. "Will your country always be at war?"

"I hope not, but we have to protect our territory, you know."

"That's what causes war, people thinking they have to protect something instead of talking to each other." Sean stood up to address the issue.

Begin smiled. "You could be right, but it isn't easy to communicate with our neighbors."

The children then asked if he would send a child to San Francisco for the Peace Prize Ceremony, but he did not seem to hear them. "Do you have children?" Raquel asked.

"I have grandchildren!" he said, coming to life. His associate reminded him he had a new grandson. "Yes, yes," he said, "and I hope there will be no more wars."

Twenty minutes later, we said good-bye.

That evening in our hotel room, we were both happy and sad because of what we had experienced that day. We thought that Begin, though warm and friendly, was not fully alert during our meeting. "He didn't agree to send a child for the Peace Prize," Kei said.

Although the youngsters appreciated meeting with the Prime Minister, they were most struck by the drawings in the Children's Museum.

Rachel observed, "The drawing that really got to me was one where a Nazi soldier was holding a naked baby by the hair with a gun pointed at its head."

Sean had been unusually silent. Biting his lip, tears in his eyes, he said, "There was this one drawing that really got to me. It was a kid behind barbed wire, wearing a patched yellow star, and crying out, 'Please don't shoot my mother!' "

The next day, as we were leaving the Arlozorov School, we were handed a letter. It was from Prime Minister Begin.

"We are happy to inform you that Israel will conduct a peace contest following your outline on behalf of your foundation and the children of our country. The winner will be sent to San Francisco for your Peace Prize Ceremony to be held June 1, 1984.

Menachem Begin,

Prime Minister of Israel

# 16.

# SEE A TEEPEE

Our trip had been intense. By now I had bonded with these children, they were part of me, as if we shared DNA. "Stay in touch, okay?" I said, hugging them good-bye. Sean would be leaving for boarding school in a couple of months, making it all the more important for me to have other kids around.

Clearing customs, bedraggled and tired, I was surprised to be met not only by Star and her mom, Mari Ellen, but also by James Borton. After my brief airport encounter with the dark-haired writer before departing for Europe, I had forgotten about him.

"Want a ride?" He held out a bouquet of red tulips. His brown eyes sparkled. "I rented a fancy car, an old Rolls, so we can travel in style."

"Wow, sure beats a taxi. Right, Mom?" Sean accepted the invitation as if it were intended for him.

"That's right, Sean, grab a suitcase. The car's just outside the door." Guys together, laughing, they helped the driver put our luggage in the trunk. Star and Mari Ellen piled into the car too, enjoying the prospect of riding in luxury.

Cruising along Highway 101, I sank into the car's soft interior, inhaling the aroma of old leather, enjoying the feeling of being cared for. I still loved the beauty of the San Francisco skyline as it came into view. But by now, life in the city I loved was becoming remote. My world was broadening, making the role of a so-called socialite seem less important than the funny papers.

I glanced at James, beside me in the back seat, noticing his lanky form, sensuous smile, refined features. He was altogether pleasing to my love-starved self.

On the jump seats, Sean and Star entertained each other. Up front, Mari Ellen, wearing a black lace dress with a red velvet hat perched on top of her cascading brown mane, kept up a stream of chatter with the driver. I hoped she was sober.

"Hey, Pat," Mari Ellen yelled, "my jewelry business is doing real good, so I can keep Star now until school starts up." In a way, I was sorry to hear the news. I would miss the adorable child who had allowed me to mother her.

I looked over at James and wondered why he was making such an effort to impress me. After all, twenty years separated us. He seemed unsophisticated, and even with the Rolls, I recognized genteel poverty when I saw it. Frayed cuffs and polished but worn shoes told a story. I was not a good prospect for romance and he had to know from news reports that I was no longer wealthy. But then everything is relative, I thought, promising myself to stay on guard.

"I've arranged a picnic, if that's all right." His actions belied a shy manner.

"I'm too tired, but thanks anyway."

"I figured that, so the picnic is for tomorrow," he smiled as we pulled up to 999 Green and the doorman ran out to help with the luggage. "Tomorrow?" James reiterated.

"Okay, tomorrow at six. But I want an early evening, okay?" I felt a thrill. Sean would be with his dad. I would not have to be alone.

"A picnic at night? You've got it." James was whistling when he left.

The next evening at the appointed hour, my would-be-swain arrived carrying a large wicker hamper. "I read your book about parties and know you like picnics." He placed the basket on the floor near the fireplace. "I like them too, especially if they're inside, away from the bug population. And," he laughed, "they suit my budget. I'm not one of your rich friends, Patricia Lou. I want to make that clear right up front." His grin was seductive. "I'm not a fortune hunter, either. I just plain admire you."

We had our meal on a patchwork quilt spread on the floor in front of a fire. James had brought a book of poetry, which we read aloud to each other. It was unabashedly romantic. But I was wary, trying not to respond to the tall, slender young man, although I wanted to open to him like a desert flower after rain. He was a Vietnam veteran and a writer, divorced, with one son. James was the kind of person I should have dated in my twenties instead of marrying Howard Groves and living on a farm in the San Joaquin Valley, I thought.

We began seeing each other, not "dating," a word I avoided, but "hanging out." When Sean was with me, we included him in our outings, and he said it almost seemed like we were a family. There was growing sexual tension between James and me, but I continued to keep my emotional distance even though he was quickly becoming the father figure my son so sorely needed.

"Hey, Sean," my beau said one Sunday when we were in his waterfront office, "I have a son named Travis. He's just a little younger than you are and lives with his mom in Boston." Sean's scowl made me wonder if he was jealous. "When he comes for a visit, I'll take you guys to a Willie Nelson concert."

"Mom plays that twanging kind of music all the time: 'Oh, honey you done, done me wrong, and that ain't right,' " Sean imitated a country western singer. "I like rock, not that stuff."

"Okay, but, I would appreciate your help when Travis comes. I haven't seen him for a while and it's hard to know what he'll enjoy."

My mother would say, "Salt the cow to get the calf" when a young "scalawag" came to call. Now it was salt the calf to get the cow, I laughed. It worked, too. Sean took a real shine to James, even imitating the way he combed his hair and affecting the thirties fashions he wore.

"Why don't you write a story about the trips you've made with your mom?" James suggested to Sean one evening as we ate at Clown Alley, a nearby hamburger place. "If you want to be a writer, well, you have to write."

"I'll bet the *Examiner* would publish your story. After all, it's not every kid who gets to talk with world leaders," I said, encouraging Sean as well. He raised his eyebrows, a habit he had when he was happy about something.

"Yea, Mom, way to go." Sean gave me a "high-five."

The story he wrote, plus photographs of him and Kei with Chancellor Kohl and Prime Minister Begin, appeared in the *San Francisco Examiner*.

For the rest of the summer Sean worked for James, running errands, having fun. My new beau was patient with him. With me, too. And James became my anchor when it was time for my son to leave for boarding school.

I sewed Sean's name into sweaters, underwear, and trousers and shopped for the things he would need. "Well, at least you'll be home for Christmas," I said, kissing him. Sean's room looked desolate. His suitcases and footlocker were downstairs, ready for Clifford, his dad's driver, to pick up the next morning. As we stood together—mother and thirteen-year-old son—surveying his room, now devoid of almost all personal effects, a deep sadness became rooted in my soul.

James and I had not yet been intimate and he wanted to stay with me that night, but I thought the two us, mother and son, needed to be alone together. Now that the time had come, I could hardly bear it. Sean was tense as well and he seemed too lost in thought for conversation. I was holding so much inside of me, how worried I was about Sean going away, as well as my personal pain over losing him, that I could say little beyond gentle reminders for him to write. Giving my progeny an affectionate hug, I finally said it was time to go to bed, that we had to get up early.

I crawled into my too large, lonely, king-size bed, assumed a fetal position, and wrapped my arms around my legs, seeking comfort. All alone in that big bed, it felt like my ex-husband was still trying to punish me, and Sean too, for I did not know what. Certainly Al had become my enemy, taking my community property, holding me up to public ridicule. But now, in the most heartless act of all, he had coerced my only child to go to a school 3,000 miles away, knowing I could do nothing to stop him.

As the enormity of my deprivation sunk in, I wondered why I had not made a scene about it. Why couldn't I express how angry I was?

"Mom," Sean stood in the doorway, "can I get in bed with you?"

"Of course you can," I pulled back the covers. He hadn't asked to do that since he was a little boy.

"I'm lonesome," he curled into a ball on the far edge of my bed.

"I'm going to miss you, Sean."

"I don't want to go."

"Well, you don't have to." I reached for his hand.

"No, it's okay. I'll be fine," he drew back to the edge of the bed. Sean always retreated when I tried to help him. Like most boys, Sean desperately wanted to please his father.

"At least you'll be home for Christmas. We'll be going on our trip to Asia then and I know you'll be happy that Kei will be along," I said.

"Yeah," he said. "Mom, I'll sure miss Mir."

Mir, the Rusian word for peace, was a cat we had adopted. When we had gone to the animal shelter to find a pet, I had worn a mink jacket. Sean, with his usual irrepressible humor, joked with the shelter manager, "My mom wants six cats. Four black ones for the jacket and two white ones for the collar and cuffs." I was happy to sell that coat.

"Mir will be here waiting for you, Sean. I will, too." He did not reply. "I sure do love you. You know that, don't you?"

"Yeah."

After Sean left the next morning, I felt as if a loved one had died. James walked six miles with me that day, from Russian Hill across the Golden Gate Bridge to Sausalito. Looking at the roiling water of the Pacific, the seagulls perched on wooden pilings, and hearing the mournful hoot of a foghorn, tasting salt spray, everything deepened my pain. I wanted to keep moving, never to return to my empty home.

"I'm staying with you tonight. Okay?" We had stopped on the Golden Gate Bridge. James held my face between his hands. "Okay, Patricia Lou?"

"Okay." I was glad he would be with me. Kissing lightly, we proceeded on our marathon walk.

That night James held me in his arms, caressing me, until we fell asleep. In the middle of the night, we awoke and made love for the first time. Our lovemaking was sensuous and fulfilling, restoring my sense of self. Never had anyone caressed me the way my young lover did, or brought out in me such a voluptuous spirit of abandon. We laughed too, reminding me that Al was incensed when I giggled during sex. With Al, it was serious business. With James, it was fun.

My relationship with James was undoubtedly temporary, I thought, but so what. After all, my "long-term" marriages had turned out to be transient. Later, when James and I were seen in public together, I was teased about our age difference. It did not bother me. Herb Caen's item, Montandon rocks the cradle, could not dent the satisfaction my romance with James Borton brought me.

One evening we went to see *The Killing Fields*, a movie about the war in Cambodia. Both of us sobbed so loudly about the children killed at the hands of the Khmer Rouge that we had to leave the theater. Sitting in my car in the glare of streetlights, we held each other, weeping still, as James gave me a hint about his experiences in Vietnam. "That war, seeing people killed, affects everything I do. I lost my youth and innocence during that awful war." He held me close. "You're right to be doing whatever you can to stop such atrocities."

Now it was my turn to console and comfort.

Even though I was busy with the foundation, and James with his job, we treasured our time together and confided in each other. Therefore, I was taken by surprise when he told me he had resigned from the *Nob Hill Gazette*.

"I've accepted a journalism job in Boston so I can be near my son for a while. James put his arms around me, "I'll miss you Patricia Lou. Why don't you come with me?"

"Why didn't you tell me you were thinking of moving?" I said, not wanting to show how unhappy I was.

"I wasn't sure it would happen and I didn't want to upset you," he said.

"That's a silly way to treat someone you say you love!"

"I'm sorry, Patricia Lou. Forgive me?"

I sighed. "I forgive you, but I still don't like it."

James held me tight and whispered in my ear, "A lot can happen in the six months before I go." We kissed gently and sweetly trying to ignore the inevitability of our eventual parting.

One day Mari Ellen called and asked me if I could come and get Star. She had moved and didn't have room for her daughter. The little girl ran into my arms happy to be going back to her yellow-and-blue bedroom. I was happy to have her back, too. She had become like a daughter to me. Calm and funny, Star was exceptional. On Sundays, James and I often took Star to a movie, a concert, or the Hard Rock Cafe.

"I'm working on a new dance for the Peace Prize," she told us as we soaked up the sun in Golden Gate Park one day. "It's called a Prayer for Peace." After finding a flat place on the grass to use as a stage, she took pink ballet shoes from a bag, wrapped her toes in wool batting, laced up the slippers and stood poised, commanding attention. Graceful as a swan she danced across the greenery, unfazed by the audience of homeless campers.

After I had taken Star back to her mother, one morning James bounded into the apartment carrying a cold bottle of champagne. "Let's sit on the balcony," he said. Grabbing two crystal flutes, he was outside before I could comment.

The bay looked like a miniature lake from thirty-three stories up. Boats were toys. We lounged back in canvas chairs. "What are we celebrating, Baby James?" I asked. Pouring the bubbly, my lover clicked his glass against mine. "To our future," he said, and then dropping to one knee, he proposed. "Will you marry me?" He reached into his pocket and fished out a white porcelain box. "I love you" was inscribed in a recurring pattern across the smooth white surface.

Lifting the hinged lid of the delicate box, I saw a ruby and diamond ring nestled on a bed of black velvet. "Oh, James. Oh, James, darling, sweetheart."

"Well?" He stood up, pulled me to my feet, and put his arms around me.

"Oh, sweetheart, you're too young, oh God." I broke down. "I can't marry you, I just can't." I loved James, but I had been married enough times, I never wanted to risk it again. "James, you've made me feel desirable again. I owe you so much. Enough to know I can't marry you."

"Patricia Lou, you have been hurt so deeply that it's hard for you to trust honest emotions from an honest man. Al's betrayal disfigured you in a way. My love for you can help you heal that wound." He walked to the balcony railing, his back to me.

"James I trust you, but I wonder if any man can be faithful to one woman." When he had not confided in me about his move to Boston, I had begun to doubt his maturity.

My lover turned away from the dramatic view and looked at me. "We can make our future whatever we want it to be, Patricia Lou." He sighed. "Maybe someday you'll change your mind. I'll keep this ring for you, always." He put the box back in his pocket. "Don't worry, I won't play the role of the rejected lover." We laughed and hugged, breaking the tension.

A few months later, James, who had often stayed at my place but always kept his own apartment, began spending less time with me. Little by little our relationship seemed to fade away. Part of me felt rejected, but another part felt relieved. I was surprised to realize that I liked being single.

On a foggy and cold January morning James invited me to have lunch with him at Pier 7. He had chosen a wharf café located on a creaky boat anchored in the bay. Our food choices were limited and we ended up eating clam chowder and drinking eggnog: a combination I will always remember. James' body language was speaking loudly to me. His right arm was placed on the table, a barrier, and the rest of his body was twisted slightly away from me.

"What's the matter James?" I asked, leaning toward him. He moved away, ever so slightly.

"Patricia Lou, I love you," he said, looking up at the coffered ceiling. "But . . . but there's something you need to know." James looked down at the table, coughed, and crossed his arms over his chest. "I'm dating someone else."

"Then how can you say you love me?" I said, suddenly feeling queasy.

"Sometimes you've made me feel like you were mothering me."

"You're kidding!"

"When you cooked breakfast for me and fussed over me, I didn't feel like your equal, Pat," James said, turning his body away from me. "I felt you treated me like a son."

"Oh! Now I get it. You think I'm too old for you!" I said, angrily. "Why didn't you just say so, James Borton, instead of beating around the bush?" I got up from the table and left the restaurant.

I was so hurt that I could not sleep for a week. I was upset that my age had become a factor in our romance. How unfair, I fumed. People thought nothing about a man dating and marrying a woman thirty years younger that he was. But an older woman and younger man was a completely different story.

That's how it ended with James, at least for a while.

A few months later, according to the *Nob Hill Gazette*, James married a woman named Marsha Munroe. I had not wanted to marry James but I didn't like being replaced so easily either. Sometimes I felt as if I was becoming a nun in a holy order of my own choosing, and not meant to have a man in my life.

A year later, James called to tell me he was divorced, his marriage had not worked out, and he would soon be going to Vietnam as a reporter for the *Washington Times*. "I love you Patricia Lou, I always will," he said. "If you ever decide that you want that engagement ring . . . let me know."

"Sure James," I said, laughing. "I'll do that. I love you too."

Alone now, with Sean away and Star with her mother, the penthouse once again felt isolated. I could not afford it anyway. It was time to let it go. Time to get on with my work, my life, and my holy order of celibacy.

Every real estate agent in town wanted the listing for the six-thousand-square-foot home. "A Villa in the Sky," *House and Garden* magazine had called it in a cover story. A pleasure dome, a pavilion in the sky," another writer said. Whatever it was called, it was too expensive for me to keep.

Once again, I did a survey of my possessions in preparation for a sale. The massive double doors from the thirty-second-floor entry opened to reveal beige travertine floors and a curved, free-standing staircase leading to the second floor. Twenty-three-foot tall windows gave me an unobstructed view of the entire bay. On a clear day, I could see all the way to the Farallon Islands, thirty-five miles into the Pacific Ocean.

My over-scale furniture by famed interior designer Michael Taylor fit the vastness of the rooms. A number of pieces were made of unfinished beige travertine, designed for the Flintstones, I would say. My gigantic round marble dining table was so heavy it was virtually immovable. Seating fourteen, it had been brought up the side of the building and tussled into the apartment by crane while neighbors gawked. I did not know how

I was going to get it out or what I would do with it if I did. I hoped who-ever bought the place would also want the furniture.

As I took it all in, chiffon-like clouds dancing a wispy waltz above the Golden Gate Bridge were suddenly transformed by the blaze of a setting sun. Pushed by a gentle breeze, the golden clouds rolled slowly toward me. Cascades of color soon reflected off mirrored walls, engulfing me in an ethereal vapor. An eighteenth-century crystal chandelier, sporting twenty-six fat candles, seemed to flare to life as if lit from within.

Where could I possibly live after all this? I wondered.

When asked by friends and the media, I would tell them I wanted a log house in the heart of the city, surrounded by trees, with a view of the bay. "Sure, Pat, but seriously, where are you going to live?" I would re-peat my answer. The warmth and beauty of wood, trees, earth, nature, appealed to me.

I was self-aware enough to know it would be hard for me to live in a small apartment after such a magnificent space. I wanted something that, though modest, would be as unique as the penthouse.

I had entered a new world, a new way of life, but part of me still clung to the old one. Then, just as I decided finally to cut the cord and accept the next offer for my home, I got a call from Pegi Brandley, Al's secretary. I was surprised that she had the nerve to call me. "Al asked me to tell you that Sean is yours for the holidays. You're to pick him up at the airport and keep him until he goes back to St. Mark's in January."

I could hardly believe the good news. Sean would be home from school and I had a surprise for him. A man called from Los Angeles, say-ing that he represented Muhammad Ali. The popular boxer wanted to become involved with our peace organization. The man asked if I could come to LA and bring a video of our work for Muhammad Ali to view. Thrilled, I arranged to go as soon as Sean got home so he could have the experience of meeting this great American icon.

Using my offspring's homecoming as an excuse, I took the apartment off the market, delaying the inevitable, sinking further in debt. After our Asia trip, which would begin in late December, I would sell my home. It was important that everything be as normal as I could make it for my son.

I carried balloon bouquets to the airport to welcome Sean home.

Watching people spill off the airplane, the blue-and-red balloons bouncing overhead, I began to worry that Sean had missed his flight. And then I saw him, with a school friend, being escorted by two police officers.

"That boy is my son," I said, pointing to Sean. "What's going on?"

"Well, ma'am, these two fellows were smoking pot on the airplane. They got pretty rowdy."

"Mom, I didn't . . . we didn't . . . honest . . . do anything, Mom . . . honest." Sean was pale, shaken.

After the boys were taken to an airport security office and an official report was filed, they were released. "What you did was a very serious offense Sean, please don't take it lightly," I said. On the way home Sean told me his version of what had happened.

"We were trying to get something from an overhead bin when a heavy speaker fell out and hit a passenger. The guy got really mad and reported us."

"As well he should," I said. "Was he hurt? And what about smoking pot?"

"No, the guy wasn't hurt, Mom," Sean said. "We were smoking clove cigarettes."

"Sean, I don't believe you. I think you were smoking pot," I said. "Pot is bad for you and it's illegal. You shouldn't be smoking at all! Do not do that again, do you hear me?"

"Okay, Mom, okay."

"What you did was a serious offense Sean, you must not take it lightly," I said. "You could end up in jail if you act that way again. I'm concerned about you."

"It won't happen again, Mom, I promise," Sean said.

Sean seemed disturbed but defiant. There was a certain hardness about him. His voice, which always blared above others, was louder still and his skin had erupted in acne. He was pubescent. Outbursts had to be expected. But he was thrilled to be going on the trip to Asia because his friend Kei would be along. And he was ecstatic when he learned he would meet Muhammad Ali, the "Great One."

The man, who met us at the Los Angeles airport, was short with a bland personality and a faintly seedy look. He seemed distracted as he drove us across Los Angeles in his old-model car. His frequent stops at phone booths were unnerving. Who was he? And what were we doing in his car?

"Sometimes my judgment is not the best," I said, telling Sean to put his hand on the door handle and be ready to jump out if I gave the word. "This guy could be Jack the Ripper for all I know."

"He's been in a lot of phone booths so maybe he's Superman," Sean said.

"Ha, ha," I said, laughing.

When the fellow returned, I questioned him. "Why are you stopping at so many phone booths? Are you Superman?"

"Ha, ha," my son echoed.

The man did not have the wit to smile. "I've been checking on Muhammad. He's not home yet, but he's on his way." A few minutes later we pulled up to a gated community and parked. "He should be along any minute," he said.

When a beige, two-tone Rolls Royce with Muhammad Ali at the wheel pulled up next to us, I was relieved. We followed the car to a huge white house surrounded by a rolling lawn. It was early evening, but the house was dark. Without a word, our driver jumped out of the car and ran to the Rolls. But with swift grace, Muhammad Ali walked over and opened the car door for me.

"You will have to forgive my friend. He is surely not a gentleman," he said, extending his hand, and with a smile, he helped me out of the car. "And you, too, young man, come on inside."

Sean was captivated. I was too.

Finding his door key, the "Great One" turned the lock and ushered us into a big, cold house. It seemed as if no one was actually living there, that Muhammad Ali had come here today from some other place where he was staying. He flipped on lights, and took us into a small cluttered library. Books of all description were scattered about, along with props for magic shows, and an old television set.

"Do you like magic?" Muhammad Ali asked Sean. My son's usual articulate self had fled in the face of glory. He could only nod.

We sat on worn but comfortable chairs while the beautiful man, with labored intensity, entertained us as if we were paying customers. Even though his hands shook, he could still perform magic tricks.

After about half an hour, it was suggested we look at the video I had brought. When the faces of our children flashed on the screen, along with Madame Jehan Sadat, Muhammad Ali asked who she was. I explained that Jehan was the wife of the slain Egyptian president Anwar Sadat. A look of concern crossed his face.

"Those who do great things often must suffer," he said, looking sad.

"We are so happy that you want to be involved in our work," I said to Muhammad. "If you need more information, I'll be glad to send it to you."

"I'll do whatever my associate says," the man said, smiling.

After we said good-bye and were returning to the airport, he said Muhammad Ali would definitely participate in our Peace Prize Ceremony the next year. What a coup! His involvement meant major recognition for our work. Now, more than ever, it was important to make the trip to Asia, and to have children from as many countries as possible involved in the Peace Prize the following year in June 1985.

Two weeks later Star joined Sean and me to celebrate at an early Christmas lunch on December 20. Little Star, so petite and delicate, was selling things for Mari Ellen during the holiday season and would have to go back to work right after lunch. Star, forthcoming as usual, said that her mom drank a lot of brandy every day and then got mad at her. "But it's okay, I don't mind," she said. I told Star she could always call me if she needed anything.

Sean didn't mention his father and I didn't pry because I knew he would resent it if I did. But our former cook, Geri Crumpler, now retired from the Wilsey household and living in Texas, sent me the Christmas card she had received from the Wilsey family. She wanted me to see for myself how Sean was ignored in his dad's home. The card was a color photograph of Al and Dede with her sons, Todd and Trevor, dressed in formal clothes, surrounded by several dogs. "Merry Christmas from the Wilsey family," the card read. How upsetting for Sean. It was as if he had been erased from his dad's life.

A week before we were to leave for Asia, Doctor Jerry Jamplosky (the man who had introduced me to the book he edited, *Children as Teachers of Peace*, and had encouraged me to continue the work), and his fiancé Diane Cirincione came to see me. Diane was fuming. Without delay, she demanded I stop using the name *Children as Teachers of Peace*. She and Jerry had decided to travel with kids the way I had and felt entitled to the name. "But Jerry," I said, "You know that I copyrighted the name for my foundation, which has nothing to do with your book. I've kept you in the loop about our activities from the very beginning," I said. "We have a Children's Declaration of Dependence scroll for world leaders to sign during our upcoming trip. Children as Teachers of Peace is embossed across the top of it! How can you do this?"

Jerry said nothing but Diane continued to berate me, so I asked them to leave. How could they suggest that I give them the name we had established? Jerry knew that the initials CATP were dear to me. Long before my vision I had had a prophetic insight around those initials. It had happened during an early meditation while being treated by Dr. Krystal. In the throes of letting go of River Meadow Farm she had asked me to find a home that would always be mine, that could never be violated. An image of an Indian teepee had sprung to the surface almost immediately.

Later, after I began my work, it took a therapist friend, to whom I had told the story, to point out the meaning of the image I was given. "Pat, look at the initials of Children as Teachers of Peace." He wrote them out on a note pad. "CATP. See A Teepee, Children as Teachers of Peace."

See A Teepee was the home that could never be taken from me, the home that would always be mine. It was that improbable story, that imagery, those initials, that made it emotionally hard for me to give up our name.

Our foundation attorney said the name was legally ours and in any case I could only license Jerry to use it or we would lose the rights to all our programs. But I was serious about my intention to live a peaceful life. After days of angst, meditating, and crying, too, I made a decision. Believing that it was not right for a peace group to fight about their name, thereby negating what they stood for, I decided to be a peacemaker. Against my board and our lawyer's advice, I licensed Jerry to use the name Children as Teachers of Peace for a period of time, and I changed our name to Children as the Peacemakers, CATP. Still, being a peace-maker was not easy.

Once again, I thought about my dad and how he had answered my mother after a "mechanic" had taken our Model A Ford for a spin to check it out and never returned. "Charlie, why do you trust everyone?" Mama had said. "Mama," Daddy replied, "that man must need our car more than we do."

Jerry and Diane must have needed that name more than I did, I thought. In any case, our initials would remain CATP.

## 17.

# THE DECLARATION OF DEPENDENCE

On December 22, 1983, intent on having children from Asian countries involved in our work, we left for a month-long journey to Japan, China, India, and Russia. On this mission children from Australia joined fifteen others including old-timers Rachel, Raquel, Matt, Star, Sean and his friend Kei Grant, an African-American boy. We carried with us our *Children's Declaration of Dependence* for world leaders to sign. The language for the Declaration had to come to me during a fifteen-minute phone meditation with Sheila Krystal:

> *We hereby dedicate ourselves, our hearts, and minds to world peace. We believe that all humankind deserves a future free from the threat of nuclear war. We will encourage peace between individuals and nations and clasp hands with the children of the world in a global effort to preserve the planet.*

On this trip our eyes would be opened to the result of war in ways we could not have imagined. In my journal, which was becoming as thick as a book—with Peace Prize Ceremonies planned for every year along with peace trips—I summarized the highlights.

The hopping, skipping, and laughter of the kids came to a halt in Hiroshima, Japan, the place where the first atomic bomb was detonated on

August 6, 1945. In Peace Park, a memorial preserve built on ground zero, we met Reverend Kiyoshi Tanimoto and his daughter Koko Kondo.

Reverend Tanimoto was revered for founding eight hundred orphanages after the dropping of the bomb, and bringing the so-called Hiroshima Maidens to the United Sates for reconstructive surgery. The reverend, a small, elegant man, his white hair blowing in wisps from under a blue wool cap, greeted us in studied English. He told us what it had been like the day the bomb was dropped on Hiroshima, changing his life and history. At the end of his talk he gestured toward a tiny woman sitting on a nearby bench. "That's my daughter Koko. She was a baby when the bomb dropped. Maybe she will tell you how she has suffered."

Koko seemed hesitant as she began to talk about what it was like to live with the legacy of the atomic bomb. But slowly, after giving us the facts, she began to tell us about the personal side of that war. "See that little girl over there?" She pointed toward a child. "That's my adopted daughter, Aki. You see," she floundered, "well, I'm sterile. I can't have children of my own because of radiation from that bomb. Ever since the bombing, I hate the man who did it. I always thought, if I ever meet the man who dropped the atom bomb I'm going to, you know, give him a punch, a real punch." Koko wiped her eyes.

"When I was about your age—ten or so," she said, slowly and painfully revealing her feelings, "I went to the United States. My father was being honored on the Ralph Edwards TV show, *This is Your Life*. I sat on the stage with my father. But I wanted to run away when Captain Lewis, the pilot of the Enola Gay, the man who dropped the atomic bomb, was announced as a guest." Koko looked across the river at the carcass of a building kept standing as a grim reminder of the bombing. "Well," she said, "Captain Lewis comes out on the stage, and I look at him and look at him, he's like any American man, not like a person who could kill people."

She told us that Captain Lewis had recalled how after dropping the bomb that day, they circled back over Hiroshima City. Seeing the monstrous firestorm enveloping the city, he said, "My God, my God, what have we done?"

"And then," Koko said, "his tears just run down and run down. Right on the television. I was so ashamed of hating this man, you understand?" She could hardly get the words out. "It . . . it . . . wasn't the man I should hate, but . . . but . . . the war itself."

"My body just quiver and quiver," she continued. "I walk over to Captain Lewis, and took his hand. We stood together, holding hands, as our tears run down."

The children leaned against each other, weeping in concert with the storyteller. "When Captain Lewis died," Koko concluded, "his doctor presented a sculpture to the public in his memory. The top was a mushroom cloud. The bottom a tear."

In Peace Park that chilly December, the melancholy sound of a gong struck over and over in memory of the dead twisted like a serpent through fog-shrouded tree branches and blanketed the river, seeming to mourn the multitudes that tried to quench their thirst with poisoned, boiling water that searing August morning.

Years later Koko told me that radiation unleashed by the atomic bomb not only left her sterile, but as a young girl, she was a specimen for medical studies. She described how she wanted to die when, as a teenager, she was made to stand on a stage in front of a roomful of doctors wearing only a diaper, as her medical condition was discussed.

Koko and I eventually traveled the world together. We had connected at the heart and felt the same sense of purpose in promoting peace.

Before leaving San Francisco I had met with the Chinese Consul General who thought their premier would meet with us, but when we arrived in China and our guide rattled off our itinerary I realized that was not going to happen.

I seldom visit the American Embassy on these trips. But on that dusty, cold morning in Beijing, I asked our guide where the American Embassy was.

"Right there," he said, pointing to a building directly across the street from where we had stopped for a traffic signal. "I'm getting off here," I told my crew. "Shelly, you're in charge. I'll see you guys back at the hotel."

Christmas was two days away and a forlorn, sparsely decorated fir adorned the embassy lobby, which was otherwise devoid of life. A lackadaisical American woman glanced at my passport, but responded with a look of surprise when I asked to see the ambassador. Within minutes an official appeared.

"What's your problem, lady, why do you want to see the ambassador?" the man said, scowling. When I told him I had twenty-five kids traveling with me, what our mission was, and that we wanted to see Premier Zhao, he laughed out loud.

"Lady, you're nuts. The ambassador has been trying to get a reply to an important message we sent to Zhao over three weeks ago." He chortled. "You're not going to see Zhao. What made you think you could?"

"Well," I persisted, "you must have his office number." While the man stared at me, a Chinese woman in a red cheongsam, hovering in the background—as if waiting for me—stepped forward. "I have number," she said, handing me a paper with the number written on it.

"May I use your phone?" I asked. Without comment the official pointed to a phone. The number I dialed was answered by Mr. Lee, an English-speaking man. I went into detail about why we were there, why we wanted to see the premier. "And," I said, "although you don't celebrate Christmas, it would be a lovely and meaningful gift to us if we could be received on December 25."

"Where are you staying?" Mr. Lee was soft spoken and polite. I told him the name of our hotel and gave him my room number.

The next day, the afternoon of Christmas Eve, we still hadn't heard from Mr. Lee. I had just sent the kids to lunch, afraid to go myself, when the phone rang.

"Miss Pat?"

"Yes."

"This is Mr. Lee. I have good news." A pause. "Premier Zhao will receive you tomorrow, December twenty-fifth, your Christmas Day, at 2:00 PM in the Great Hall of the People."

On Christmas Day, as I walked side by side with Premier Zhao over lush red carpeting with large murals of Chinese landscapes all around, I wondered how such a thing had happened; that I, Patsy Lou, with no official credentials, was walking beside the premier of China, and being treated with dignity and respect. The contrast to my life in San Francisco was startling. I was the butt of jokes at home but a respected diplomat in the rest of the world.

During our two-hour meeting, Premier Zhao said he would instruct the All-China Women's Federation to conduct a peace contest in all the provinces of China, and to send the winner to San Francisco for our Peace Prize Ceremony. He went on to tell us he would be in San Francisco in a month and that he looked forward to seeing me there.

Beau Basse, a Chinese-American boy, was chosen that day to read our Children's Declaration of Dependence and to ask the premier to become the first world leader to sign it.

The head of the powerful People's Republic of China rose from his chair, and with a flourish of blue ink, signed the Declaration. It was a joyful moment.


In India, Prime Minister Indira Gandhi was the next to sign the Children's Declaration. Walking onto the prime minister's private grounds in Delhi, the early morning stillness broken only by birdcalls, inhaling the swirling aroma of wood smoke, I felt as if I had come home into that imaginary place of dreams. And, as if in a dream, small groups of people were clustered under jacaranda trees, cooking. Campfires were scattered throughout the spacious garden. Apparently this was not unusual, as I also saw Mrs. Gandhi, accompanied by two uniformed guards, visiting with the campers. She was wearing a blue wool coat over her sari to ward off the morning chill, the distinctive white streak in her black hair unruly in the light breeze.

Shown into what appeared to be a small dining room, the first thing I noticed was a portrait above the fireplace of Jawalhara Nehru, Indira Gandhi's father and India's first prime minister. There was no other ornamentation. Seated at a rectangular wooden table, we were told to wait. Fifteen minutes after our arrival, Prime Minister Gandhi joined us. We stood up, palms together, greeting her in the traditional manner of her country.

"I'm so sorry to be late," she said, removing her coat, "but I have to look after my people, you know. They camp on my grounds from time to time, and are almost like family."

When a child asked Indira Gandhi what world leaders could do to ensure peace, her answer was thoughtful. "It isn't the world leaders, you know. No one listens to us. It isn't until the people themselves raise their voices that we will have peace. That's why I think what you are doing is a wonderful thing. God bless you all."

Before the end of our hour-long visit, Indira Gandhi agreed to send a child for our Peace Prize Ceremony, and became the second world leader to sign the *Children's Declaration of Dependence*.

A Sikh bodyguard shot Prime Minister Indira Gandhi to death on October 31, 1984, ten months after we had met with her.

The relaxed and colorful stop in India was the respite we needed before once again facing what was often referred to by American politicians as "The Red Menace," Moscow. Sean and Kei, who had filled the hall of our hotel with feathers from a middle-of-the-night pillow fight in India, had settled down a bit, and everyone was getting along well.

It was January 1984. The Cold War had intensified. The leader of the USSR, President Konstantin Chernenko, was suspicious of President Reagan and convinced of an impending American nuclear attack. When the Korean airliner, KAL-007, flying over Soviet territory, had been shot down by the Soviets in 1983, the arms race had escalated as never before. President Reagan used the deaths of the 268 passengers as justification for pushing production of MX missiles, for deploying Pershing and cruise missiles in Europe, and for escalating funds for his new Star Wars project.

Tension was palpable from the moment we boarded our Aeroflot flight from Delhi to Moscow. Our Soviet hosts greeted us with scowls. In Moscow's Cosmos Hotel, I had a terrifying feeling of impending danger. Unable to talk to anyone about my fears, I went into the dingy bathroom and ran water in the sink so Sean couldn't hear me cry. Then, dimly over the sound of running water, I heard the telephone ring.

A phone call in Moscow? At that time it was virtually impossible to get a telephone call to or from the United States. "Hello." I heard a crackling sound, a faraway voice. "Patsy, Melba. Dear heart . . . concerned . . . important." Her voice faded in and out. "*Pravda* . . . you hate U.S. Don't . . . get . . . burned by curling irons."

Melba Beal's cryptic message carried a code we had established earlier. Curling irons meant we were in danger and the Soviets were trying to use us for propaganda. ". . . News bureau chiefs . . . monitor your official meetings. My church group . . . praying . . ."

A sharp snap, the line went dead, leaving me with a lot to think about.

Being granted an audience in the Kremlin was not nearly as easy as it had been on our first trip. However, when the day finally arrived, our bus pulled up to a four-story yellow-and-white stone building; we were ushered inside, and urged to walk quickly up a wide staircase to the second floor.

Chairman Ruben with Yuri Zhukov greeted us with hasty handshakes, and led us into an opulently appointed room dominated by a mammoth painting of Lenin addressing a mob. His background was the Kremlin where we now sat. It was the original painting of the one I had seen at the Soviet Consulate in 1982. Despite the décor the atmosphere was frigid.

Glancing around, I saw Soviet television and film people as well as the news photographers. But Melba had done her homework—ABC and CBS crews were also present. I was seated alone at the far end of a gleaming mahogany table, relegated to a Siberian gulag.

Standing at a podium, all pretense of geniality gone, Ruben welcomed us and then, with a thick sheaf of notes in his hand and frequent glances at Zhukov, he launched into an anti-American denunciation that had us cringing. His face flushed, Chairman Ruben finally wound up his bombast. He was saying good-bye.

I would not let our meeting end this way. Seizing the moment, I stood up, and acting as if I had been invited to do so, began to speak. "Thank you, Chairman Ruben, for once again receiving us."

Zhukov and Ruben looked startled.

"Many people have said to us, 'The Soviets are using you,' " I said, looking directly at the Russian men. "I want you to know that is exactly

why we are here. To be used. But we are to be used for peace, not l̶
itics—by any nation. And sir, we look forward to a day when w̶
longer recite negative statistics about each other, but recognize and embrace our common humanity."

Ruben started to say something. "Excuse me sir, but I'm not quite finished," I said, smiling. He looked confused but he sat down. I quickly
wound up my little speech.

"Chairman Ruben, we well remember your graciousness during our
first visit here. That day, outside the windows in your study, I saw soft
snow falling onto the golden onion domes of a cathedral. Later, when I
mentioned this to a friend who had been sitting opposite me, she said, 'I
didn't see that. I saw a painting.' Perhaps, Chairman Ruben, that's the
way truth is; everything depends on where you're sitting. And now,
please, our children would like to speak."

Ruben looked uneasy, Zhukov glared. "Let them come up here with
me," Ruben said, rising to the occasion.

Joining us now, trying to save face, Zhukov motioned for twelve-year-
old Lisa Grant to speak next.

"Chairman Ruben," Lisa said, "I want to read our Children's Declaration of Dependence to you." Kei, Rachel, and Sean helped Lisa unroll
the scroll. "It was signed by Premier Zhao in China and Prime Minister
Gandhi. We hope you will also sign it," Lisa said. Taking a deep breath
she began to read.

"We hereby dedicate ourselves, our hearts and minds, to world peace.
We believe that all humankind deserves a future free . . ."

"Nyet, nyet," Ruben said, interrupting Lisa. "No, I cannot sign."

Lisa looked as if she was going to cry.

A look of consternation flashed across Ruben's face. A sotto voice
conversation with Zhukov ensued. "Nyet, nyet," he reiterated, "I cannot
sign." Clearly Ruben wanted to sign, but Zhukov was giving the orders.
"It's a matter of protocol," Ruben said. "I cannot sign."

"Well, we can't force you to," I said, as a disappointed Lisa rolled up
the scroll.

After effusive good-byes, we could see that Chairman Ruben was embarrassed about not signing the scroll. I think that because of his chagrin,

he gave us an hour-long tour of the House of Parliament of the USSR Supreme Soviet within the walls of the Kremlin.

Back in San Francisco we were greeted with positive accolades, and at my apartment building I was greeted by Star who was waiting for me in the lobby. She gave me a note from Mari Ellen who said that Star could stay with me for a while. Sean had been picked up at the airport by Clifford and was already on his way back to school, and with Star in the house, even for a short time, I knew I wouldn't be lonesome.

Jet-lagged, with my sense of time skewed, I would awaken at three in the morning, concerned that something awful had happened to one of the children, until I realized I was home. Finally I hit on a solution. Star helped me outline large characters on white construction paper, saying, "YOU ARE HOME. THERE ARE NO KIDS HERE. GO BACK TO SLEEP." Knowing that message was next to my bed was enough to ensure a good night's sleep.

Premiere Zhao arrived in San Francisco, just as he said he would, the day after our return. The Chinese Consul General called to tell me an invitation from Premier Zhao was being hand-delivered for a reception that evening in Mayor Dianne Feinstein's office. I was pleased he had remembered me, but so jet-lagged I could hardly think.

Passing through security, invitation in hand, I arrived at the designated room ahead of schedule. Many of my former acquaintances and friends were there. Foremost among them was the mayor's Chief of Protocol, Charlotte Maillard, a woman I had known for years.

Waiting for Premier Zhao, I was talking with Cyril Magnin, my former boss and now a friend, when Charlotte approached me. "You don't belong here," she said. "Only people who paid for the privilege are allowed in this room!"

"What are you talking about?" I asked. "The Chinese Consul General requested I be here, Charlotte. Furthermore, I've been on the mayor's host committee for years." Charlotte was unmoved. "You belong down the hall with people who haven't paid," she said, piloting me toward the door.

I decided to leave before causing a scene by telling Charlotte off, which the press would have loved. But the next day Herb Caen wrote that I had tried to crash the event. Later that same day, I received a phone call from Deputy Mayor Tom Eastman who said Premier Zhao had asked for me and left a gift, the video of our meeting in Beijing, which would be sent to my home. Tom also said that the premier spent barely five minutes with those gathered in the mayor's office and I was the only person he asked to see.

I had been deeply hurt by Charlotte's verbal assault and her jealousy that Premiere Zhao wanted me there. Out of a misguided definition of what it meant to be a "peacemaker," I swallowed my anger and did not confront my "friend" about her actions. It was getting pretty crowded inside me. I did not know that unresolved anger could damage my health.

Shortly after that incident, I ran into Cyril Magnin who told me that Al Wilsey had said he would no longer support any politician who granted me access. Now I understood the reason for slights from former friends at City Hall. That knowledge did not make me feel better about our city or our country.

# 18.

# A TRIP IN
# THE DARK

I longed for Sean. Although I saw him for school breaks and holidays and our trips abroad, it had been more than three years since we had spent any real time together as a family. He was now fifteen and with his dad for the summer before returning to St. Mark's boarding school. It seemed like the emotional distance between us had become as big as the physical one and I didn't understand why. Sean seldom responded to my letters or phone calls to him at school. But recently he had written me a letter that had thrown me into a tailspin. His communication was printed in distinctive block letters on Lowell Hotel letterhead. It was short, curt.

*"Dear Patricia,"* he wrote. *"I call you Patricia because I don't consider you a mother. Dad says you will understand."*

What was he talking about? Understand what? I picked up the phone and called the Lowell Hotel in Manhattan.

The reservation clerk spoke guardedly with a British accent. "Mr. Wilsey? Mr. Alfred Spaulding Wilsey?"

"Sean . . . Sean Patrick Wilsey. My son. Is he there?"

"One moment please."

I hung on, palms sweating. What would I say to my child? The stranger to whom I had given birth, the boy who had rejected me in favor of the woman who had broken up our family.

The disembodied voice of the gatekeeper came back on the line. "I'm sorry Madam, but the Wilsey family checked out yesterday morning."

"The family?"

"Yes Madam, Mr. Alfred Wilsey and Master Sean Wilsey. They checked out yesterday morning."

"You're sure?"

"Certainly Madam, their car and driver picked them up promptly at eleven o'clock."

"Do you know if they were leaving the country?"

"Madam, I cannot divulge Mr. Wilsey's schedule."

"I'm Sean's mother. I very much need to know where he is."

The man cleared his throat, and then spoke in a lower register. "I think they mentioned their pilot was waiting for them, Madam."

Slamming the phone back onto the receiver, I tried to kill the messenger. Or at least deafen him. My inability to talk to Sean when I needed to threatened to propel me into another depression. I had to snap out of it. I tried to be calm about Sean's "Dear Patricia" letter. I knew he was parroting his dad, but even so I was deeply hurt. It had only been a few months since I had visited Sean at St. Mark's when he had been loving and sweet.

As soon as Sean returned to school from the summer with his father, I called and arranged another visit.

I rented a car and drove in heavy Friday-night traffic from the Boston airport to a hotel near the school. I got lost trying to find the Mass Pike, which turned out to be the Massachusetts Turnpike. I cursed Al. I cursed the traffic. I cursed myself. By the time I got to the Sheraton Hotel where Sean was meeting me, it was after eleven and I was an anxious mess.

Sean was waiting for me in the lobby. I was happy to see him and he acted happy to see me too, but he also seemed nervous. I decided to wait until I was rested to talk to him about the letter. The next day I took him to Boston and after dinner I finally asked him about what he had written to me.

"I'm sorry, Mom." He laughed. "I guess I'm just your crazy teenager son."

"Sean, crazy teenager or not, that was extremely hurtful. Do you honestly think I'm not a mother to you?"

"Well, you'll never be the mother I want," he said, not looking at me.

I tried to remain calm because I didn't want to push Sean further away from me. Maybe this was a teenage thing, maybe all parents had to go through such rebellion.

"Sean," I said, "that may be true but you're stuck with me. And I insist that you show me respect."

"Okay, Mom," Sean said. "I love you anyway."

"I'm glad to hear you say that but it's actions that count, Sean."

"I hope we're going on a peace trip Christmas after next, when I'm with you," he said, changing the subject.

"We'll see," I said, wishing I had help parenting Sean.

All the way home my chattering mind replayed my conversation with Sean. I wished I were wiser and more secure about my role in Sean's life so I could shrug off the hurtful things he said to me. But I wasn't. My only comfort was in meditation and childhood hymns, which in times of duress played over and over in my head, becoming a meditation. *Rock of ages, cleft for me, let me hide myself in thee.*

On a Saturday in November 1984, I was in a fabric store when a stranger began to talk to me. Her deeply wrinkled face was thin. She wore a brown, out-of-style coat that hung loosely on her body. Her accent was thick.

"Are you her? Patricia Montandon?" She touched my arm.

"Yes," I acknowledged.

"You work for peace and *people's* rights, yes? You go to Soviet Union, yes?"

"Yes," I said.

Her gaze was penetrating. "My country, Poland, is so sad there. Fear, no freedom. Such is true all over Eastern Europe."

"I'm sorry. But I hardly know anything about Poland or Eastern Europe."

"All is controlled by USSR. Like prison—go there if you want to do something good. Read, please," she said, pulling a dog-eared newspaper article from her voluminous bag. "Our wonderful priest murdered by Stasi-like police, because he preached human rights." She thrust the article into my hands. "God will bless you if you make one little difference," she said. The woman touched her lips to my hand and then quickly walked away.

The story said that freedoms were so suppressed in the Eastern Bloc nations that those who defied the Soviets, even now in the '80s, were exterminated or sent to relocation camps. "The citizens of Eastern Europe are isolated in their struggle," the author wrote. "The world does not seem to know or care what is happening in Poland, Czechoslovakia, Bulgaria, Hungary, or Romania, where children are starving to death and their parents are powerless."

A month later, while Sean was with his dad for the Christmas holiday, I was on a train sliding across the frozen fields of Eastern Europe during the coldest winter on record there. Star and fourteen other kids, along with a documentary crew from a CBS affiliate, were with me. It felt good to have something important to do.

Our steam-powered Karpati Express, with its melancholy whistle and no dining car, was carrying us across a snow-covered landscape to Prague, Warsaw, Bucharest, Sofia, Belgrade, and Budapest, cities that seemed to be decaying under the communist system. On a small finger of land at the Polish border, our train had been lifted overhead to change its wheels. "While on Soviet land, we must change wheels. Track is different size in USSR," our conductor informed us in a simpering monotone. What was routine for him became dramatic adventure to us.

The monotonous click of train wheels had finally lulled me to sleep when the Karpati Express shuddered and came to a halt. "What now?" I muttered, straining to see through the thick ice curtaining the window. This must be a Soviet border, I thought. My breath clouded before me as I beamed a flashlight into the upper bunk to check on Star and the three other girls sleeping there. They were sound asleep, wrapped in a tangle of coats and blankets. Suddenly, I became fully alert as footsteps in the corridor sounded as if the entire Russian army was arriving. A loud knock on the door was followed by a harsh command.

"Open!"

Sliding the door open, I was greeted by a phalanx of Russian military men. Guns held loosely, the ornamentation on their gray overcoats glinting in the dim hall light, they stamped thick-soled boots against the floor. "Papers. Your papers." Gloved hands reached for the requested passports.

"Out of bed!" they said, as they shined bright flashlights into the upper bunk.

"They're just kids," I said, pulling back the covers to reveal the small faces, flushed with sleep, looking like delicate roses.

The guards did not care that these passengers were children. "Out of bed, all." Gently, I awakened the girls, and helped them put on their coats and boots. They were groggy as they left warm nests and stepped into the frosty corridor. The other children and adults from our group joined us, also heavy-lidded.

The youngest of the children was nine, the oldest thirteen. Two had re-entry permits only, not passports, as they were not U.S. citizens. Orathay was a refugee from Laos, and Nguyen (Win), twelve, was a so-called boat child from Vietnam. Before leaving California, I had received a phone call from the pastor of the Baptist church that Win and his family attended in Atlanta, Georgia. "We're very concerned about this boy being taken into communist countries," he said. "We're afraid he won't be allowed back into the United States."

Their concern surprised me. "I've never had trouble on other trips," I said.

"I know you've taken kids to Russia before," he continued, "but have you ever taken a child who wasn't a citizen of the U.S. and who had fled communism?"

"Well, no," I admitted.

"Do you realize that Win was in prison in Vietnam? He's very precious to us."

"Yes, I know. He's special to me as well." The boy had been awarded our Peace Prize the previous June along with twenty-five kids from other countries. Win's photograph had appeared on page one of *USA Today* and as a result he had received a scholarship to a private school.

"I give you my word," I said to the pastor. "Win will be all right."

But now, here we were, lined up in the middle of the night, cold and sleepy, not knowing what to expect. The Soviet border guards pointed bright flashlights in our faces, checking passports again and again. Telling us to stay in the corridor, the soldiers left, taking our passports with them. Half asleep, Star leaned against me. Orathay clung to my hand. Win looked pale.

"Are you all right, Win?" I asked.

"Yes, ma'am," his reply was soft, polite. "I'm fine." However slight his body, Win's heart was that of a fighter. He and his parents attempted to escape from Vietnam three times before finally making it. He had been imprisoned, and starved.

"Come stand by me, Win," I said. Making a space next to me, I told him that everything would be all right. I had checked with the State Department before we left and his re-entry permit was in order. "We're protected in some mystical way, Win," I said, trying to reassure him.

The child's body, so close to mine, tightened when the guards reappeared. "Are you leader?" The man's expression was as cold as the temperature.

"Yes."

"Papers are not in order." He held Win's permit out in front of him as if it were a viper. "This not passport. Not proper papers. The boy must leave train."

Win leaned into me, his coat pulled tight.

"That's a re-entry permit. It is legal. I checked before leaving the United States." I hoped my voice did not betray my alarm.

"Is . . . not . . . passport!" He emphasized each word by slapping the permit against his hand. "The boy comes."

"No!" I held Win close.

"You cannot proceed trip." It was a standoff. Handing me the stack of passports, minus Win's permit, the man growled, "You and boy wait. Others to bed."

The weight of responsibility was overwhelming. I silently prayed, and I wondered once again why God had chosen me, if indeed I had been chosen, to carry on this work for peace.

"Now," I said, "all of you, scurry back to your warm bunks. I'll stay with Win. Don't worry."

Donna and John Velasquez, traveling with their son John, cast quizzical looks at me. "John, I need your help," I said. He was a lawyer and I knew he would be responsible. "Take all the passports except mine. If anything happens and we have to get off the train, you're in charge." John took the passports and squeezed my hand reassuringly. But I could see his concern. I was their leader; it was my personal faith and belief in the power of children to open doors and create a peaceful world that had led us here. I had to appear strong and sure.

The doors of the various compartments slid closed as the group settled down again. Draping my bulky coat around Win, I held him close, feeling the hard thump of his heart through his clothing. Putting my cheek against his coarse black hair, I attempted to comfort him. "Everything will be fine, you'll see." But I wondered why Win had been singled out and Orathay had not.

Approaching footsteps alerted me to the return of the patrols. They loomed in front of us, a battalion of power and authority. "The boy comes," a soldier said.

"Then, I'm coming, too."

One of the guards made a half-hearted attempt to wrest Win away, but seemed to change his mind. Keeping my arms tightly around the child, we followed the soldiers to the end of the car. As we stepped off the train, separated from our base, my heart sank.

Our boots crunched in the snow and icy wind tore at us. We followed the soldiers into a small wooden building near the tracks. The room was lit by a single bulb dangling over the desk of a man who was clearly in charge. Cast in shadow, his face was obscured. Whatever he was holding looked like a letter. I could see Win's white re-entry permit lying next to one of three telephones.

"This is not passport." The man thumped the document with tobacco-stained fingers.

"It's a re-entry permit."

"Is not legal."

"Yes, it is. I checked with the State Department before we left the United States."

"You, you are Paytreeseeya." It was not a question, but I nodded.

"You spent two days in Assisi, met mayor, was with pope in Rome, da?"

A chill, quite different from the one produced by the weather, caused my knees to shake. How did he know this?

"Yes," I said.

"You saw pope."

We had seen the pope again, only six days before, but it all seemed remote now. I had to pinch myself to make sure I wasn't hallucinating.

"In Warsaw, you went to Popieluszko church!" He pounded his desk with a closed fist, "against official orders."

Yes, we had gone to the church of Father Jerzy Popieluszko, the priest who had spoken out against the Soviet-controlled government. He had been brutally assassinated by the Polish secret police two months before we arrived in Warsaw.

In Warsaw, we had only just arrived at the Victoria Hotel when a burly, dark-haired man introduced himself as our host. "Do you have plans for tonight?" His manner was brusque.

"No, we have no plans for tonight," I said. We were tired after our long train ride from Prague.

The man looked relieved. "Good. I'll see you tomorrow. Have pleasant sleep."

After dinner we revived and the filmmakers suggested we go to Popieluszko's church. "We can get some good shots there."

"Okay," I said, not dreaming we could create an international incident by doing so.

As soon as we got out of the cabs, we were led by an elderly priest past the long lines of people and into the church courtyard. Thousands of candles were burning there, melting the snow and creating a halo of warmth around masses of flowers mounded on the grave of Father Popieluszko. Inside the church, thousands were praying as six priests officiated at the last Sunday mass of December 1984. The intense emotions of the devout, the weeping, and the sense of danger affected us deeply. I was glad when we were finally outside again, in the crisp, cold air.

When we got back to our hotel, the man who had met us earlier was pacing in front. He was furious that we had gone to the murdered priest's church and he warned us we were being watched. "Under no circumstances are you to go see Lech Walesa (the steelworker leader of Solidarity and later president of Poland)," he said.

We had been glad to leave Poland but sidling up to me as we boarded the Karpati Express, a man had whispered to me in English. "Get children back to U.S. fast, or trouble."

Was he the person who had supplied this Soviet border guard with such detailed information about us, I wondered? How dare they try to scare us, to follow us, and threaten Win!

The face of the officer behind the desk was almost obscured by a veil of smoke. "Do you have children?" I asked him. He fanned the gray smoke away with his hand and gave me a quizzical look. "Do you have children?" I asked again.

He exhaled and the wall of cigarette smoke grew thicker again.

"Dyeti?" I used the Russian word for children. "Do you have dyeti?"

"Da, da," he said with a smile. His gold front tooth glinted in the dim light. Pulling open a drawer, the officer took out a black-and-white photograph of two young girls, and handed it to me. Alongside them stood the man in front of us, their father.

"Natasha, Marina, six, eight." He beamed.

"They are beautiful girls. You love them very much, da?"

He took the picture from me and kissed the photograph. "Da, da," he said.

"Do you want them to be allowed to grow up, and not be killed in a war?"

"Da, sure." He glanced at me.

"We also want your Marina and Natasha to be able to grow up without fear of a being killed in a war." Unpinning the CATP pin from my coat, I handed it to him. "For your girls. For Natasha and Marina."

He took the pin in his massive hands and slowly read it aloud. "Children As The Peacemakers. Good, is good. Spasiba, thank you." He lit another cigarette. "The boy has no passport." He drummed his fingers on the desk.

Suddenly, Win moved from my protective arms and with courage few show, addressed the man, speaking softly. "Sir, thank you sir, I was in a war, a prisoner, when I was six, and sir, I hope your children are never in a war. We should love each other." There was a hint of emotion in the boy's voice.

The bureaucrat looked at Win, as if seeing him for the first time. He turned the pin I had given him around in his hands, gazed a moment at the photographs of his children, and then back at Win. Abruptly, he scraped his chair back and stood up. Speaking rapidly in Russian, he handed me Win's permit, and then walked across the room and opened the door. "Go. Have peace," he said, not looking at either one of us.

A wave of relief engulfed me. Once again I felt the assurance that we were protected by an unseen power. As we stepped back on the train, I smiled at the guards. "Mir," I said, the Russian word for peace.

"Mir," they replied, smiling ever so slightly, as if unaccustomed to doing so.

Knocking on Win's compartment door, I was startled when it slid back to reveal our entire group scrunched together in the tiny space. Seeing us, they broke into applause. Amid a wild tumble of arms, legs, and relieved giggles, they hugged Win.

"You are my family," the boy sobbed into his cupped hands. "You didn't leave me."

"Yes, we are your family, Win," I said. "We would never leave you."

"This is the first time I feel I belong since leaving Vietnam." His voice was muted. "You don't show prejudice or think I'm different. You show love."

Star, who from the start had decided Win was her brother, said with simple truth, "Win, it's you who loves us. That makes us love you."

Back in the United States, in Washington, D.C., we once again attempted to be received by President Reagan. Again, we failed. So instead, we arranged for the children to lay a wreath on the Tomb of the Unknown Soldier at Arlington National Cemetary.

That January morning at Arlington Cemetery was freezing cold. Taps, the poignant respect for the dead, chilled us even more. The sound drifted across the fields of white tombstones in a reverberating lament. A pause, and then a quartet of Marines in lockstep—with highly polished black shoes and sharply pressed uniforms—led the children forward to the Tomb of the Unknown Soldier. Somber, dignified, their small hands touching a wreath of yellow chrysanthemums, they carefully placed it on the memorial.

The words engraved there were no less effective in Hebrew, German, Chinese, Russian, Arabic, or any language. "Here rests in honored glory a Soldier, whose name is known but to God."

I stood there reflecting on the path that had led me to this cemetery on a hillside outside our nation's capital. Looking past the white markers, I viewed landmarks that link us all the way from George Washington to the Vietnam War: the Curtis-Lee Mansion, the Lincoln Memorial, and the Capitol dome.

With a cannon salute, the choreographed ceremony ended. The children clustered near as the shivery ether resonated once again with the sound of taps. That haunting salute traveled over the graves, lingered around the eternal flame, and finally came to rest on the white marble Tomb of the Unknown Soldier.

Unknown child.

Unknown mother.

Unknown father.

Unknown.

It was our mission to give a voice to this soldier and the victims of war—to make them, the father, the mother, the child, known. We had traveled the world to do it, met leaders from every country we visited— but on this somber day, we were leaving our nation's capital having been spurned by our own.

# 19.
# THE MYSTICAL ROCK

The following spring in 1985, I opened the *Examiner* and there on page one, staring out at me, were pictures of the gaunt faces of children in a famine camp in Ethiopia. I turned away from my breakfast and began to read about the famine and Colonel Mengistu Haile Marriam, the dictator who ruled the country.

The report said that when the famine first hit, Mengistu used the disaster as a pretext to forcibly relocate hundreds of thousands of villagers. The "villagization" campaign was meant to relocate people from food-deficient areas in the north to the fertile plains of the south. In reality, I read, the move was meant to empty rebel-held areas of potential supporters. The government especially targeted young people. The families of those killed were required to pay for the bullets used to execute their children.

Impulsively I got up from the table and went to the phone. I was going to Ethiopia, I decided. I couldn't stand to see those faces staring out at me over the breakfast table. David Myers, my travel agent, said he couldn't book a flight for me because the United States did not have diplomatic relations with Ethiopia. After numerous phone calls and false starts, I arranged to join two men from World Vision who were taking supplies to the famine camps.

Once I knew I could get there, I decided to auction my last major work of art, a Rodin sculpture called *La France*, to buy aid to take to the victims of the famine. During the decade we were married, Al and I had enjoyed buying a handful of great works of art and they had special meaning for us. But now, it's only use to me was to fund my work. Al heard about my intent to sell the Rodin and purchased it himself. That was fine with me. I wanted to take aid to the famine victims to salve my conscience for having so much when children were starving.

The two men I was with largely ignored me but I could tell they were uncomfortable with me. In Kenya we got our visas and then flew to Addis Abba, and a few days later to Idnap, a famine camp on the northern plains of Ethiopia. In Idnap, I was thrown into a world I could have scarcely imagined.

Forty thousand famine victims hardly moved as they sought shade under swaying rag canopies. Waves of heat undulated across the corrugated tin roofs of the feeding stations. Surely, this was Hell, I thought.

Why such heartbreaking inequities in life? I wondered. Even though my childhood had been one of relative poverty, in Idnap, Ethiopia, the cruel reality of real need was brought home to me. Poverty was not a strong enough word to even begin to describe such circumstances.

Sweat ran down my sides, leaking through my white cotton underwear, staining my khaki pants as if I had lost control of my bladder. My long blonde hair was pulled up and tied with a frayed red ribbon I had torn off my suitcase.

I was wondering what to do to help when a relief worker approached me. "You can work in the dying hut," she said, as she pulled open a canvas flap and led me inside a tin structure. The stench of death was overwhelming. The room was crowded with stick-thin women and children lying on mats. It was eerily quiet. I wanted to run back outside. But if I ran away, I would prove to be as inept in this famine camp setting as my traveling companions expected me to be.

"What can I do?" I asked, feeling weak.

Before she left, the relief worker said, "Just hold their hands, help them die."

I inhaled, trying to keep my emotions in check, and knelt on the dirt floor beside an emaciated young child, cradled in the arms of her equally wasted mother. They lay, unseeing, on sour-smelling straw mats the same color as the earth, the landscape, the room, and the tatters that clothed them. They already could have been dead, so hollow were their eyes.

Their coal-black skin was pulled gaunt against skulls that seemed too large for such frail bodies. Other people lay in rows along the walls of the hut duplicating the dying mother and her dying child, a madman's illusion.

Even my unusual appearance in such a setting failed to elicit a single spark of interest, although I smiled and hummed while stroking the soft, feverish arm of the little girl. I was surprised that her skin was so soft. I had expected it to feel scabby, callused like her mother's feet, which were splayed out with inflamed legs no bigger around than a silver dollar. A relief worker had told me that those limbs had carried her emaciated daughter, slung in a length of cloth across her back, over a hundred miles across the cracked earth of her homeland to reach this place.

Singing softly, as I had to Sean when he was a child, I shooed away the flies feeding on the mucus from the little one's mouth. "You are my sunshine, my only sunshine . . ." The child reached up and wrapped her scrawny little fingers around my thumb. She held on to me, to life, trying to live against all odds. My voice cracked with emotion as I continued my tune. "You make me happy, when skies are gray . . ."

Spontaneously I released my hair from the red ribbon I had used to keep it in a ponytail, and crooning still, fastened it around the girl's wrist. The scarlet glowed like a distress signal in the stillness of decay.

Then, penetrating the walls of the dying hut, came the sound of an Ethiopian chant. I had seen the small group of singers earlier, near what looked like a gravesite. Now, their falsetto voices, rising and falling, pierced the space, undermining my simple tune, unnerving me. Those haunting lamentations, those plaintive cries, sounded like the forlorn soul of a lost tribe. It felt like an arctic wind had blasted through the scorched atmosphere and slithered down my spine.

"Auggh . . . auggh." Gravelly sounds coming from the mother's throat made me flinch. With visible effort the woman took a breath, her skeletal hands clutching her baby.

"Auggh." She suddenly stared at me, her eyes fixed, she made another guttural noise, and thrust the child at me.

There was nothing to do, short of letting the child fall, but to catch her in my arms. She felt no heavier than a rag doll.

The worn-looking mother, probably no more than twenty-five years old, uttered yet another cry and then, as if she had nothing left to do, let her head fall back onto the mat. In seemingly choreographed movements, she drew her legs up under her body, arched her right arm out toward the child and me, made a slight noise, and through cracked lips, seemed to smile. Then she stopped breathing.

Two men arrived almost at once with a rawhide stretcher, covered the woman's body with a dingy cloth, and carted her off. The only sign of mourning was the ongoing funeral chant from outside the hut.

Until now I had shut off my emotions. Crying would interfere with the work I was there to do. It would cripple me. But the barrier I had erected to hold my tears was crumbling. If my hard-won sense of control gave way to tears, I feared they would never stop. Staring down at the frail child in my arms, so alone and sick, and dependent upon a stranger, I began to pray. "Oh God, help me to keep my tears dammed up, help me to help this baby, help . . . help . . . help."

A pallid, plump, white woman, a nurse, her daisy-print dress clinging to her body, her brown hair cut short, appeared at my side and took the little one from me. The woman reminded me of a missionary who had spoken at my dad's church when I was five.

"Go outside, Pat. Find the people you came here with, take a breather." Her skin was the color of ashes. She could stand a break herself. "There's food and tea in that building over there," she said, her voice weary. She pointed across the esplanade to a place near a scorched vegetable garden.

"But the child?"

"She won't live long. Poor little thing, she's hardly breathing." She held the girl loosely in her arms. "I've seen hundreds die since I've been here. Over a year now." She sighed then coughed.

"Can't we do something? Anything?"

"No. She's in the hands of God now." She glanced at the baby, then at me. She said,"Aren't you a preacher's daughter? From Oklahoma, right?"

I nodded yes. "Texas and Oklahoma. A long time ago."

"Well, even if it was a long time ago, you should know God works in mysterious ways. Now go, take a break." She walked away, limping slightly, the child's arm with the red ribbon dangling like a toy. I stared after her, uncertain what to do, but finally decided to make my escape through a droopy canvas opening.

Outside the dying hut, in blinding glare, I stumbled through the encampment, determined to ignore the misery surrounding me on every side. But sick children, wearing donated t-shirts printed with ironic slogans such as Fun in the Sun, continually stopped me. With circular motions, they rubbed distended bellies, put grimy fingers into ulcerated mouths, letting me know they were hungry. A little girl, no more than four years old, turned and lifted her skirt to show me pustules erupting in a frenzy of pain on her inflamed buttocks. Her eyes, fringed by crusted lashes, begged me to do something.

There was nothing I could do. The aid I had brought, blankets for the often-chilly nights, flour, and sugar, were kept track of and given out from a central location. I had no control over it.

I covered my eyes with sunglasses and tied a scarf around my hair as I began a game of pretend. Humming a show tune, I tried to distance myself from the viscous web of despair.

"Send in the clowns . . . where are the clowns . . ." A lone and mostly barren tree on the far edge of the campsite beckoned. The tree, like the only survivor of a ferocious battle, stood majestically erect, silhouetted against the sky with limbs lifted toward heaven as if honing in for a message from God. For rain.

A few limp leaves among brown thorns hung from the tree branches, a testament to the indomitable will of all living things to survive, to grow, however harsh the environment. Propping myself up against the rough trunk, I bent my knees, put my head down against them, and let my tears flow. I poured out the sorrow I felt for what I had just witnessed, the sick children, the orphaned baby, and the dead mother.

Leaning back against the tree, my eyes closed, trying to get more comfortable, suddenly I had a feeling that I wasn't alone. I opened my eyes. Surrounding me, staring, were a dozen children. They clustered together as if for protection from a blue-eyed alien. Their skin, hairless heads, mahogany eyes, colorless shreds of clothing, and beige teeth blended with the earth and the mud-colored sky.

"Hi," I said.

"Hi," they replied.

"You speak English!"

"You speak English!" They repeated.

"Do you speak English?"

"Do you speak English?" They were perfect imitators.

"I love you."

"I love you."

"Selam," I responded.

"Selam," they echoed.

With each word they moved closer. One unsmiling boy shifted so near, leaning in, seeking affection, I thought he might crawl onto my lap. The child wasn't wearing a shirt. His sharp ribs were laid bare by starvation, each breath obvious. His knobby knees were exposed in ragged shorts unlike his companions whose loose garments, tied across scrawny shoulders, covered their legs. Smiling, I took the child's hand and tried to pull him onto my lap. He leaned toward me, but then quickly drew away and laughed, to my surprise, showing polished white teeth.

"What is your name?" I asked.

"What is your name?" He replied, his brown eyes rimmed by thick black lashes.

"Pat."

"Pat."

"No, your name?"

"No, your name?"

"Hello."

"Hello."

"Love, peace, love."

"Love, peace, love." It was a game.

Getting to my feet, I began like a pied piper, to lead the kids in a dusty dance across the bleak landscape. We waltzed, ran, square danced, and hollered a litany of English words. An audience materialized on the rise above us. They watched, leaning on tree limbs, propping each other up to gaze at their children—children still—as they played with me.

"Love. Selam. Peace. Love. Peace. I love you. I love you. Love. Love. Selam. Peace. Peace. Love. Love. Hello. Hello . . ."

Oh, how I wished I could speak their language. We held hands, ran in circles, walked in a straight line, zigzagged, and laughed in the face of death.

My energy flagged, but the undernourished children had the stamina of the healthy. They were starved, not only for food, but for play and diversion as well.

After a time, I saw the men I had come with waving to me from the dusty field we used for a runway. It was time to leave, to go back to the comfort of a hotel room in Addis Ababa. Holding my hands up, I indicated the children were not to follow me. Bare feet rooted, their toes clutched the earth as if they grew there. They dared not move. They had seen the soldiers from President Mengistu's military government, guns drawn, guarding the aircraft.

I thought about the dictator as I waved good-bye to the children. I hoped they would be safe. If only I could gather them to me and whisk them away. Waving and then blowing a kiss, I turned away resolutely, my eyes stinging.

I was about fifteen feet from the aircraft when a soldier, his gun pointed in my direction, yelled. I stopped. But the man, his green uniform soaked with sweat, his face intense, walked past me. His target was the shirtless boy, the one who had been holding my hand minutes before and who, evidently, had followed me. The child looked terrified as the soldier bore down on him.

Without a thought of danger, though I could hear shouts from the pilot, I intercepted the man. With a smile and forced casualness, I greeted him as if we were out for a Sunday stroll. "Hi, thanks for taking care of our plane. My name is Pat, and I'm so glad to be in your country . . ." I said, panting.

To my astonishment the soldier stopped his forward thrust and answered me in English. "You U.S. lady?"

"Yes, yes I am. How wonderful that you speak English. I was taking this boy to get something for him from the airplane and I truly

appreciate . . ." My babbling stopped when the armed man smiled, showing beige teeth worn down from malnutrition. He was not much more
than a child himself.

"Okay, U.S. lady, okay," he motioned toward the airplane with the
butt of his gun.

"Cigarette?"

"Sorry, no," I said, grasping the shirtless boy's hand. I began thinking
about the things I had in my backpack. Lipstick, sunscreen, aspirin, prescription medications, underwear, pajamas . . . pajamas . . . yes, of course,
the boy needed a shirt. I had a pajama top. Okay.

Everyone, including the boy and the soldier, watched as I retrieved
the garment from my bag. The name of French designer Givenchy was
emblazoned in a paisley pattern across the soft jersey fabric. The irony
did not escape me.

The boy gave me a shy smile when I put the top on him and tied the
drawstring neck into a bow. I felt like a mom again.

This hapless young refugee from hunger was not without grace
and a sense of appreciation. Digging into the pocket of his threadbare
Western-style shorts, he withdrew a gift. With a broad smile he handed it
to me. It was a rock. A rock as black as midnight, one end touched by the
color of a golden sunset. Turning his pocket inside out, the boy laughed
aloud when he revealed a further treasure. How odd, I thought. His treasure was a bit of red ribbon. It was the ribbon I had untied from my hair,
the one I had placed around the wrist of the dying child.

"Selam," he whispered, tucking the tag of color back in his pocket before running to join his friends.

I stared after him. He resembled a man in a photograph my therapist,
Dr. Shelia Krystal, had shown me—an Indian guru of some sort.

"Hurry it up, Pat. We gotta' get goin'." The pilot clearly was annoyed
as were the men with whom I had come to this tragic land. Hands on
hips, they radiated disapproval. They had tolerated my presence because
of the money I had given to their organization for supplies, and they
probably thought there was more where that came from.

Three nights earlier, through thin hotel room walls, I had heard them talking about me. "She's nuts, you know. Meditatin', thinkin' she was guided to come here. Thinkin' she had a vision. A rich divorcee woman, nothin' better to do, I'll wager." They didn't need to know that I had sold a work of art to buy food and medicine for the victims of the famine.

Over the drone of engines, seat belts tight across bellies, chewing gum in their mouths replacing toothpicks, the men probed. "What did that kid give you? Back there, you know, when you put that shirt thing on him? He gave you somethin'." They exchanged winks. "Didja tell him how to meditate?"

"He gave me a rock, a plain old rock," I said, slipping the gift into my purse without showing it to them. Even then I knew it was much more than a plain old rock. As we flew away from the camp, across the headlands of the Blue Nile, into lush green countryside, I wondered out loud why the whole area couldn't be irrigated like California's desert. There, row after row of fragrant orange trees grew before being uprooted for ranch-style houses.

"The long rains didn't come and they don't know how to dig for water," one of my traveling companions said. "But look over there." The pilot flew the rattling plane low, over a big square of green. "That's the North Koreans' doins'. They're testin' for the government. Rice fields. Piped the water from a long ways away. But the politicians don't want the natives to know nothin' either. You know?"

How could a leader be so cruel to the very people he was supposed to protect? I wondered. Just like personal relationships, those we trust—those who know us best—can hurt us the most.

My thoughts were still gloomy when I got back to San Francisco. Back in my penthouse, before unpacking, I pulled open the apple-green silk draperies in my bedroom and flopped down on the king-size bed in my tired-looking travel clothes, oblivious to the silk spread and hand-embroidered pillows. No one had met me at the airport. There was no one to whom I could tell my stories of the famine. No one to hear about the baby whose mother died or the boy who gave me a rock after I put my pajama top on him. Who could I tell about my traveling companions, the men who barely tolerated my presence?

Why had I cut myself off from so many people?

Perhaps it was because of the change within me. My social friends, for the most part, seemed to care only about the latest fashions or the next party. Things that no longer interested me, so I was no longer interested in them.

Gazing out my bedroom window, I watched soothing gray fog finger under the Golden Gate Bridge and linger in smoky swirls over Alcatraz Island. The panorama of water, fog, and seabirds eased my mind. But the emptiness I felt, knowing I could die right there, and no one would find my body for weeks, made it hard to get off the bed to unpack.

My bags challenged me to unpack and my large purse was a mess. Dumping its contents onto the bed, I dispiritedly sorted through the debris. Lipstick, melted chewing gum, foreign coins, and then, like a forgotten friend, the ebony rock.

Rubbing it lightly against my face I fancied I could smell the plains of Ethiopia and the innocent aroma of the child who had given it to me.

The rock meant something to me. I did not want to lose it. So I began to search for the perfect place to stash it. As I walked down a hallway over soft carpeting and descended a winding staircase into the mirrored foyer, I caught the reflection of the large and ancient wooden Buddha ensconced on a table. It was a prized possession, which I had purchased three years earlier when I had taken Sean on a vacation to Japan for a month, trying to bond with him again.

From the moment we found it, almost hidden behind a screen of painted birds in a small antique shop in Kyoto, Sean and I both loved the Buddha. The striking sculpture was made of a black tropical wood and bore traces of a gold border on the robes. The Buddha's countenance radiated such serenity that I bought it on the spot.

And now the Buddha's outstretched hand, fingers gently curved, seemed a likely spot, a resting place, for the gift I thought special because of the child who had given it to me. But it wasn't until I placed the rock in the Buddha's hand that I realized how truly unique it was.

It was amazing. As if designed to go there, its shape nestled perfectly within the fingers of Buddha. The ebony hue of the rock matched the Buddha's color, making it appear that the rock and the figure were carved from the same substance. Even the golden shade on one end of the rock harmonized with the faded gold trim of the Buddha's robe. The rock and the Buddha were one.

Taken aback, I thought of the child who had given it to me. How strange that he had reminded me of a man I had seen in a photograph in my therapist's office.

Pondering the unusual happening, I picked up the rock to inspect it again. My hands tingled. It was as if reinvigorated blood surged through my veins, strengthening muscles, healing my heart.

Placing the rock back into the hand of Buddha, I noticed something more. Two engraved lines, shadowed by gray within the black rock, co-joined and continued the exact same dusky stripes in the hand of the Buddha. It was an unbelievable coincidence.

I reflected on the hopelessness I had felt six years earlier when my married life was in shambles. That crisis had led to a vision and saved not only my life, but perhaps my soul as well. A soul in danger of being smashed by the weight of material possessions: homes, jewels, limousines and private jets, trips, parties, and unlimited shopping, until I had lost sight of the reason I was given life.

It had taken a rock from a field in Africa, given to me by a hungry child in rags, to reawaken me.

# 20.

# THE HUNDREDTH MONKEY

A few days after my return from Ethiopia, I got a call from the FBI, which was followed by a visit. "Hello," I said to the buttoned-up fellow at my door. "May I see your badge?"

"Oh, sure." He flipped a leather case open and flashed an honest-to-goodness FBI badge. Feeling like a suspect on a television series, I invited him inside.

"Now Ms. Montandon, I just want to ask you a few questions," he said, proceeding as if I had said it was okay." He sat down and crossed his legs in sharply creased trousers, and then opened a briefcase and pulled out a file.

My file? I wondered.

I didn't have to wonder for long. The agent began to quiz me about various people I had met in my travels and especially about my connections in the Soviet Union. He knew so many details about me, and the trips I had taken, it was obvious that I had been followed and my activities reported to the FBI, probably for years. I needed to talk to a lawyer, I thought, so I asked the agent to leave.

The man got up from the chair and moved slowly toward the foyer. "Call me if anything unusual occurs. We are only trying to protect you," he said.

Putting the FBI out of my mind, unafraid, I increased the mortgage on my penthouse and went about the business of paying bills and financing my work.

Sean was still in boarding school and we spoke on the phone from time to time. Star was living with me again, which meant school lunches and homework. Star was practicing for our big Peace Prize Ceremony that would be held in February 1986, in the glorious rotunda of City Hall. It was a big deal.

Children from forty-four countries selected by organizations in their nations would be there to accept their peace awards. And a special award would be given to Jane Smith on behalf of her daughter Samantha, killed in an air crash three months earlier.

Samantha was ten when she had written to Soviet leader Yuri Andropov, asking why he wanted to start a war and take over the world. Andropov had replied with an invitation for the girl to visit the Soviet Union. Samantha captivated the Russians. They had adored "Samantha Smeeth."

When we found out that Muhammad Ali would also be present for our Peace Prize Ceremony, I was elated. But a few weeks later a friend in Los Angeles called with unsettling information. "Pat, there's a story in the *Los Angeles Times* about a Children's Peace Prize event. Lots of movie stars are involved," she said. "The honorary chairman for the inaugural fund-raiser is Muhammad Ali."

"No! I was told that everything was on track for our ceremony," I said, aghast.

"Well, Pat, the awards are to be, and I quote, 'bestowed' on John Lennon and Samantha Smith! I'll send you a program," my friend said.

When the elaborate printed program for the First Annual Children's Peace Awards arrived, I was stunned.

"As its initial project, Muhammad Ali and other prominent personalities will accompany fifty children, each from a different country, to meet the world's superpower leaders and the pope. This unique event that unites the world's children and leaders will be known as the Children's Peace Journey and will take place in the summer of 1986."

As it turned out, no ceremony took place nor did Muhammad Ali make a trip with kids. After the tickets for the ceremony were sold, the money for the event was nowhere to be found. Muhammad Ali and I had both been used.

But regardless of what happened in Los Angeles, nothing could dampen our excitement over our Peace Prize Ceremony. On the night of the event, two hundred people in formal attire sat at tables that were centered by peace lilies and aglow with candlelight. An orchestra played as a large movie screen at the top of the marble staircase showed children arriving in San Francisco from across the planet. When the picture became live, and the forty-four Peace Prize winners in native dress ran down the red-carpeted stairs to take their places at a long table, they were welcomed with enthusiastic applause.

Leila Gilday, an Inuit child from Canada, wearing a buckskin dress and moccasins, summed up my feelings about children and peace with this story. "When I was little," she said, "my mom told me legends. One was about a bear that stole the sun. It was a raven, in the form of a child, that brought the light back to the world. I think we children could be the raven that brings the light back to the world."

When I introduced Soviet Consul General Kàmanev that evening, the audience murmured in surprise, "The Soviet Consul General?" Standing at the mike, wearing a tuxedo, unusual for a Russian at the time, the Consul General read from a prepared text: "It gives me great pleasure to announce the peace award for a Soviet girl to travel with Pat Montandon to five cities in the United States, in memory of Samantha Smith."

This was a first. Members of the media surged forward, wanting to know more. I was excited but did not have an inkling of the magnitude of the idea that had just been launched or of the challenges we would encounter.

Seven months later, eleven-year-old Katerina (Katya) Lycheva, a beautiful child actress with huge green eyes and brown hair cut in an up-to-date style, came to the United States from Moscow for what became a historic peace trip. I had chosen Star to be Katya's traveling companion because I knew she would be able to handle the pressure and would not be jealous of the attention the Russian girl received.

We thought we were prepared for Katya's visit, but we were not. As soon as the first press release went out, we got requests for her to be on

THE HUNDREDTH MONKEY                                    225

everything from the *Today* show, the *Tonight* show with Johnny Carson, and it seemed, every radio and television show in the nation. They all wanted Katya. The excitement began even before she left Russia. On *ABC Nightly News*, anchor Peter Jennings had pictures of Katya boarding an airplane in Moscow. "A little girl from Moscow is winging her way to the United States," he said.

When Katya arrived in Chicago on a Sunday evening, accompanied by four adults, over one hundred members of the media were waiting for her. It was that way for her entire tour. I felt as if I were traveling with a rock star. McDonald's closed so Katya could have a hamburger there and the police blocked off streets as people strained to see her. The child became a major celebrity in the U.S., and in the USSR as well.

Everything was hectic but seemed to be going well until we reached New York. We were touring the United Nations building when my assistant Barbara came running up to me. She was out of breath, her face was flushed "Pat . . . quick . . . hurry . . . there's been an assassination threat against Katya! Call Gladys Boluda at the State Department!"

I dialed the number I had been given and Gladys answered.

"Pat," she said, "there's been a death threat against Katya. The State Department is taking it very seriously."

"What should I do?"

"You should get the Russians back to the Soviet Union. We are working on it, but you should get Katya back to the Soviet Union at once. Keep me posted," Gladys said, hanging up.

While I was on the phone, Barbara was pacing back and forth in front of the sofa where the Soviets were sitting. I surveyed the area. Was an assassin lurking behind that door? I wondered, sweating. Dimitri Agratchev, our interpreter, asked me if something was wrong.

"Dimitri, please tell Katya's chaperone, Alevitina, that I need to talk to her right now. Over there." I indicated a phone booth on the far side of the room. Alevitina quickly walked over. The three of us huddled together, partially inside the phone booth, as I continued to glance around.

"Katya's life has been threatened," I whispered. "Our State Department recommends Katya return to Moscow. If you want to stop the tour, I'll pay your way back to Moscow. It's your call."

Alevitina appeared unruffled, but her face was ashen. Dimitri was blinking so fast that I wondered how he could see. The politburo chaperone was the first to speak.

"How will you protect Katya?" she asked in Russian, and Dimitri translated.

Thinking fast, I hoped my credit cards were still good for cash. "I'll hire bodyguards and ask the hotel to close off our floor. Other than that, I don't know what to do." The responsibility for Katya's life was staggering.

"We will stay," Alevitina said with certitude. "Da, we will stay. But Katya and her mother Marina are not to know."

"Da," I answered. I wasn't about to tell Alevitina how to handle her end of this stressful turn of events.

Almost immediately we had two police cars escorting us as we drove around New York City. The Hyatt Hotel closed off floors for us. Bodyguards were hired. Our car had blacked-out windows. I was scared silly that some nut would try to become famous by shooting Katya.

Events were moving so fast that there was no time for reflection on the international impact of what we were doing, which I learned later was huge. In Washington, D.C., the State Department called the minute we checked in at the Hyatt, wanting to know every detail of our itinerary. FBI agents guarded us around the clock. They accompanied us everywhere we went and sat outside our rooms at night. They even answered our phones. With sirens blaring, Washington police ushered us around the capital.

Katya was a superstar. Crowds had to be contained behind police barriers even when we took her sightseeing. Yet, through it all, the years of work, the entreaties, and now this historical breakthrough, our own government still proved to be the most resistant to our peace efforts.

"Are we going to see President Reagan?" Katya asked. "I have a present for him." She showed me a cloth doll in the shape of the earth and wearing a babushka scarf.

We had tried every avenue to get an appointment for Katya with the president. Nothing worked, although prestigious news agencies were calling on him to see the child. The day before we were to leave for

Texas, we got a phone call from the White House. President Reagan would see us at nine the next morning.

At the White House the next day, we were taken away from the tourist areas and asked for any gifts we might have for the president, so they could be x-rayed. We waited. I wandered over to look at something and then suddenly, Katya, Marina, Dimitri, and Star were gone. They had been spirited away for a meeting with Reagan. I was not invited, nor was Alevitina or the press entourage that had followed us to the White House. Afterward, we were given an official photograph of Katya presenting her babushka earth to the President of the United States.

An official press release said that President Reagan accidentally ran into the Soviet child as she was touring the White House. I wondered if the administration thought they would be perceived as going soft on communism if they acknowledged meeting with a Soviet child on a peace trip.

Al was quoted as saying the Katya trip was a stunt and an ego trip for me. I was upset with myself that I allowed his criticism to affect me. Why did I still hear his censorious voice in my head?

A year later, I came up with the idea and coordinated the first Soviet/American copublication: a book, *Making Friends*. Photographs by Morton Beebe accompanied the story that Katya and Star wrote about their remarkable journey together. *Making Friends* became a historical record of a giant breakthrough by ordinary citizens during the Cold War. I did not put my name on the cover of the book I had created. The harsh criticism I had received from Al caused me to retreat from, instead of embrace, my gifts. It would take a while for me to wake up and stop allowing others to dictate how I should feel about myself.

A few months after Katya's trip, Star and I were treated to a celebratory tour of the Soviet Union. In Moscow we had been given an appointment with the ballet mistress of the famed Bolshoi. My lovely surrogate daughter donned black leotards and stood poised with her long neck extended, her arms graceful, and with piano accompaniment performed her Prayer for Peace. Afterward, Star was given the opportunity to study with the Bolshoi, provided she did specific exercises that would enable her to do high leg lifts.

"Star, if you really want to be a ballet dancer this is a great opportunity," I said.

"Do you want me to?" Star nervously laced her fingers together. "I don't think I can do those exercises," she said.

"Star darling, it's not my decision to make. It's up to you and Mari Ellen, but I'll support whatever you want to do. You can decide after we get home."

Later, Star admitted that she was afraid to live so far away from home. I understood her feelings, but I was disappointed. Training with the famous Bolshoi was the opportunity of a lifetime, but Star didn't see it that way.

When someone sent me *The Hundredth Monkey* by Ken Keyes, it resonated powerfully with me because of what we were trying to do. The story is about monkeys that were being studied by scientists on islands off the coast of Japan. The scientists observed that when a young female began to wash the sand off her sweet potatoes before she ate them, the adult monkeys soon began to imitate her. Then something startling took place. Monkeys on one other island began to do the same thing. Soon, colonies of monkeys on all the islands and on the mainland began washing their sweet potatoes before eating them as if communicating directly from mind to mind, like ESP.

The theory is that when a critical number achieve awareness, this new awareness seems to be communicated—mind-to-mind. When only a limited number of people know something, it remains the conscious property of those people. But there is a critical point at which, if only one more person, the hundredth monkey, tunes in to a new awareness, a field is strengthened so that awareness reaches almost everyone.

My curiosity was piqued when I learned that numerous peace groups sprouted at the same time I received my vision. How did that happen? Did the Universe, God, or some force say, "Okay, you guys, if you want to destroy the earth, go ahead, this will be the result," and with that knowledge, we could act, or not? And many of us chose to act.

I believed it was true that if enough of us worked in concert to create change, we could reach critical mass and prove "The Hundredth Monkey" phenomenon.

## 21.

# TESTOSTERONE DRUMS

In 1986 the penthouse was once again on the market and probably would be sold soon, but before that could happen Sean got kicked out of St. Mark's for poor academic achievement. From there he went to Woodhall, a private school in Connecticut, and then to Cascade, a harsh summer camp. Sean ran away and called me to pay his bus fare home. I enrolled him in Urban, a private high school in San Francisco. When he flunked out there, Al said that Sean was my responsibility from now on.

It was as if the boy I had nurtured no longer existed. His normal gentleness and rambunctious humor had evaporated, replaced by a remoteness and loud hostility. Every other word was FUCK. I was afraid he might be on drugs. When I asked him if he was using drugs, he became angry. He was always angry.

"Get off my back," he said, and grabbing his ever-present skateboard, he stormed out. I was afraid his attitude reflected more than the normal teenaged rebellion. I didn't know where to turn. In desperation I called Al.

"I'm worried about Sean. He's hostile and seems very disturbed."

"That boy needs to apply himself. He's a goof-off and a troublemaker, Pat," Al responded. "I told you that a long time ago. He's a liar and a thief."

"I don't believe it. Sean is basically kind and sensitive. If he has emotional problems I think they were brought on by the way he's been treated since our divorce." And then, as sweetly as I could muster, I made a request. "Al, will you meet with Sean and me . . . just the three of us . . . anywhere you say, and only for a few minutes, to talk to Sean?"

"Why?" Al asked.

"It's important for us to tell our son that we love him unconditionally. We need to work together for Sean. He needs to know he had nothing whatsoever to do with our divorce. Will you do that, please?"

There was only the briefest pause. "No, I won't do that. Sean is your problem now," he said, and hung up the telephone.

And what a problem Sean was that summer. Kei lived some distance away, and Sean's other friends seemed as confused as he was. I took him to see Dr. Krystal, who had saved my life, and I hoped she could help him as well, but he wouldn't cooperate with her. I rarely knew Sean's whereabouts. Although I gave him strict orders about my expectations, I didn't know how to enforce them. At the same time, I was trying to continue my work and sell my home. My head hurt all the time from the stress. I simply did not know what to do with Sean, although I asked my friends and doctors for advice. They said to relax, that he would grow out of it.

I couldn't relax. Sean would slam in and out of the house, loud, cursing, his pierced friends in tow. One day, when I was in Sean's room checking for drugs, I found four nude Polaroid pictures of me that Al had taken to check my body changes while I was losing weight. They had been in my safe. I was furious with Sean.

When Sean came home I confronted him. "Why did you take those nude pictures from my safe? You've humiliated me!"

"You have no right to snoop around my room, Mom," he jeered.

"I have every right!"

"I showed those stupid pictures to Spencer and Blane. We laughed at you."

"Sean, your disrespect of me is shocking. Tell those boys they are not welcome here ever again and you are not to see them either!" I screamed.

Sean pulled a duffle bag from the closet and began stuffing his stereo equipment into it. "I'm outta here," he yelled, heading for the door. "I'm going to live with friends who care about me!"

"I never want to see you again, Sean!" I yelled, not meaning a word of it.

My son left and moved in with two friends; the apartment was unnaturally quiet and I felt an inexplicable emptiness. What was I going to do about Sean? He desperately needed a father in his life.

A few days later, Sean came home to pack more of his belongings. I found a gun in his suitcase. He pretended it was a toy. I was angry and frightened. "A gun is serious business, Sean. Where did you get it?"

"It's Dad's," Sean said, not looking at me.

"You are never to bring a gun into this apartment again. Do you understand me?" I said. "Now I'll have to call your dad. Thanks a lot!" I called Clifford and asked him to come and get the gun and return it to Al.

Sean was in and out of the apartment. I became afraid of and for him, but I didn't know what to do. The decision was made for me late one evening when I received a call from an official at Juvenile Hall informing me they had Sean in custody. They called Al, but he had told them to call me, not him.

Driving through thick fog to the detention center near San Francisco's Twin Peaks was the loneliest trip I had ever made. The mist gave my headlights an otherworldly glow, and I had an eerie sense of being disembodied, floating somewhere in time.

The clank of metal as a cell door opened alerted me that Sean was on his way to the small room where I was waiting. Black curls hung over his eyes. He was pale.

"Oh, Mom, I'm so sorry. I'll never get into trouble again, I promise."

While a guard told me that Sean and a friend had stolen a motorcycle, Sean sat trembling, trying to look composed, but failing miserably.

"I guess Dad and Dede can say they're right about me now. They've always said I steal things." Hanging his head, my precious troubled son made a futile effort to stem the tears sliding down his cheeks.

After being warned about the severity of his crime, Sean was chastened and meek once he was released into my custody. My heart ached for him. On the way home, I said, "Since they got married, your dad and Dede keep saying you're a thief, but Sean that doesn't mean you have to steal," I said.

"Oh, Mom, I'm so ashamed."

"You should be ashamed. I hope you've learned something from this."

In the darkened car, I could feel tears steaming down my own face. Here I was, calling myself a peacemaker, taking care of other people's children, escorting them across the planet, actually changing their lives, as I learned from the letters they wrote to me. Yet I was failing with my own son.

I called Al and told him he had to help with Sean or I would take him to court. He said he would help if I would agree to send Sean to Amity School, a reform school in Tuscany, Italy. I agreed. Sean left the following day. He was to have no communication with outsiders for a year. The rules were stringent. I found out that Sean could only write to two people, and I was not one of them. When I protested, Al told me once again that I was not the one paying the bills.

"Al, you've used money as a reason for shutting me out for the last time! I intend to find out about my son!"

After giving Sean time to get settled, I called Amity and spoke with the headmaster. I said that I wanted to visit the school and see where Sean was living, but he said that Sean could not have visitors for a year. The headmaster said I could write to Sean but I had to keep my letters bland and not refer to the past.

I was glad to be able to send Sean letters and packages. Within the school's limitations, I enjoyed selecting his favorite things: beef jerky, Mrs. Field's cookies, and books. Sean had always been an avid reader, but I was told not to send publications that might "subvert" his lessons at Amity School. I selected innocuous reading material, wondering if it would interest him. After all, he had delved into *The World According to Garp* when he was ten. At least, I thought while wrapping his packages, he will know I'm thinking about him. I would go to Italy to see Sean as soon as I was allowed to do so.

As always, the year continued to pass and the financial burden of my penthouse was staggering, but I still procrastinated about selling it. I fought depression every minute of every day. My energy was sapped. I couldn't have planned a move if my life depended on it. But I was determined to keep CATP afloat. It was the only thing that gave meaning to my life. I also wanted to strengthen myself for whatever was to come next.

. . .

Next proved to be a journey of a different kind. It would be a personal journey across a jagged chasm to visit my son in Italy. He had been gone for a year and I desperately wanted to see him.

At the villa where Amity School was located in the beautiful Tuscan countryside, Sean and I greeted one another as if we were strangers. Our discomfort was evident in the stiffness of our conversation, in the careful wording of our feelings. I felt as if I were walking on the slippery deck of a ship during a hurricane, afraid I would say or do something wrong. Sean's anxiety was also apparent. He was tentative, overly polite. As he showed me around his home and school, all under the roof of the lovely old chateau, his hands trembled. His room was a model of neatness, a place for everything and everything in its place.

I was worried. Was Sean being brainwashed like a Moonie cult member? He was not allowed to leave the grounds and only could talk about specific subjects. Amity School seemed like a prison to me.

When I tried to discuss my concerns with the American headmaster, he said, "Mr. Wilsey said that Sean doesn't have problems with him or his stepmother, only with you. Sean's afraid of your anger. If you don't shape up, Ms. Montandon, you will never get your son back."

I wanted to prove the man right by hitting him, by screaming, and yelling. I wanted to get my son and take him to an island where no one could ever find us. I wanted everything to be the way it once had been, when we were a family. Instead, I did nothing.

The headmaster's words set off a chain reaction of unequaled anguish. I thought I was dying and did not care. There are no guidelines for dealing with this kind of guilt, nor are there timetables, rules, or boundaries for grief. The man's words pierced my fragile sense of self, ripping up what few anchors I had forged, creating questions about the meaning of my life and work.

Why had Sean said that he only had problems with me? Was it to please his dad and Dede, or did he actually feel that way?

Burdened by guilt, I left my son to go to a place of healing—Lourdes, France—over the New Year's holiday. Again, my life had become a long, lonely search for meaning, love, and healing. It did not matter if the place was Catholic or Muslim or Buddhist or Christian. What mattered was the degree of peace I could find there.

My prayers were for enlightenment as well as restoration. In Lourdes, my nun-like cell with a wooden cross over the narrow bed and a peg for my clothes suited my mood. Most visitors make their trek in the summer when five million pilgrims and fifty thousand people suffering from various maladies converge on the shrine. I was among the few who braved the icy weather, the shuttered buildings of December. There was plenty of time for introspection. Other than the soft sounds of the rosary or "Ave Maria," it was silent at Lourdes.

On my last day at the shrine, I sat in the natural grotto of Our Lady of Lourdes, reading about Bernadette Soubirous, who had been given the vision of the miracle of Lourdes when she was fourteen. An illiterate country girl, she had been singled out for this vision in a grotto that had since become known throughout the world as a sacred place of healing. I washed my face with the curative water, leaned over the fountain and drank deeply, and then I filled a bottle to take home with me. I also decided to light a candle for my son. It would burn for a very long time, sending my prayers upward in its flame. It gave me hope that the insight and message I longed for would come.

Returning to San Francisco on a flight out of Paris, I was glad to find an English-language magazine in the seat pocket. I was ready for light reading. But an article on grief caught my attention. A previous reader had highlighted a passage with a yellow marker: "It isn't until you go down into your own depths and recognize the dark empty places where grief is buried that you can let it go and new life can come bubbling forth. You must have faith. This is your lesson."

Deciding to focus on the positive things about my relationship with Sean, I created a short video called "A Message of Love" for him as soon as I got home. With music under pictures of him on various trips, the last frame showed us comforting each other as we sobbed over the wounded Vietnamese children we had met at a peace village in Germany. The end of the video showed me lighting a candle with a message printed on the film, "I light a candle for you, my son, every day of my life. Love, Mom."

I mailed the video off to Sean, but before he could have received it, as if my communication reached him by mental telepathy, he called. "Mom, I love you so much," he said. "I'm sorry to have given you a bad time. Someday, I'll make it up to you. You are a wonderful mom and I really, really love you."

His phone call made me wonder if my positive thoughts were somehow communicated to him. Whatever the reason, I felt as if ballast had been removed from my heart.

# PART THREE
# FORGIVENESS

# 22.

# FORGIVENESS

Seven years had passed since my divorce and the beginning of my work with children. Sean was almost nineteen. We corresponded, pretending everything was all right, but I feared that the lightning bolt of divorce had shattered our bond. With Sean torn away from me at ten, sent by his father to boarding school at thirteen and then to Italy to a reform-type school just after his seventeenth birthday, we had both missed out on the familiarity that comes from living together on a daily basis. But at least I could now call him.

Whenever we talked, I felt as if I were trying to cross the Grand Canyon on a balance beam: one false step and I was history. I tried to find out about his life, but Sean's brief answers did not encourage communication.

"Sean, how's it going?" I would say.

"Fine."

"What are you studying?"

"Journalism and art."

"Tell me about your classes."

"They're okay."

"Is there anything you need?"

"Mom, I've got to go."

"Sean, please tell me something about your life."

Reluctantly, he told me he had worked as a waiter in a Mexican restaurant in Florence, spent the summer in Venice, Italy, as a docent at the Guggenheim Museum, and as an apprentice gondolier. When he said he had fallen into the canal during one of his attempts at controlling a gondola I suggested he update his tetanus shots.

"Mom, I've gotta, go!"

I love you, Sean."

"You, too."

After these exchanges, I was so frustrated that I beat pillows and screamed, trying to release the tension in my body. Sean's unwillingness or disinterest to put forth the smallest effort to communicate with me was excruciating.

It felt like I had never had a husband or child. That luxurious period of family life seemed a *Wizard of Oz* dream. But for seven years I had experienced horrific nightmares of abandonment and babies being brutalized, which bound me to the past like razor-sharp wire. Without the pain I would not have sought peace. But now it was important to forgive, to get on with my life and let go of my divorce hangover, but wanting to forgive is different than being able to forgive.

We're told that time is a great healer. But I wondered exactly how much sand had to pour through the hourglass before Sean and I could heal.

Apart from my feelings of loss, I was helpless in the face of my ex-husband's ability to manipulate bank officers administering my divorce allowance. My income was dependent on Al's whim and at times, without warning, it dropped by as much as 80 percent, forcing me to go to court to request more money in order to pay the bills.

"That trust agreement is the most convoluted contract I've ever seen," Charles Morgan said. "Al, his daughters, and Sean, have more to say about your money than you do. You should never have signed such a document."

"You and Larry Beil and Marvin Michelson advised me to sign it," I said. Charles changed the subject.

Even though I was feeling stronger, I had no power to effect a change in my financial life. Judge Isabella Grant granted me an increase in the amount of money I received for a period of one year but said the matter was not to be presented to her again.

I dealt with my frustration by getting lost in sleep. But sleep was not comforting. It was filled with nightmare terrors.

"My nightmares are wearing me down," I said to my niece Linda.

"Have you talked to Dr. Krystal about them?" Linda knew my therapist.

"Sheila says my dreams are a way of processing my pain and then she talks about Sai Baba, an Indian guru of some sort who manifests Vibutti, a gray ash that means everything can be reduced to ash except the soul, and rings and stuff!" I laughed.

"Do you believe that?" Linda asked.

"No, of course not. But hey Linda, just in case it's true, let's go to India and have Sai Baba manifest a dozen big diamonds. I could have another jewelry sale!"

"Pat, I think you should go to India to see Sai Baba," Sheila said when I spoke to her about it. "I think it would help you a lot."

When I told Linda what Sheila had said, she surprised me by saying she would accompany me to India. "Okay," I said, "let's go next week."

"Well Pat, it's not that easy," Sheila said, when I told her what we wanted to do. "You'll find that you go on Baba's time, not yours. Nothing will work until the time is right."

"Oh please, Sheila," I said. "All I have to do is call my travel agent."

I was not arrogant for long. For the next two months, David, my travel agent, could not get a reply from Indian Airlines. He couldn't understand it, but Linda and I had become somewhat ambivalent about the trip anyway. And then David called. "If you still want to go to India, I have two, free, round-trip tickets for you."

"You can't be serious! Really? How?"

"An official with Indian Airlines said they want to give you two tickets to India because of your work with kids. They liked it that boys from Delhi and Bombay won a Peace Prize from you. Still want to go?"

"You could also visit Mother Teresa in Calcutta. I know how much you admire her," Linda chimed in.

"I'd love to see Mother Teresa," I said.

"You have the time now. It will do you good," said Linda, who was pushing the trip.

A week later, Linda and I were in the heat and clamor of Bombay en route to Sai Baba's ashram in Puttaparti, India. An ardent admirer of

Mother Teresa, I wanted to try to see her before going on to the ashram. So I called Missionaries of Charity in Calcutta to find out if she was there and if we could come to see her. After several unsuccessful efforts to get a call through to Calcutta, Linda went to ask for help while I continued dialing. I had just dialed for the fifteenth time when Linda came back and told me that all the telephone operators in Calcutta had walked off the job. "They were getting electric shocks from their old equipment," she said.

"Well, that's odd. The phone's ringing now," I replied.

"Hello," I said, screaming to be heard above the static.

"What do you want, what are you saying?" The woman's words competed with the scratchy noise.

"Is Mother Teresa there?" I shouted.

"Who?"

"Mother Teresa!" I yelled. "Mother Teresa!"

"This is Mother Teresa!"

I continued with far less bravado. "I'm sorry, uh, Mother Teresa, my niece and I are in Bombay and we would like to come to see you. I want to interview you about forgiveness."

"Come, come," she replied. "But no interview. I'm busy."

Early the next day, we stood in an alley teaming with sari-clad woman, crying babies, cur dogs, and beggars, outside the walled compound of Missionaries of Charity, the home of the dying and the destitute. Knocking on the heavy wooden door, we were greeted by a rotund nun in the blue-and-white habit of their order.

"Mother will be along in a bit," she said. "You can wait for her on the second floor. I'll show the way."

She led us up a flight of cement steps. The two-story compound was built around an open courtyard, where a group of nuns were washing pots and pans, laughing, breaking the quiet. A mantle of calm enveloped me as we settled on a rough wooden bench to await Mother Teresa.

Noticing a chapel, I asked a nun if I could pray there.

"Of course," she said, "God will always listen."

Slipping off my sandals, I walked into the clean cool room. Sunlight fell softly across the floor, which was covered by straw-colored matting.

A whitewashed wall displayed wood-framed drawings of Jesus and the Stations of the Cross. A simple white altar was the only furniture. I knelt on the floor and gave thanks for the path I had been shown and for the grace of my life. "And God, if you exist, watch over those kids in Ethiopia," I prayed. Then, getting to the point, I asked God to help me get an interview with Mother Teresa.

When Mother Teresa—this "Saint of the Gutters"—appeared, her walk was quick. Everything about her personified purpose although she was no taller than a ten-year-old child. It was hard to imagine how she could work so tirelessly.

"You wanted to see me?" Mother Teresa's Albanian accent was guttural. All business, she brushed off the hug I tried to give her. My words stumbled over each other, as I said things she must have been hearing from others for years. "What is it you want?" she interrupted my chatter.

"Mother Teresa, I was in the chapel just now, praying, asking God what I could say to you to get an interview about forgiveness."

"And what did God say?" There was a twinkle in her eyes.

"That I tell you about my prayer."

"Well, then, I must do it," she said. Darting behind a green-curtained doorway, she dragged out a rough wooden chair and sat down. Linda and I sat on a bench that was already in place. With my tape recorder humming, Mother Teresa talked about forgiveness. With her gnarled hands clasped, she spoke by rote, only occasionally looking at me.

"Forgiveness always gives a new life, new strength, and a new beginning. We know from the life of Jesus, but we forget, that even the last words on the cross were 'Forgive them for they know not what they do.' The beginning of forgiveness began on the cross. This is the sign of greater love and that's how he showed his love for us, by forgiving those who tortured him."

I studied the face of Mother Teresa. A network of coarse lines crisscrossed her face. Stooped, she was eighty and looked older. Her feet, in mended sandals, were cracked and calloused. Her toes were crooked. They must hurt, I thought.

As Mother Teresa continued, I internalized her words. "When Jesus was asked how many times we must forgive one another, he replied:

'Seventy times seven,' " she said. "You must forgive not just once or twice but seventy times seven. We need a clean heart to be able to forgive, and we need a humble heart to be able to ask for forgiveness, and we need a very deep love. Write down your forgiveness seventy times seven, do it with love and humility and a clean heart." Mother Teresa repeated phrases and words, as if to be sure I understood.

Taking my hands in hers, she looked deep into my eyes. "Faith is the most important. Faith is a gift of God. Unless we have faith, we will not be able either to forgive, either to love, either to feel the fruit of love, which is service. The fruit of service is peace."

"Mother Teresa, what about all the wars fought in the name of religion?" I rushed my words afraid she would soon tell us to leave.

Mother Teresa assumed a prayerful attitude, her hands folded together as she answered. "War is the same as what can happen through uncharitable words and actions; we destroy the very heart of love, peace, and unity, and so break the beautiful buildings of our society, which was built with so much love by Our Lady," she said, looking up at me. "We must pray, and in our own way create peace in our own place, in our own home first. Love begins at home. Peace begins at home. If you, in your home, and I, in my home, if everybody begins like that there will be peace. We are always counting the multitude and we forget to begin with one. Ourselves."

I cleared my throat, wondering if I should mention Sai Baba. "From here, we're going to an ashram in Puttaparti," I said.

"To Sai Baba?" she smiled.

"You know who he is?" I was astonished.

"Yes, yes, there are many Babas in India. This one has a hospital for children."

"Are we doing a bad thing to go there? In God's sight, I mean?"

"God dwells in all of us, even in those we do not always agree with. The beggar, the king, Sai Baba, we are all the same in the sight of God."

Before we said good-bye, I asked Mother Teresa if she would participate in our Children's Peace Prize Ceremony.

"I will pray for you and all the children, and for the unborn, too," she said as a Sister ushered us out of the gentle harmony of the compound and into the swarming, clamorous multitudes of Calcutta.

Later, Mother Teresa sent a message for our Peace Prize Ceremony. "I am sorry I will not be able to be with you. But I will pray for God's blessings on all of you, so that your work will be for the glory of God and the good of our children, and their work for peace."

I began to correspond with her. She wrote on lined tablet paper in a light, flowing script. Once she sent me a magnet engraved with the face of Jesus. "To keep you safe," she wrote.

Before leaving Calcutta, I purchased a notebook and began to write over and over, "I forgive Al and Dede." I would do anything to be free from the nightmares about those two. If writing forgiveness would do it, that was fine with me.

Even during the bumpy five-hour taxi ride to Sai Baba's ashram, I continued to write. "How can you do that when we could be killed by this crazy driver?" Linda said, hanging onto the seat as we outpaced top-heavy buses, screeched around donkey carts, and missed an elephant by inches.

"There should be a Disney ride called 'The Road to Sai Baba,' " I said, laughing.

Just outside the pink, blue, and beige entrance to the ashram was the clamorous world of India. Beggars, flower vendors, children, mangy dogs, noise, dust, monkeys, snake charmers, cobras, camels, pungent odors, and carts mingled in a psychedelic symphony, punctuated by women wearing swirls of magenta, gold, purple, and yellow butterfly-like saris. I loved it.

Inside the walled enclosure of the ashram, it was clean, quiet, and calm. There was no traffic on the paved street that was bordered by a bookstore, bakery, community dining hall, and an office. On a cliff overlooking the compound was Sai Baba's hospital and school.

Because Linda and I are blood relatives we were allowed to share a cement room that had a moldy-smelling bathroom with a showerhead over the toilet. We rented cots and mosquito netting at a store outside the gates and bought clothesline on which to hang our saris.

The spicy food served in the dining room, which we ate with our fingers, presented a challenge until a fellow seeker came to our aid.

"What do you expect for four dollars a day?" she asked. "Where else could you get room, board, and blessings for such a small amount?" she said, giving us each a fork and spoon, which she carried in a straw bag. The woman had white hair, green eyes, and a creamy complexion. We had spotted her from thirty feet away, tall, slender. Wearing an electric blue sari, she exuded sex appeal.

"I've been here many times. Sai Baba is truly an avatar, you'll see. Relax, let his spirit wash over you." Friendly and helpful, the woman would not tell us her name.

"Just call me 'the lady in blue,' " she said.

"Have you ever had a private audience?" Linda asked.

"Oh, yes, several. Each time I was so overcome I could hardly answer Baba's questions." She held out her hand to show a silver ring inset with a picture of the Indian avatar. "Baba manifested this for me as well as a medallion. I know it's hard to believe, but he really did. It wasn't a trick, you know."

No, I did not know. The Lady in Blue, as we began to call her, seemed to be nuts.

She read my thoughts. "I realize I sound crazy and would have thought so myself at one time, but now I know better. At the morning and evening darshan [blessing], you will find out for yourselves. That's when Sai Baba manifests the ash, Vibutti, and indicates who is to be given a private audience."

Linda and I exchanged glances of disbelief as she began to walk away. "Oh, one more thing," the Lady in Blue said, "be prepared for unusual dreams. Baba visits you in your dreams." A pause, then a shocker. "I'm over eighty and I know my good health and vitality is due to Sai Baba."

The Lady in Blue looked forty.

"Over eighty? My God, Linda, let's see what she eats."

"And who she sleeps with," Linda said, with a laugh.

The setting for darshan was exquisite. The clear blue sky was alive with acrobatic black birds calling out nosily to each other. Lofty palms cast elongated patterns across the sand. The temperature was mild. We sat quietly in rows with other sari-clad women, on the warm sand, legs crossed, breathing the heavy, still air.

Sai Baba appeared so suddenly and noiselessly that I was startled. His skin was dark; his heavy features were crowned by a huge Afro hairdo. Taking in the very foreignness of it all, Sai Baba seemed to change to a more radiant person right in front of my eyes. As he walked among us, devotees gathered the grains of sand holding his footprints. With each step bringing him nearer, I hoped he would single me out for a private audience. But he passed me by without a glance.

Every night, tossing restlessly on my narrow cot, I had nightmares about River Meadow Farm. First, the house burned down, then it was under water or covered with mold, and cobwebs; drifts of sand buried it; it was filled with decay and death. The occupants were made of shells, painted and dressed to look alive.

The last night at the ashram, I had a different kind of dream. A cool breeze ruffled my gown as I stood on top of a towering mountain. The wind became a zephyr, pulling threads from my robe, unraveling it. The strands drifted skyward, leaving me naked on the mountaintop. I lifted winged arms, and in a lazy pattern, flew across the countryside. I awoke refreshed, and cool—filled with the joy of life.

The week in the ashram had gone by quickly, and now we only had time for one final darshan. Sitting on the warm sand, no longer expecting anything, my hands were relaxed and open. With closed eyes, I soaked up the tranquility of Puttaparti.

With a nudge, Linda told me to open my eyes. "Look in your hand, Patsy," she whispered. A mound of Vibutti was in my open palm. I had not felt a thing. I licked my finger and dipped it into the ash. Putting a small amount on my tongue, savoring the taste of muted sweetness, I placed a dot of it on my forehead and throat as Sheila had taught me to do in her office before I embarked on this trip, and then I shared the rest with the women around me.

"You received a true blessing today," the Lady in Blue said that evening.

"But I didn't have anything manifested, like a ring or medallion."

"Vibutti is a manifestation," she said. "Maybe next time you'll get more solid evidence as a reminder if your faith wavers," she said, and wafted away.

Our return flight from India to New York was delayed by a fierce snowstorm, causing us to miss our connection to San Francisco. "We'll put you up at an airport hotel and you can leave tomorrow morning," an airline representative said.

Boarding the Hilton van in a stupor, wanting to fall into bed, I overheard an Indian woman with a baby talking to her seatmate. "I have a hotel room but no money for food," she said. Impulsively, I reached into my purse and handed her twenty dollars.

"Oh, no, I can't take your money," she said, pulling back into her seat.

I was embarrassed. "Please, take it. People have helped me all my life, and it's really very little . . . please." She reluctantly took the money.

The next morning as we boarded the van for the airport, eager to get home, the woman from the night before dressed in a neon blue sari, came running up to me.

"Excuse me." Her voice was soft. "I have a gift for you." Taking my hand she closed my fingers around an object. Before I could see what it was, the van pulled away.

"What did she give you?" Linda asked. Opening my fingers, I saw a silver medallion nestled in my palm. An intricate design of an om, written in Sanskrit, covered the silver. Engraved on the back of the medal was the face of Sai Baba.

"You got your manifestation," Linda said in her soft manner. "Do you suppose that woman had anything to do *with* 'The Lady in Blue'?"

"Of course not." I put the medallion in my purse. "Such things are not possible."

"Are you sure? You, of all people, know the power of meditation and prayer. Just look at the things that have happened to you since you started meditating."

Back home, after unpacking, I decided to put the medallion with the Buddha. The Ethiopian rock was still nestled in his hand when I placed the new object alongside. It was then that I realized that Sai Baba's features were similar to those of the child in Africa who had given me the ebony stone.

Before I could absorb this new insight, the phone rang. It was Tore Nareland, a friend in Oslo, Norway. "Pat, he said. "You've been nominated for a Nobel Peace Prize."

# 23.

# THE ENCHANTED COTTAGE

Was it a dream? Me, nominated for a Nobel Peace Prize? I might never have known if my friend in Norway had not called me. Nominees are not notified; only the winner is announced to the press.

"You have a good chance," Tore told me. Later when he called to say that Corazon Aquino, the president of the Philippines, had been nominated, I realized that the odds of my getting the prize were slim. Even so, it was gratifying to know that others had faith in our work.

On a more humble level, I received a different kind of sign; my ceiling fell in. Surely I thought, fate is telling me it is time to sell my home. The roof of our building was being repaired when an unexpected and heavy rain began. Within hours, the roof flooded and a rush of water cascaded into my home. Portions of the ceiling fell in soggy lumps on to beds, tables, and rugs. As soon as repairs were made, I accepted an offer and sold my Villa in the Sky.

Wanting to make a grand farewell gesture, I arranged a *Gone with the Wind*, Part Two party. Part One had been the *Gone with the Wind* soirée Al and I threw at River Meadow ten years earlier. This party would be an entirely different matter.

Empty of furniture now (Charlotte Maillard Swig Schultz, who bought the apartment, did not want the furniture; I gave my huge dining table to the Delancey Street Foundation), the penthouse was turned into an enchanted ballroom. The glow from city lights merged with those strung through five large indoor trees, magnified and replicated by mirrored walls. An orchestra played show tunes as my guests drank champagne. My niece Linda was there, as well as my sisters Faye and Glendora. Before the evening was over, we sang a rendition of "Amazing Grace" that had the crowd clapping along with us. After singing "Give Me That Old Time Religion," we segued into "Swing Low, Sweet Chariot," whose last line is, "coming for to carry me home."

Home—I no longer had one—so I arranged to stay with my friend and new assistant, Anne Thomson, while looking for my "log house in the heart of the city." Anne rented two rooms to me, and let me equip a small space off my bedroom with a microwave and a tiny refrigerator. Without running water in my makeshift kitchen, I washed my few dishes in the bathtub. What a transition. From penthouse to the poorhouse. I laughed.

When I was not traveling, I trudged in and out of houses, trying to find a place to live. My heart was set on a house that would be the opposite of the penthouse, with its marble, mirrors, and memories.

Late one evening, a policeman and a social worker came to Anne's house with ten-year-old Star in tow. They said they took Mari Ellen into temporary custody and that I was the only person Star wanted to be with. I was in an awkward position to take care of her but I loved Star, I couldn't turn her away. She told me that Mari Ellen had been drinking and in a drunken rage had trashed their apartment and cursed her. With pleading eyes she asked if I would adopt her.

"Star, I'm so glad you came to me," I said, hugging her. "There's nothing I would like more than to adopt you, but I'm not sure it's possible. Tomorrow I'll figure out what to do," I said. "But right now you need to get to bed." I got her a cup of milk and some graham crackers, and made a bed for her on a sofa.

After driving Star to school the next day, I called family services to find out if I could adopt her. With a living mother it would be difficult, they said, unless I could prove she was being abused. Star said she hadn't been abused so I had no grounds to pursue an adoption. Star lived with me for a month. When she went back home to Mari Ellen, I prayed she would be okay.

After months of fruitless searching for a house to buy, I received a phone call from Althya Youngman, an elderly woman who had been honored by our foundation for her work fostering peace.

"Pat dear, your log house is just across the street from me, right here in the geographic center of San Francisco," she said, making a quasi–sales pitch.

"Thank you, Althya, but I don't see myself living in that part of town," I said, somewhat brusquely. "The Haight Ashbury doesn't do it for me."

"Oh, it's not like that in this area. We're above the Haight," Althya said. "I can look over at that little house right now, at the beautiful Monterey cypress trees bending over the driveway, and see you living there. It will be so wonderful having you for a neighbor.

"Well, okay. Thanks Althya, I'll take a look," I said, not feeling optimistic.

Not wanting to rely solely on the opinion of Adelle, my real estate broker, I asked my friend Marilyn Rose to look at the house with me too. None of us were thrilled with what we saw. The "log" house, painted muted orange, and covered with moss, was a rundown shanty.

"Don't waste your time, Pat," Adelle advised. "This place is a pile of junk."

I wasn't sure I agreed with her quick dismissal. At least Althya was right about the trees. Two enormous California cypresses were sentinels at the entrance to a narrow brick walkway. Their enormous branches canopied over the street. Elsewhere, scrubby trees and bedraggled ferns gave the property a rural look. All the other houses in the neighborhood were built flush with the sidewalk. This one had a long driveway leading to the house.

Marilyn laughed. "I drove all the way from Hayward for this? But we're here, so we might as well look."

The three-story cottage had rotting floors, mildewed windows, plywood walls, worn linoleum, narrow stairs, an antiquated and smelly kitchen, and a defunct heating system. The floors swayed when we walked across them. "Althya sure knows my taste," I chuckled, picking my way around holes big enough to swallow a cat.

But the basic structure had good lines, and there was a charm, an indefinable quality, that kept me looking in spite of Adelle's negative refrain. "Pat, I have a perfectly beautiful penthouse for you in Pacific Heights. Don't waste your time here."

"If I had wanted a penthouse, I would have kept the one I had," I snapped. Perhaps it was my pig-headedness, but something about the house appealed to me. It reminded me of myself in a way. Conceivably, by rediscovering its beauty I could also reclaim my own. Standing in front of an upstairs window, Marilyn noted the view. "The natural light is amazing," she said. "And with those huge trees, it's like being in the country."

There was something mystical about the place. And it was secluded. Quiet, too.

Sensing a sale, Adelle changed her tune. "You have lots of wildlife here, squirrels and raccoons from Sutro forest." She pointed toward a densely wooded area a block away. "From the top floor, you have a view of the city and the towers of the Golden Gate Bridge."

"There's your old home, Pat," Marilyn said. In the distance, directly in our line of sight, was my old "Villa in the Sky."

"It's on the same elevation as this place," I said, stepping around a door that was leaning crookedly into the room. I wondered why I was even considering this badly damaged house in what I once would have considered an unfashionable part of town. Maybe it was because it reminded me of the ramshackle houses I lived in as a child, and had always wanted to make beautiful.

I was still sorting out my feelings when we descended scabrous steps to a ground-level bedroom. It was then that I became like Alice in Wonderland and fell down the rabbit hole. The small space was an island of calm and beauty, like a house that survives unscathed when a tornado decimates the neighborhood.

"A holy man, Sherman someone, lives here," Adelle whispered. "He's staying here until the place sells."

Hardwood floors sparkled. A cot, made up as neatly as any drill sergeant could demand, was positioned against a wall. Sunbeams danced through clean panes of a wide window. Directly under the window, flooded by sunlight, was a linen-covered altar. Neatly printed implorations were propped up on it, and votive candles and incense gave further evidence as to the nature of the inhabitant.

But it was a picture taped to the center pane of the window that got my attention. It was a photograph of Sai Baba. The steady gaze of the Indian avatar seemed centered on me, his outstretched arms as beckoning as the cypress trees. Under the picture, taped to the window, were penciled written messages on white, lined paper.

> *"Build of your imaginings a bower in the wilderness ere you build a house within the city walls.*
> *For even as you have homecomings in your twilight, so has the wanderer in you, the ever distant and alone.*
> *Your house is your larger body.*
> *It grows in the sun and sleeps in the stillness of the night; and it is not dreamless. Does not your house dream? And dreaming, leave the city for grove or hilltop?*
> *Would that I gather your houses into my hand, and like a sower scatter them in forest and meadow.*
> *Would the valleys were your streets, and the green paths your alleys, that you might seek one another through vineyards, and come with the fragrance of the earth in your garments."*

We stood there, Marilyn and I, reading aloud, transfixed. The words from *The Prophet* seemed prophetic indeed.

Looking out the paned window, I could see flowers and tomato plants struggling to grow, providing evidence that once upon a time a garden had flourished in this soil. In my mind, I could see a lush garden, flowers, tree ferns, a waterfall, and the warming sun. Could I wear the "fragrance of the earth on my clothes?" Could this be my "valley" and my holy mountain? Nestled on the side of a hill, this disintegrated cottage, nevertheless, seemed to hold the serenity for which my soul yearned.

"I'll buy it," I said to Adelle.

• • •

Anyone who has remodeled a house knows that it is not a simple matter. As I coped with an uncooperative city planning department, a dishonest contractor whom I ended up suing, out-of-control budgets, and all that "money pit" stuff, I reminded myself that I had chosen this demented renovation. Intent on overseeing this project myself, I moved into a small apartment across the street from my new house. At the same time, I was still trying to forge a link with my son and keep CATP functioning. I also kept tabs on Star, who, according to her teachers, seemed to be doing all right.

But not only was I working on my home, I was also working on myself. Consulting Dr. Krystal in a further effort to clean out my mental closet, I rebelled at what she suggested. "Do you suppose that on an unconscious level you wanted your marriage to end? After all, Pat, we write the script for everything that happens to us."

Outrageous! My marriage had been perfect. I loved my husband. I did not want a divorce. "Sheila, how can you of all people suggest such a thing?"

But just as I had to fumigate my house, and repair the dry rot, I knew that if I wanted to heal and get on with my life, I had to be honest with myself. What were my real feelings about that marriage? Had I been happy? Had I hidden the truth from myself? I had to concede that I had been bored attending so many social events, flying every weekend from the city to the country, and forgoing the challenge for growth for which my spirit longed.

Grudgingly, I admitted to Sheila that Al and I had different values. He wanted sex but spurned intimacy. After we began hanging out in the Napa Valley, Al had begun making fun of almost everyone we knew. I had laughed with him, although this kind of behavior was not my true nature. Known for pouring oil on troubled waters, Al actually enjoyed striking a match to the fuel, igniting chaos, and then watching the havoc, while he quietly smiled.

During the first few years of my marriage, I had pretended to myself that Al's antics were clever rather than mean-spirited and cruel. It was difficult to acknowledge my own culpability in supporting my husband's judgmental attitudes toward people. I wondered what had become of the loving man I had married. Perhaps Al was incapable of loving anyone, I thought, not even his own children. I was the one who had insisted that his adult children and young grandchildren be included in our family gatherings. Al did not seem to care if they were there or not.

Yes, maybe I had written part of the script, but I had not created the characters that had caused the nonstop suffering over the loss of my son. No, I would not accept that. But I did acknowledge my responsibility in making my relationship with Sean worse. I would sometimes lash out at him, identifying him with his dad. In a misguided effort to get his attention, fearful that he was using drugs, and frustrated, I once told him I never wanted to see him again. I had hoped he would be frightened into listening to me. Instead it only served to alienate us further.

I realized that I was angry with Sean because he had rejected me in favor of the woman who broke up our family. It hurt like a fresh wound to know that Dede had taken my son, as well as my husband, away from me. My only hope was that when Sean became an adult he would recognize the truth and come back into my life.

And what about Dede? Was her role also one I created? All along I had known that she used people, and that she was sarcastic and snide, but I had ignored my inner wisdom. One Sunday when she and John had come for lunch at River Meadow, after returning from the powder room, she lay down on the dining room floor and wiggled from side to side in a suggestive way to show how hard it was to zip up her oh-so-tight pants. Her eyes were on Al as she pulled at the zipper on what she called her "Dede" green jeans, showing her "Dede" pink underpants. Years ago, I'd laughed when she told me that she'd appropriated the rainbow as her personal colors. I wasn't laughing now.

Was Sheila right? Had I unconsciously wanted to end my marriage? I didn't know. I had begun studying the works of Eastern philosophers, mystics like Lao Tzu, Confucius, Buddha, Mahatma Mohandas Gandhi, the Dalai Lama, and reading the Bhagavad-Gita. I also listened to new-age tapes by Dr. Deepak Chopra and Dr. Wayne Dyer. As a result I had come to believe that we create everything in our lives and also that everything happens to us for a reason, although at times it is hard to fathom that reason.

I understood that I had to experience the painful ending to my marriage and a dark night of my soul to go forward, to grow. My entire life, being poor, being rich, learning how to present myself on television, giving parties, writing books, and losing my family had been the building blocks for my work in the world and made it easy for me to relate to people from all walks of life.

So, after all, it was good to know that Al and Dede had presented me with a priceless gift: my true self.

Just as my home needed studs and nails, retrofitting and a new foundation, paint and a whole new look, so did I. I was twenty pounds overweight. My face showed the ravages of stress.

So, I thought, if I'm writing the script, I can change my external appearance just the way painters are creating a fresh façade for my house. I changed my lifestyle. Every morning, rain or fog notwithstanding, I took a brisk forty-minute walk up and down the steep hills of San Francisco. I began eating nonfat vegetarian food with fish and chicken added occasionally.

Within two weeks the needle on the bathroom scale started a slow descent. My energy level increased, and the chronic depression I had experienced for ten years lifted. With all the activity, I continued to look tired, and I thought about getting a face-lift. But as absurd as it sounds, I wondered if a person who is being considered for a Nobel Peace Prize should have cosmetic surgery. I had turned myself into a kind of missionary, as if atoning for the breakup of my family. I couldn't remember reading about any "real" missionaries having face-lifts. So, I postponed the procedure. Unfortunately, my sacrifice did not impress the Nobel committee. The prize that year was awarded to Elie Wiesel.

Still, it was gratifying to know I had been considered for such a tribute. During the next three years, I learned from friends that I was nominated again by people in the USSR, the USA, Hungary, and Bulgaria. What a long road I have trod, I thought.

By late spring, as my new house neared completion, I, too, was refurbished: refreshed, more or less thin again, and with a face that belied the stress I had endured to get to this point. The house and I were integrated in a harmony of regeneration.

My new home matched the new me. It was exactly as I dreamed it would be, with a stone fireplace, log beams, and hardwood floors; as far removed from the glitz of my former life as a monastery is from Cartier.

One morning, as I worked in the garden, blossoms from a peach tree rained petals over an open deck. They fell like pink snow onto delicate maples, ivy, and wild fuchsias, creating a carpet of dawn-tinted foliage.

I was content.

# 24.

# HOPE FOR
# THE HOPELESS

Shortly after I settled into my new home, I once again had visitors from the FBI. They asked for the names and contact numbers of my Soviet friends. They also wanted to know how I had managed to be received by so many heads of state.

I asked them to leave and then called my attorney to request that he get my FBI records under the Freedom of Information Act. I received a form reply saying they were processing the request. The next correspondence asked for my social security number. There were other letters of this ilk and then I got a notice saying that my file contained sensitive information that could endanger national security and it could not be released.

I called Senator Barbara Boxer's office for help. Three months later, on a rain-soaked afternoon, I got a call from the senator's office saying what little of my file they could obtain had been mailed to me.

I didn't know what to expect when I opened the envelope containing my FBI records. Each of five pages was stamped: "All information on this page is classified secret unless indicated otherwise." The first paragraph identified me as a wealthy, divorced socialite. It said that I worked for the *San Francisco Examiner* and listed my old address. Then the report got to the substance of their interest in me.

"The CATP Foundation came to public attention in San Francisco during late 1982 in a meeting with the wife of the late Anwar Sadat, stressing peace and nuclear disarmament through print and TV news media."

The *San Francisco Chronicle*, a major newspaper, reported on January 5, 1983, datelined Moscow, that:

"A group of Northern California children who brought messages of peace to Pope Paul II in the Vatican last week met yesterday with Kremlin officials and presented them with letters and posters from American children . . . calling on their cooperation in the search of peace . . . 'Vremya.' Soviet television evening news featured a segment on the children and their five adult escorts meeting with officials.

"The narrator of the news program said it was probably the first time a delegation of children had been received at the Kremlin and that 'The number of anti-war organizations in the USA is growing. Young partisans for peace, on behalf of their peers, are coming out against the arms race.' "

The third and forth pages of the report were blacked out, marked with solid black as SECRET.

I had been under surveillance by my own country, but not only that, an additional thirty-three pages had been withheld from me.

Instead of fretting, I felt there was nothing to be afraid of, and I put the record aside; it was time to enjoy my home. From a cozy chair in the living room, looking out over the glowing city, I poured myself a glass of champagne and toasted my future.

It looked as though the future of our planet had a chance of becoming more peaceful, too, when Mikhail Gorbachev became president of the USSR. When it was announced that Gorbachev and Reagan would have a summit meeting in Iceland to discuss the elimination of nuclear weapons, I, like the rest of the world, was overjoyed. Perhaps, at last, the scary arms race with a reputed U.S. arsenal of 23,490 nuclear weapons and Soviet nuclear missiles estimated at 38,859, would end. High hopes were soon dashed however, when President Reagan refused to sign the treaty to eliminate nuclear weapons.

A quote from Martin Luther King, Jr., came to mind: "Returning violence for violence multiplies violence, adding deeper darkness to a night already devoid of stars. Darkness cannot drive our darkness; only light can do that."

It was the time, I thought, to give more children a chance to cast their innocent light into a dark world and so I planned a trip with an international delegation of children. On January 5, 1987, children Peace Prize winners from eleven countries gathered in Oslo, Norway, to begin our journey. From Norway, we would travel to Moscow, India, Hong Kong, Japan, and China. The youngsters would beseech those in places of power to support the elimination of nuclear weapons. Perhaps they in turn could influence President Reagan to cooperate with Mikhail Gorbachev.

I was especially glad that Mari Ellen had let Star come along. Win (Nguyen), a Peace Prize winner, was also on the trip.

Our beginning in the peaceful capital of Norway set the pattern for an astonishing journey and one that became a benchmark in how diverse people, not speaking each others' languages, can get along. In Oslo, we were received by Prime Minister Gro Harlem Bruntland, who supported our initiative, and Norway's beloved King Olaf. That night, policemen on horseback stopped traffic as we carried flaming torches through the icy streets singing "we shall live in peace someday."

In Moscow, Andrei Gromyko, a member of the Politbureau and Chairman of the Presidium of the USSR Supreme Soviet, received us in the Kremlin. The warmth of his greeting belied the man's reputation, which could be compared to the blizzard that was blowing in freezing gusts off the snow-covered Caucasus Mountains.

In India, we went to Mahatma Gandhi's cremation site where Win declared his life path as he placed marigold garlands on the large square of black marble. "Mahatma Gandhi," he said, "I honor you as my hero, my teacher, and someone I will shape my life after." Prime Minister Rajiv Gandhi met with us in the evening in his garden. We sat in chairs under a full moon as we waited for him. Wearing a white tunic, he shook our hands with warmth and a quiet calm and then sat in a chair and addressed the children's concerns about nuclear war.

"We need to look at how we see each other," he said. "We still see each other as different people. We don't see each other as one human family. We still see solutions in violence or war. We don't see final solutions across the table and this is really much more disturbing than just nuclear weapons, but that's born out of this. And unless we get down deeper, you might get rid of the nuclear weapons, but you'll get something else, chemical, biological, or some new technology that will be more devastating. To get rid of that we have to change the attitudes we have toward each other."

Win read a document asking that a major weapon of war be demolished in a public ceremony on behalf of the children of the world.

"It has to start with the big powers, " Rajiv said. "I'll help you."

Six months later, at the Indian Embassy in Washington D.C., I once again met with Prime Minister Gandhi. We planned an international children's summit. Rajiv said he would ensure that major powers would be present to listen and respond to kids from around the world. Before he could act, Prime Minister Rajiv Gandhi, like his mother before him, was assassinated. On a personal level, his death deeply saddened me.


Returning home after having the camaraderie of a loving surrogate family was a lonely experience. I would think of Sean, his birth, his first steps, and our exuberant happiness during his childhood. For years I had not allowed myself to think about the good times of my marriage. Remembering the good times made my pain more acute.

But a song on a kids' television show would set my mind reeling into the past. "Oh, do your ears hang low, do they wobble to and fro . . ." Sean was four and we were in a camper parked in a state park on a family vacation. Sean was in a bed pulled down over the driver's seat. Al and I were in narrow bunks on either side of the vehicle. Drifting off to sleep, content, I heard Sean begin to sing softly to himself. "Oh do your ears hang low, do they wobble to and fro, can you tie them in a knot, can you tie them in a bow, can you throw them over your shoulder like a continental soldier, do your ears hang low?"

"That's great, Sean," I said. Al and I applauded.

Sean giggled and sang the song five more times before going to sleep.

• • •

Casting aside memories, I plunged ahead with my work. Before becoming enmeshed in remodeling my house and the last world trip, I had been working on the Banner of Hope, a memorial for children killed in war. It had come about because of something my former lover James Borton had said to me when I told him how affected I had been by the Vietnam Veterans' Memorial in Washington D.C.—that long, black granite wall with row upon row of names of the dead chiseled on it.

"There should be a memorial for children, too," James had said. "I saw so many dead children in Vietnam." He looked away.

His words created a picture in my mind. I saw a river of blood flowing through the villages of Vietnam, Laos, Korea, Cambodia, China, and Japan. The swirling current was filled with dead children. Innocents caught in the crossfire of adult wars.

A week later I was working with Ariel, a theatrical artist, to come up with a design for a Children's Remembrance. We decided on panels of red silk, four by ten feet, that would be inscribed in black with the names and ages of children killed in war from World War II to the present day. White silk doves, symbolizing hope, would be sewn across the crimson in random patterns of flight. Other panels would be silk-screened with black bombs evolving into red flames and finally into redemptive white birds. When completed, the three hundred panels would be sewn together and taken on a "wake-up" tour around the world. I sent out the instructions, blueprints, and silk to people I had met from every corner of the globe.

Barbara, my former assistant, now close friend, was skeptical. "You're going to be responsible for a lot of red silk dresses in the world," she said with a laugh.

"Maybe, but I'll bet we have a memorial too," I replied. I was accustomed to having my ideas doubted.

When the first envelope containing a banner panel came back to us and we opened it, it was a gripping feeling, as if the spirits of the dead children were being released with the unwrapping of the parcel. I realized we could not be alone when the next ones came. I was alone, however, the day a packet arrived from Hiroshima, Japan. With unsettled feelings, I opened the pouch and extracted four lengths of red silk. The material slipped from white tissue paper and rippled from my lap to the floor in a scarlet tide. Thousands of names, written in tight script, covered every inch of the fabric. A letter from Koko Kondo explained how difficult it had been to find the names.

"No one in Japan wants to admit they were present when the atom bomb was dropped or that they had a child killed by it. I put an ad in the paper and several women called begging to have the name of their child written on the banner, but not wanting to give their own names. I went to a cemetery and with friends we copied the names from tombstones for the dates the bombs were dropped. Many names were sent to me anonymously. Thank you for giving us a chance to mourn our children."

When my phone rang at two in the morning in the spring of 1987, I knew it was a call from Moscow. All the calls began the same way.

"Aello, Paytreeseeya, aello, so sorry, I've awakened you, aello, aello, are you there?"

Eventually, through repeated apologies, static, and many "aellos," I got the message. Alevitina Fedulova, who had traveled with Katya Lycheva and had just been on the world trip with me, was head of the Soviet Women's Committee. She was inviting me to bring children from seven countries of my choice, along with the Banner of Hope as a work in progress, to Moscow for an International Women's Congress in July. "You are to present your banner, and address the Congress just after Mikhail Gorbachev speaks. You are being honored also, Paytreeseeya."

"Me? Why?"

"For the Katya trip and getting the first Soviets into Hong Kong in 1987."

Once in Moscow I was nervous. Being a featured speaker in the Kremlin was a momentous occasion for me although I was struggling in a quagmire of self-doubt. Here I was—Patsy Lou Montandon, a grassroots American citizen with little formal education—being celebrated in the very heart of the so-called Evil Empire. The thought of addressing six thousand people filled me with anxiety. It seemed a fantasy that I was to be a speaker at such an august gathering. But the event was real, all right, just as my meetings with heads of state in twenty-six countries was undeniable. I had a passport with more supplementary pages than a lawyer's brief to prove it.

I was glad that Koko had come from Japan to join me and that the seven children I had invited were all accompanied by adults. I didn't have to be concerned about them this time, I thought, as we boarded the bus taking us to the Kremlin.

The earlier trips had been marked by the fear and paranoia of the Cold War, but today the talk was of "glasnost," openness, heralding a new era in the rebirth of the Soviet Union. The hammer and sickle snapping overhead, a symbol of fear for a generation of Americans, now seemed benign. Congress Hall, our destination, was alive with hoards of women streaming through the doorways. Several surged forward to greet us and to take charge of my delegation.

Back stage, tuxedo-clad waiters served champagne, wine, and vodka, which I declined, being mindful that I would soon be giving a speech. The hubbub of languages overlapped, reminding me of sermons about the Tower of Babel. I was glad to spot Alevitina Fedulova hurrying my way. Often told we looked like sisters, both blonde with blue eyes and a bit overweight, neither of us was flattered. But through the years, although we could not speak each other's language, we had forged a bond of love and respect. I hugged Alevitina and then made my hands tremble, to let her know I was nervous.

"Alevitina, brrrr, nervous," I said.

"Ahh, Paytreeseeya, da, da." She grabbed a glass of red wine from a tray and made drinking motions. "Paytreeseeyaa, iss gudit. Nurvs."

"Sure, Alevitina, just what I need to ensure I'll make a fool of myself," I said, but she was not the least interested. Mikhail and Raisa Gorbachev had entered the room.

Alevitina grabbed my arm. Red wine sloshed down the front of my white dress.

"Oh Lord!" I exclaimed, attempting to blot the spreading stain. Alevitina made swipes at my dress with a napkin, all the while eyeing the president of the USSR. "Paytreeseeya . . . Gorbachev . . . Raisa . . . comeit . . . Gorbachev . . . Paytreeseeya . . . comeit!'

An indomitable force, she pulled me toward the president. Arriving at her destination, Alevitina summoned all the English at her command. "Paytreeseeya Montandonit . . . General Secretary . . . Mikhail Sergeyevich Gorbachev . . . Raisa Maximovna Gorbacheva." She beamed, mission accomplished!

The butterflies I had been trying to suppress took full flight. ". . . Mr. President . . . I appreciate . . ." I tried not to stare at the birthmark on his head. ". . . what you are doing to create peace. It's a goal I also have been striving for."

President Gorbachev smiled, "Yes, Patricia," he said through his translator, "we know of your work with children."

Interrupting my awkward sentiments, Raisa addressed more immediate concerns. The simultaneous translation by her talented translator made it seem as if the words came directly from the First Lady. "Alevitina says you have a small difficulty, Patricia, yes?"

"Yes," I gulped, "I do."

"Soda water!" Raisa took charge.

A waiter materialized with the requisite soda water. Cosmonaut Valentina Treshkova, the first woman in space, standing nearby, joined Raisa to help clean my dress. I was being spot-cleaned by the First Lady of the Union of Soviet Socialist Republics and a celebrated Cosmonaut. Cascades of giggles erupted.

My dress was still damp when we were told to go on stage.

With the president and first lady leading the way, we walked onto the stage. A resounding ovation for the two of them swept over me like a tidal wave, engulfing my own frail ego, sublimating my concerns.

Seated on stage in a chair upholstered in the omnipresent red, I savored every detail. The long, burnished table where we sat had translation equipment at each place, along with silver carafes of water and blue-covered plastic note pads embossed in Cyrillic and English "Toward 2000—Without Nuclear Weapons! For Peace Equality Development." Fifteen women, renowned in the communist world, were also seated at the table with the president and his wife. Another fifty dignitaries were in a tiered section behind us.

Three balconies overflowed with people from around the world. On the main floor, standees spilled into the aisles. Rows of television cameras were banked across the back of the auditorium. Then President Gorbachev was announced. I knew I would be next and wondered if I would be able to rise up out of my chair.

Following thunderous applause for President Gorbachev, my musical cue enveloped the auditorium. I rose from my chair as if in a dream and walked down the red-carpeted steps to the lectern where President Gorbachev waited. Smiling, he shook my hand and then presented me with a bronze plaque. The images and names of four young girls were embossed on its round surface.

> Sadako, poisoned by radiation from the atomic bomb dropped on Hiroshima. Tanya Savitchiva, dead of starvation during the World War II siege of Leningrad. Samantha Smith, killed in a plane crash following her historic visit to the USSR. Anne Frank, a victim of Hitler's ethnic cleansing of Jews.

After the president returned to his seat on the dais, a musical cue resounded throughout the hall and five hundred Russian children came streaming through a series of double doors, down the aisles, waving flowers, singing "Mir, Mir, Mir . . . Peace, Peace, Peace." The audience was electrified.

Another musical cue and the children I had brought from Japan, Mexico, Norway, Africa, America, India, and Russia walked out on the stage and to my side.

Leaning into the microphone I spoke about children and death. "There is no greater pain than to lose a child . . ." I said, feeling the truth of my words. The children spoke of their fear of nuclear war and then, accompanied by violins and a choir singing "Ave Maria," two hundred youths carried the scarlet Banner of Hope with the thousands of names of children killed in wars written on it, into the auditorium. Standing, weeping, the thousands gathered in Congress Hall that day acknowledged the message so painfully inscribed among white silk birds.

Vegard Thomassen, a boy from Norway, his voice quivering with emotion, said, "On the banner we have brought into this hall are written the names of children killed by the violence of war!" And then, in unison, the children shouted.

"We want To Live, We Want To Grow, We Want To See, We Want To Know, We Want To Live!"

Delicate eleven-year-old Aki Koko ran around the table on the dais straight to Mikhail Gorbachev. In her hands she carried a crystal globe of the earth. "President Gorbachev," she said, "this crystal ball is like the earth, it's easily broken." She handed him the globe. "Will you help keep us safe?"

At that time, the president of the Soviet Union, one of the most powerful men on earth, reached down and in one smooth motion lifted Aki up into his arms and held the transparent symbol of our fragile planet aloft. Putting Aki down, he used a handkerchief to wipe his eyes.

"We must heed the message of these children," he said, wiping his eyes again. "If we care about our children and the future of the world we must become nuclear free."

Standing there, looking into the faces of the future, I embraced the moment. This was an illuminating moment on the transcendent journey of my Joyous Life After Divorce.

## 25.

# HUMPTY DUMPTY

It was September 1988. Koko, her adopted daughter Aki, Win, Barbara, and children from four countries had joined me on the Banner of Hope tour. We were in Leningrad, our first stop before going on to East Berlin, West Berlin, Belfast, Ireland, and the United Nations in New York.

Two hundred Russian children had just made a dramatic presentation of the banner in Piskariovskoye Memorial cemetery, where four hundred thousand victims of World War II lay in mass graves, covered by green lawn and red roses, when Win got my attention.

"Pat, you need to talk to that woman over there." He indicated a grandmotherly looking person wearing a black coat and white babushka, staring straight ahead as if in a trance. During the ceremony she had stood apart from the dignitaries, dwarfed by a granite statue of Mother Russia on the marble platform where we had gathered, gazing at the names written on the banner. Win and I approached her with a translator in tow.

"Are you looking for a name?"

"My baby son, all family is buried here, all, all. In the siege of Leningrad they died. Now no one gives me a seat on bus even. Young people today do not care."

I touched her arm. "Will you tell us your child's name? We'll write it on the banner." We had anticipated such an eventuality.

"Nyet," she said. "No one cares."

"We care," Win said, holding out paper and a pencil. "Please give us the name of your son."

"Nyet," she said. But in spite of herself the woman wrote down the name of her child.

As the woman watched, her expression frozen, the children placed a plastic tarp on the ground and on top of it a length of red silk. They chalked in the letters, then dipped small brushes into black paint and painstakingly printed the baby's name onto the silk: "VLADIMIR SERGEVITCH CHIKAROV—AGE 2. LENINGRAD 1946."

Weak sunlight filtered through the leaves of birch trees and fell onto the scarlet, creating dappled patterns of brightness. Attaching two poles to either end of the silk, the children lifted the panel into the air where it fluttered over fragrant rose bushes and the towering mounds of green sod. The woman gazed at the name of her dead child floating softly in the wind and her tears were finally released from their forty-two-year prison.

"Spasiba," she mumbled, burying her face in a sopping handkerchief. "Spasiba."

We left Leningrad for our next stop carrying the image of that grieving mother with us.


Back home at the Enchanted Cottage, I felt lonely. Sean was still in Italy. He wrote occasionally, but would not commit to a visit home. Star was with her mom and working at the Wharf after school, although she stayed with me occasionally. The kids who had traveled with me were in school, most in other cities and countries. Rachel and Win were involved in their studies. My siblings were busy with their own lives and lived some distance away from me.

Added to that, my income from my divorce trust, which was sold by Bank of America to Wells Fargo Bank, suddenly was cut by 85 percent. Once again, I was floundering in financial crisis. I feared I would lose my new home. The officials at Wells Fargo Bank said the trust money was being invested, as Al instructed, for his adult children even though Al and I had created trusts for all his children during our marriage. Once again I had to go to court, to try to get what was rightfully mine.

Neil Eisenberg, my new attorney, was the kind of man who wore suction soled shoes that made him look as if he could walk up the sides of buildings. His suits were rumpled and his ties unfashionable. Neil's office overflowed with papers in seeming disorder. I liked the guy. He had saved my skin when he rescued my Enchanted Cottage from a flimflam contractor, winning a lawsuit for me without taking a single deposition.

"I wish I didn't need Al's money," I said to Neil.

"That's been your mistake all along, Pat. You look at it as his money, when in fact, it's yours. You have every right to your money. If you had had better representation, you wouldn't be going through this. You would have millions free and clear. But it's too late now. I have to try to convince bank officers to enforce the original agreement. To do the right thing."

"Yeah, and he even used my money and invested it in properties but gave me no equity, the bastard!" I said, resigning myself. It was too late to do anything about it now.

I borrowed money from my family to pay bills and began thrashing about trying to get my income back to a level that would support me.

Neil was able to get my divorce trust moved from Wells Fargo Bank—where they refused to listen to me (saying they invested according to Al's instructions)—back to the Bank of America, now in the trust business again. Finally, my income was restored—for one year. A promised cost of living increase did not materialize.

"Neil," I said, when I learned that my income was restored for only one year, "at this rate, I'll be going to court every year for the rest of my life. It's disgusting when you consider that Al is worth at least $250 million. He and Dede want to obliterate me for some reason!"

"It's control, Pat. That's what it's all about. Al wants to stay connected to you. He also wants power over you." Neil shook his head. "Otherwise, a man worth that kind of dough would not do this to the mother of his son."


"Patricia, Werner here, Werner Rumpel from the GDR." It was November 9, 1989. The telephone call was such a surprise it took me a few minutes to place him.

"Werner Rumpel from East Berlin?"

"Yes, Patricia, Werner Rumpel from East Berlin. The Berlin Wall is being torn down now, right now!"

"The Berlin Wall is coming down?"

"Yes! Come, Patricia, come and pull your banner through Checkpoint Charlie! Bring Rachel."

"The wall is coming down? Really Werner?" He said yes, and while I could not comprehend the magnitude of what he had told me, I said we'd be there.

"Call Honi Schmidt when you get to West Berlin. She'll help with logistics."

As soon as I got off the phone, I turned on the television set. My God, it was true. Stories about the Berlin Wall being dismantled dominated the news. Part of the graffiti-covered structure was being pulled down as I watched. People were going crazy, celebrating.

I had gotten a firsthand education about the Berlin Wall on our trip there in 1983 when we put our hands on the wall and meditated that it would come down, and again on the banner tour in 1988. And now, it was hard to believe that the Wall was coming down.

I immediately called my friend and assistant Anne Thomson, and Marilyn Rose, and Susie Raferty, who had sewn the banner together, and asked them to go to Berlin with me. We had to leave within twenty-four hours and would only be gone two days. They all said yes. My next call was to Rachel.

As soon as she heard my voice, she squealed, "Pat, have you heard about the Berlin Wall? I knew it would come down! I knew it! I knew it!"

When I told her we were going to Berlin and wanted her to go, too, she was so thrilled she could hardly contain her joy. But her teacher, a shortsighted man, would not let her leave school. "He said he will flunk me for the whole year if I miss even two days," Rachel wailed.

"I'll bring you a piece of the Wall, Rachel honey. But you really should be there."

From our West Berlin hotel, I called Honi, who had helped us with our banner presentation nine months earlier. She came right over. When she arrived, I expected her to be elated, thrilled that the barrier was being dismantled, but instead she was nervous.

"Patricia, perhaps it's better if you have our kids unfurl the banner in East Berlin."

"No, Honi, no. The only reason we're here is to have East Berlin children join their peers in the West to carry it through Checkpoint Charlie."

"But, maybe that's not a good idea. The kids are frightened. They've never been to the West, you know."

"There's nothing to be afraid of, Honi. Nothing."

Reluctantly, my German friend agreed to cooperate. "Okay, Patricia, okay. I'll have a hundred kids at the East side of Checkpoint Charlie tomorrow at eleven o'clock, but you have to get the children from the West."

"How am I going to do that?"

"I don't know, Patricia. Our kids will also have parents with them. They are very afraid, the parents and the children. This is so sudden, so sudden."

The moment Honi left, I got on the phone trying to locate youngsters from West Germany to carry the banner with those from the East. The whole endeavor was in jeopardy unless I could find kids to help with the unfurling.

My first call was to Mayor Walter Momper. Someone from his office suggested I call an American military base. The officer of the day advised me to call a school, which in turn gave me the phone number of the Martin Luther King School near the border.

Five hours later, I had a commitment from the principal of the Martin Luther King School to have fifty kids at the western side of Checkpoint Charlie at 10:30 the next day. I was elated and exhausted.

En route by taxi to Checkpoint Charlie the next morning, I was caught up in the excitement of the crowds. The Brandenburg Gate was still closed, and bets were being made as to when the wall surrounding it would come down, reopening the historic portal between the two Germanys.

"Pat, we've got to get a piece of the wall before we go home." Marilyn was gazing at a horde of people chipping away at the structure. "We only have today."

"Our ceremony should be finished by two, so we'll have all afternoon, Marilyn," I said.

The border guards from East and West wore yellow flowers in the armbands of their olive green uniforms, and looked relaxed, visiting and laughing together like old friends. They knew about the children's banner and seemed as excited as we were, ready to help. The heavy wooden box housing the Banner of Hope was delivered to the West side of Checkpoint Charlie for us. Placing the box in a fenced-off area just inside the wall, my helpers began getting it ready for the unfurling. Soon youngsters from the Martin Luther King School arrived and stood a few feet beyond the barrier. They seemed to be trembling with excitement at the prospect of seeing their peers from behind the Berlin Wall. Their colorful jackets and permed hair, earrings, and running shoes identified them as children from the prosperous West.

Then, from my vantage point on the West side of the Berlin Wall, I saw the kids from the East, moving toward us as if in slow motion, each child held the hand of an adult as they advanced in an orderly, but timid column. One hundred kids, one hundred adults—crossing for the first time a barrier they grew up seeing every day. It was a fortification that had separated them from the rest of the world, from life. The children looked small and vulnerable in their caps and out-of-date clothes, bunched close to each other, holding tightly to the hand of an adult. Their fear was palpable.

They gave the impression of being ready to flee. I started toward them. They stopped. I smiled and waved. No one returned my greeting. No one smiled.

The Western youngsters yelled something in German. The group from the East came to a halt, and then slowly, stumbling, looking over their shoulder, began to turn back.

I saw my friend Werner Rumpel at the head of the line facing me. "Werner!" I yelled. "Tell them it's okay," I screamed. "Tell them it's okay!"

Werner turned around and saw what was happening. He held up his hands and, like Moses parting the Red Sea, stopped the exodus and turned the group back toward the West.

Then Werner reached me. We rushed into each other's arms with tears flooding down our faces. Embracing, we conveyed without words the joy we felt. My dear friend. My lovely East German friend had lived to see this glorious day. And he was sharing it with me.

Poles with the red silk memorial, dipping toward the ground, snarling, then flying free, were placed into small, unsteady hands. The children in West Berlin screamed encouragement, beside themselves with excitement. Little by little those from the East began to relax; they were not going to be shot, they could walk in freedom. At last. At long last.

Throngs surged around us, cameras clicked, people wept, as children from the East and West became partners. Linking hands and then holding the rippling red silk with the names of memorialized children high above their heads, they yelled, "Friede . . . Friede . . . Friede . . . Peace . . . Peace . . . Peace . . ." as they walked together, for the first time in their young lives, through the barrier that was called Checkpoint Charlie, into the West.

Afterwards, back at our hotel, we scurried to get going again, to dig out our piece of the Berlin Wall. There was precious little time before our flight back to the United States.

Climbing into a taxi, we asked to be taken to the Wall. "We want to get a piece of history," Marilyn said. The driver muttered something in German, not understanding our request, just sitting there, confused. Frustrated, the clock ticking, we debated what to do, when there was a knock on the taxi window.

"You're supposed to be in my cab," said the slim, clean-cut young man, who was dressed in jeans and a blue sweater.

"Don't ask him how he knew to rescue us, Pat, just go!" Marilyn said, scrambling out of the taxi. We were thrilled with this providential turn of events.

"I know exactly where to take you," the man said, and drove us to where the first block of wall had come down. "I'll wait and then take you to an even better location." He smiled. "Besides, you'll need tools. I'll go by my house and get some for you. And then, I'll take you to my church, Saints Peter and Paul, near the Potsdam Bridge, where spies were shuttled across."

What a twist of fate. Saints Peter and Paul was the name of the church in San Francisco where I went to light candles and pray before every trip. It had special meaning for me.

Our driver parked and we walked over to a section of the Wall. Along the length of the barricade were hundreds of colorful drawings, cartoons, zany slogans, as well as profound messages. A quote from Mahatma Gandhi, printed in black block letters, resonated with me.

"If we are to reach real peace in this world and if we are to carry on a real war against war, we shall have to begin with children; and if they will grow up in their natural innocence, we won't have to struggle; we won't have to pass fruitless idle resolutions, but we shall go from love to love and peace to peace, until at last all the corners of the world are covered with that peace and love for which consciously or unconsciously the whole world is hungering."

Next to the excerpt was a drawing of children standing hand-in-hand around the curvature of the earth. It was a universal image, one I had seen many times in the art of children.

Above a white-painted graffiti message, "Love is thicker than concrete," there was a gash in the wall where we could see through to the East.

"Pat," Marilyn handed me a votive candle. "I thought you might like to light a candle."

After I stuck the candle in the opening, and just as the match ignited the wick, I had a flash of insight that something more awaited me in Berlin.

Leaving the site to go with our driver, I was filled with anticipation. Our enigmatic chauffeur secured hammers and sharp instruments so we could pry out pieces of the wall from a location near the Potsdam River. As we chipped away, I broke into the center of the structure and found barbed wire and wood, as well as cement. Winding a length of the wire over my gloved arm, I put the rest of my piece of the infamous Berlin Wall into a large purse. Then the next part of our adventure unfolded.

"Now, I'll take you to my church," our driver said, turning off of an asphalt road onto a narrow rutted lane in a deeply wooded area. "There it is, Saints Peter and Paul Church, over there under the trees." He pointed toward an old-world, cream-colored brick building.

The moment we entered the sanctuary, as if illuminated by a spotlight, my eyes went to a circular bas-relief of the face of Christ. I could hardly move. "Marilyn," I whispered, grasping her arm. "That's the image from the dream that I told you about."

In that dream, the face of Christ was in a golden circle with a ring of barbed wire around his head. Now, in Saints Peter and Paul Church, on the border between East and West Berlin, the same image was reflected in the glow of candlelight. And encircling my arm was a ring of barbed wire from inside the Berlin Wall.

Sinking into a pew, Marilyn beside me, I leaned my head against the bench in front of me. My friend sensed the wonder of the moment and rubbed my back as I tried to absorb the synchronicity of events across time and space. "During all these years," I said to Marilyn, "I thought the reason I had to hurry to finish my work was because I was going to die."

"The rush wasn't that you were going to die, my friend, but that you had to hurry to play your part in world events."

I had not thought of such a possibility. Could that be true? Are we given signs when we're on our path? "Maybe you're right, Marilyn. I'd like to think so."

Marilyn said, "My Mother had this saying engraved on her headstone, 'Life is a mystery to be experienced, not a problem to be solved.' You have traveled a long way my friend, hold close this moment. Hold it close."

But what of my own walls, my personal confines, so thick and tall, still filled with loneliness and anger, as prickly as the barbed wire I had extracted from the Berlin Wall? Mahatma Gandhi said, "The only devils in this world are those running around in our own hearts, and that is where all our battles should be fought." I battled the Lucifer in my heart a lot. When I returned from Berlin, I wrote Sean a letter and sent him a piece of the Berlin Wall. He replied that he would come home for a visit on his twentieth birthday, May 21, 1990, two months away.

I prepared for his homecoming and the date of his birth as if he were a Pasha king. What could I do to please him? Years had passed since I had had the opportunity to spoil my son, to do something special for him. Sean had a Triumph, an English motorcycle that he loved. He kept it at a friend's house and spent every free moment tinkering with the machine when he was home. So, resurrecting my party-giving skills, I decided to surprise him a few days after he arrived, with a celebration in a motorcycle shop in San Francisco's Mission District. In an effort at good will, to make it better for Sean, I even invited his dad and Dede. They turned down the invitation but a lot of other people came, my sisters Glendora and Faye and Al's secretary, Pegi Brandley, the woman who had testified against me in court; Michael and Lad, Al's sons by his first wife; Geri Crumpler, our former cook; driver Clifford Mooney; Star, wearing makeup and looking like the teenager she was; and fifteen of Sean's long-time friends.

I was making a major effort to give my son a sense of family, trying to put Humpty Dumpty back together again. Yet, after the party, Sean said he appreciated the thought, but added that he didn't like parties and did not want me to give another one for him.

I was deeply hurt. "Are you trying to punish me?" I asked. "Do you feel you must reject not only me, but the things I like to do?"

"I live life differently from you, Mom, that's all," Sean replied.

I knew Sean also was torn by our relationship. A letter he wrote to me from Italy revealed his conflict and innate sweetness. "I remember things about the past that have been buried. A special memory of how you used to rock me in the big old green rocker and tell me stories about the future, about my adolescence, about how my voice would change and my future girlfriend . . . the tea parties we had together . . . how you took me everywhere with you . . . You are the best mom and the best friend I ever had. I want that same love we had for each other then, back again."

So did I.

Life continued at a steady pace following Sean's brief trip home. In 1990, when Mikhail and Raisa Gorbachev made a much-heralded visit to our city, I covered the story for the *Examiner*. Everyone in town was working to get close to the pair. When socialite Ingrid Hills announced that a Friends of Raisa group had been formed and that they were going to meet with her, "and that doesn't mean Pat Montandon," I laughed. On the day of that supposed meeting Raisa was having tea with me. Later, Dodie Rosekrans, an acquaintance, became one of the sponsors of the Raisa Gorbachev Partnership in Learning at Stanford University.

Mikhail Gorbachev was intent on normalizing relations not only between the United States and the USSR but also with South Korea and China. In San Francisco he had the first of several meetings with the president of South Korea, Roh Tae Woo. The USSR's policy in Asia aimed at two ends: first, to reduce security threats posed by such powers as the U.S., China, and Japan, and second, to integrate the Soviet Far East into international economic relations of the Pacific. To do so, however, he first had to make a breakthrough in Soviet relations with South Korea so that it could serve as an impetus to improving Soviet–Japanese relations. Mikhail Gorbachev was an amazing visionary.

That same year Win called to tell me he had gotten into Harvard. "My grades weren't that great," he said, "I wrote an essay about my travels with you. That's what got me accepted at Harvard."

Win was one of the jewels provided by the universe. Later, he worked in Calcutta with Mother Teresa, caring for the dying. In a letter, he told me of holding the hand of a dying man, of feeling inadequate, not knowing how to help. "I held his hand and sang, 'we shall live in peace someday.' It was so little, but it was all I knew to do," he said.

When the United States threatened war against Iraq, in 1991, I had not wanted or expected to go there. But on a gloomy day in December, Dan Rather reported on the CBS evening news that Saddam Hussein had targeted American students living in Florence, Italy. At that moment, Sean, who had always been my motivation, was attending a school in Florence. I felt as if Uncle Sam was pointing his finger at me and saying, "I WANT YOU."

Therefore, ten days before the Gulf War, on January 3, 1991, I was in Amman, Jordan, with fourteen teenagers from ten countries attempting to get visas for Baghdad. A potential war zone was not the place for young children, so I had invited teenagers and I made it clear that they were to be accompanied by an adult.

For a week, we had been cooling our heels in Amman with no movement in the direction of visas until we ran into King Hussein's wife, Queen Noor, in the lobby of the Marriott where we were staying. Wearing a red Chanel suit, her blonde hair cascading past her shoulders, she asked what we were doing in Jordan.

"We're trying to get visas for Iraq," I told her. "We hope to somehow be an influence for peace." Queen Noor smiled and wished us well.

The very next day we were summoned to a poorly lit room at the Iraqi Embassy where a man fastened pins bearing the likeness of Saddam Hussein to our jackets. He dispensed the pictures as if they were prizes at a county fair.

Back at the hotel, with our visas securely in hand, I gave everyone an opportunity to opt out. "This is a serious situation. If you decide not to go to Baghdad, no one will think any less of you," I said.

Koko, my stalwart friend, spoke for us all. "It is our duty to go," she said. "Our duty."

Katya Lycheva, the Soviet child we had brought to the United States in 1986, wanted to know if we were going to meet with Saddam Hussein.

"It's always iffy when you're dealing with a head of state," I answered.

In Baghdad we went to an elementary school where a bulletin board had drawings of the United States as a hand, denoted by an arm of stars and stripes, with a claw dripping blood over an oil well. The words "No Milk, No Medicine," were interlaced with baby bottles and medical syringes on the pictures. "Down Bush, Down Bush," was written along the borders in English and Arabic.

A teacher, her thick black hair coming uncoiled from a knot on the back of her head, led us into a classroom that was dominated by a portrait of Saddam Hussein. The children immediately jumped to their feet. "Down Bush. Down Bush," they recited. And then they sat down. That routine was repeated in every classroom until the last one. The kids there spoke English.

Standing up from his desk, a fine-looking boy with black hair and brown eyes, was passionate, "Bush is trying to kill children by stopping medicine and milk for Iraqi babies. The United States is evil," he said, and sat down.

Katya rose to the challenge. "I am from the USSR and I used to feel the same. I thought Americans were horrible. But then I took a peace trip there and saw it was a great place and the people were really nice."

The boy was having none of it. He stood up again and began a diatribe worthy of a politician.

"I know what to do about this," Katya said, smiling. She walked over to the boy, leaned across his desk and, with a loud smack, kissed him. The boy's face turned scarlet; his classmates pounded him on the back, giggling. Soon they began to act like children everywhere, sniggering, and passing notes. They also began talking—about war, its causes, and how to keep it from happening.

"If we could get to know each other," a girl wearing a Mickey Mouse t-shirt said, "we could learn to get along."

We did not meet with Saddam Hussein, but we did meet with his First Deputy Prime Minister, Taha Yassin Ramadhan. (In 2005 he was the ten of diamonds in a deck of playing cards of the Most Wanted officials in Iraq.) The Prime Minister wore a green military uniform and carried a pearl-handled revolver.

"Do you always carry a gun when you talk to children?" Aki asked, shyly.

"Only when we expect a war against our people," he replied.

The First Deputy Prime Minister told us he had eleven children, to which Katya said, "Then you should not want them killed in a war."

"No," he acknowledged, "I do not want them killed, especially not for oil. You should talk to President George Bush about that," he said.

Not wanting our meeting to be a total failure, we gathered around the man, as he idly fingered his gun, and proceeded to sing a peace song. Iraq's First Deputy Prime Minister must have either wanted to shoot us, or to surrender on the spot!

## 26.

# THE LAST TRIP
# TO MOSCOW

It was 1992 and Sean was still in Italy. We did not see each other often, but I was pleased that he now called with some regularity.

The world had changed enormously since my vision about a nuclear holocaust ten years earlier. The Berlin Wall was dust, and the powerful Soviet Union had crumbled. Having ousted President Mikhail Gorbachev, Boris Yeltsin was now the head of the Russian Federation. Gorbachev had survived a hard-line coup attempt in August 1991, but resigned four months later when the Soviet Union ceased to exist.

A vast land with a wealth of natural resources, but paradoxically a nation of anxious, angry, hungry people, Russia was a country in transition. Looted by a greedy government (before Gorbachev took power) with a failing infrastructure, the new Russians were not equipped to handle our brand of democracy or philanthropy.

With increasing apprehension, I read about Moscow's starving children, and hospitals that were overwhelmed with abandoned kids. It was not unusual to find babies buried alive in snowdrifts. The situation was so desperate and weighed on my heart with such ferocity that I set about getting donations of food and medicine to take to Russia. Overseeing distribution was vital or the aid could end up on the black market. Therefore, I promised the donors that I would personally deliver their largess to Moscow.

I was only dimly aware of the Russian Mafia, a violent bunch who, without a second thought, would kill anyone who got in the way. My vague awareness was to be jolted into sharp focus.

Two months after beginning our campaign, seventy tons of food and medical supplies had been contributed for the children of Russia. The hard part was getting the aid delivered to the Russian capital. After trying every avenue, I grew frustrated, thinking I could not make it happen. Then a man from the Russian consulate called with good news. A military cargo plane from St. Petersburg would be arriving in San Diego with a yacht for the America's Cup races. Because it had no other cargo on the return flight, they would take the food back to Moscow for me without charge.

The next day, the United States Army was working alongside the Russian military to help Russian children, a goal I had not even dreamed of in 1982. A U.S. Army truck took the food, now shrink-wrapped and on wooden pallets, to San Diego, where it was loaded aboard a huge AH-123 cargo plane, headed for Moscow. The aircraft was due to arrive in Moscow on December 31. I would get there, on Delta Airlines, on New Years Day, 1993.

I invited Nathaniel Rossin to accompany me. He was a handsome widower in his late fifties whom I had met at a health center a year earlier, who had been courting me. Our fledging romance did not have the fire of my affair with James Borton, but it helped fill a void in my life.

When I called Sean to tell him about my latest sojourn, he said he and his school chum, Leandro, would come to Moscow to help distribute the aid. I was delighted and told him I would be staying at Moscow's Leningradskaya Hotel on January 1.

When our Delta flight landed at the birch-and-evergreen-bordered Sheremetyvo Airport, I thought of my first trip there. No one had met us then, but now a TV news crew recorded our arrival and Tatiana Domracheva, a longtime cohort with the Soviet Peace Committee, greeted us with smiles and red carnations. We would wait in the VIP lounge until our passports and visas were processed and our luggage cleared customs.

The drab lounge sported two brown upholstered sofas, a coffee table, and a snack bar. "I'm sorry dear, but there's no coffee," Tatiana said, seeming anxious. She kept looking over her shoulder, into the gloom of a hallway, as if she was expecting someone.

"Patricia dear, no coffee," Tatiana looked everywhere except at me. "But I've ordered tea and a little red caviar." She sighed. "We must have a serious talk about your program, dear."

"What do you mean, Tatiana?" Russians often called the most minor change in one's schedule "serious." A written agenda did not necessarily have validity.

"Yes, dear, your food did not arrive, you know, and so, well, you might as well enjoy . . ."

"The food didn't arrive? What are you talking about?"

"Well, the food you sent wasn't on the airplane."

"That food was loaded onto a Russian cargo plane in San Diego, the one that brought a yacht for the America's Cup races." I rummaged in my purse for the paperwork. "It arrived in Moscow on flight AN-124 on December 29. Two days ago."

"No dear, Boris and Sergi took trucks to the military base to get it, but the pilot said your shipment wasn't on the plane, so . . ."

"Nonsense, Tatiana. Of course it was."

"No, dear, it wasn't. I'm very sure."

"But I know it was loaded on that plane, Tatiana." I made a quick decision. "I'll find out for myself. Where is that airport located?"

"Oh, you can't do that. It's twenty miles from Moscow." She waved vaguely toward the north. "You could never gain entry to a Russian air base, never. Forget it, have fun. We have a lovely schedule planned. You're going to the Danilov Monastery for a blessing by His Holiness Alexiy II, the Patriarch of Russia and a party . . ."

I was angry. "Tatiana, as much as I respect the Patriarch, we didn't come all this way for his blessing. I came to deliver seventy tons of food and medicine, and that's what I intend to do!"

"Patricia," Nathaniel squeezed my hand so hard I feared nerve damage, "she has a good idea. Let's relax and have fun. I've never been here before. I want to see the sights." Leaning near, he murmured, "Cool it," before continuing the conversation. "Anyway, you don't have to do everything yourself. The stuff will probably show up in a few days."

I pretended to agree.

Tatiana smiled and assigned a car and driver to us, as well as Yan, a young translator. He would accompany us to our hotel where we were guests of the government.

As we were driven to our lodging—Yan, his football player bulk crammed into the small car—bombarded us with questions about the "States." With straight brown hair and green eyes covered by thick lenses, he said he had applied for a visa to the United States. As a Jew, he said he feared persecution if he stayed in Russia.

"Yesterday, I met your son and friend at airport." Yan, not the best translator I had ever met, struggled with our language. "Same age, me." I returned his smile, happy to know that Sean and Leandro had arrived safely.

In Russia there was no choice as to where you were to stay so the two young men were housed across town from us at the Rossia Hotel, a five-thousand-room monstrosity near Red Square. They were waiting for us in the dank lobby of the Leningradskaya when we arrived. "Yo, Mama, when do we start delivering the food?" Sean said, giving me a hug. It was a breakthrough in our relationship that he greeted me in such a friendly manner. Sean was equally sociable when I introduced him to Nathaniel.

"You're so tall, Sean. Thin, too!" I kissed my son, feeling the sharpness of his ribs, noting the springy curl in his black hair.

"Guess I need a little fattening up, eh Mama?" He assumed a twangy, sing-songy, southern accent. "Maybe you can cook up a mess of your southern fried chicken, gravy and biscuits. I'll be coming home, soon."

"You will?"

"Yep, I've enrolled at The New School for Social Research in New York in the fall, but I'll be visiting you first. You can turn me into the fatted calf!"

Sean knew how to make his mama laugh.

During the time we waited for the creaky wheels of Soviet hotel bureaucracy to turn, we sat in the dismal lobby talking. I told the boys what Tatiana had said about our shipment of aid. "I'm sure it arrived. I can't imagine why I was told it hadn't."

Nathaniel and I were fighting jet lag as we listened to the young men discuss ways to find the missing provisions. The only concrete information I could offer was a card with the name of the person who delivered the yacht to San Diego, written on it. VEK, Vladimir E. Kulbida. There was also an address in Moscow.

"Who's this VEK guy, Mom?" Sean asked.

"According to his card, VEK is Vladimir E. Klubida, the president of the St. Petersburg yacht club," I said, rifling through my papers. "But, Sean, I was also given the names Viktor A. Kudrayashov and V.I. Ikonnikov, from Yeltsin's office, all using the initials VEK. How strange."

"Yan, do you know the address on that guy's card?" Sean asked.

"Well, so, yes, that's very old Intourist hotel address . . . and . . ." A hotel employee interrupted Yan. The woman, whose brown dress fit snugly over a lost shape, had a face full of bitter memories. Without a word, she handed our translator a large wooden paddle from which hung a bronze room key. Yan stood up. "Please. Is ready now. Your room."

We agreed to meet for breakfast.

It was always surprising that however lacking in towels, there was usually a grumbling refrigerator and a piano in Russian hotel rooms. "As if we're going to give a concert," Nathaniel commented. We were so weary that even the lumpy mattress did not faze us and we quickly fell asleep. Two hours later, there were loud knocks on the thick wooden door. Nathaniel, a pillow over his head, continued to snooze.

"Mom, Mom, it's me, Sean." I could hear Russian epithets from the floor lady.

Throwing a coat on over my pajamas, I opened the door to three ashen, agitated young men. Sean, Yan, and Leandro. All but falling into the room, their distress tumbled out in a cascade of words; they were gasping for air.

"Mom, we found" . . . gasp . . . "the headquarters of VEK. Yan took us there, to that address you gave us." Gasp. "It's a big old Intourist hotel." Another gasp. "Mom, they have tons of electronic equipment. They threatened us." Sean was sweating as if it were July.

"In English. Russian, too," Yan added. His thick hands shook so hard he had trouble guiding a cigarette to his mouth.

Leandro jumped in. "Yeah, Pat, this big, I mean enormous, guy came barreling out the door and grabbed us. They have surveillance cameras all over the place."

"You boys went snooping around in the middle of the night?" My travel-fogged mind could barely cope with what they were telling me.

"Yeah, but wait, you haven't . . . heard it all. This gigantic guy took us inside this old hotel, yelling the whole time. 'Tell your mother to leave Moscow . . . or . . . or . . . you're all dead meat! Got it?' He said that over and over."

"No, seriously? How did he know who you were?"

"I swear, Mom. He said something about you being followed. I don't know." Deflated after telling their story, the boys, an unstrung mass of dampness, sagged onto the horsehair sofa.

"Is serious, very serious. He, the guy, is Mafia." Yan, no longer trying to smoke, was pulling his gloves off and on, off and on. "Is very, very serious."

I was so exhausted I could not concentrate on the immensity of the problem. "Okay, go to your hotel," I instructed. "Lock your door, put a chest in front of it, and don't open it for anyone. I'm getting the two of you out of Moscow tomorrow."

"No way, Mom. We're okay," Sean wheedled, suddenly composed. "I'm twenty-three Mom, and I know how to take care of myself."

"You're out of here, no arguments." I kissed Sean and Leandro good-night and crawled back into bed, but not to sleep. Nathaniel continued to snooze, oblivious to the fuss. In my head, I kept replaying the scenario the young men had described. Shortly before dawn, I fell into a fitful slumber.

Threats made during the night were much less scary the next morning. Using the cracked plastic phone in our room, a red phone at that, I attempted to call Sean at the Rossia. After eight tries, I got through to him on the notoriously malfunctioning system. The boys agreed to return to Italy that evening, but before departing they wanted to explore the famous subway system. We would meet for an early supper.

Nathaniel, even though he was eager to see Moscow, nevertheless said he would accompany me to the American Embassy. Dealing with a faceless person on the embassy intercom, I asked for assistance in finding our missing foodstuff and supplies. The man's indifference was disheartening, but he did tell me how to get to the Russian military base, chortling, "Lady, you'll never get inside the front gate. Never."

"Maybe not, but I'm going to try."

Nathaniel wasn't enthusiastic, either. "Can't we wait a day before colliding with a bunch of army brass?" He nuzzled my neck, attempting to distract me. For a moment my anger melted. I, too, wanted to relax and enjoy the day. A delay, however, would be a blunder we could not afford. With a sigh, I kissed my beau and said no.

The road outside Moscow was a jostling, pothole-filled, icy nightmare. The journey of twenty miles seemed like fifty. Unsure that he should be involved in our problem, Yan, our youthful interpreter, was nervous. He bounced up and down in his seat, moaning that he would get into trouble. "Tatiana will, you know, not hire me again." He refused consolation.

"Don't worry, Yan, I'll talk to Tatiana after we find the food."

"That food's worth a million hard-currency big U.S. bucks on the black market. You will never see it again," Yan said. "That's the way it is in our country now."

Two enormous gray gates, a crimson star on each half, identified our destination. I climbed out of the car. Beads of moisture poured off Yan as if he was in a sauna. Nevertheless, he hunched his shoulders, lowered his head into his coat collar, ready to help me talk to the guards.

Our tortoise-like translator communicated my words to the sentries. After lengthy discourse using walkie-talkies, and with Yan's liberal use of my name, "Paytreeseeya," the gates swung slowly open. It would have been unthinkable a few years earlier for an American citizen to be ushered onto a Russian military base, but it was 1993 and here we were. It felt like a dream.

"What did you say to those guys?" Nathaniel asked Yan. His eyes never strayed from the army vehicle we were following.

"I said Paytreeseeya is, well, you know, movie star in USA. She, she wants officer for film." He allowed himself a smile. "Mink coat, dark glasses, good boots, well, only famous, or new rich, wear such in USSR, uh, Russia." Our translator's laugh was contagious.

With theatrical flourish, an officer ushered us into an antiquated building and then into a cramped office. We were soon offered glasses of hot tea in silvered filigree holders, and thick slices of buttered bread, which we gratefully accepted.

Because of my high profile on Soviet TV for many years, I was a curiosity, a "movie star." Using my presumed celebrity to advantage, I flirted, employing my few words of their language to elicit a response. All the while I was asking for the manifest for our aid. An hour after our arrival, full of tea and bread, the lieutenant in charge, smiling broadly, gold teeth glinting, handed me the bill of lading. All the supplies I sent were listed and had arrived as expected on the AN-124. The official said the foodstuff was stored on a nearby paratrooper base. "The Commanding General will meet you at the gate," he said.

Thanking him, ready to depart, the officer smiled and handed me a card with his name scribbled on it in English. Bowing, he raised my hand to his lips. "Would be good, me, for film? Da?"

"Da. You bet!" I gave him a thumbs-up.

Half an hour later, at the paratrooper base, the commanding officer, a large man wearing a chest full of ribbon decorations, greeted us, "General Schwarzkopf?" I flirted. He did resemble our Gulf War hero. Smiling, he took my arm and guided me over a frozen walkway to a large Quonset hut. Inside, guarded by five armed paratroopers, was my food and medicine. Some of the shrink-wrap with my name emblazoned in red had been removed, but most of the larder was there, still on wooden pallets.

"May I take a photograph?" Yes, but I was not to include the paratroopers or any of the vehicles housed there. And the aid could not be released to me without orders from VEK, because that was the name on the manifest.

We sat in the commander's office playing the game tic-tac-toe with him, a common language, waiting for a promised emissary from VEK's office. After Sean and Leandro's experience, I wondered if we were dealing with the Mafia.

A respite from tension arrived along with the Mafia representative. I could not suppress a giggle. "He's seen The Godfather," I whispered to Nathaniel. Dressed in a black suit, vest, white buttoned-down-shirt with French cuffs held together by heavy gold links, a florid tie, Gucci loafers, with a bowler hat on his head, the man was a movie mobster. With a flourish, he placed a leather attaché case on the table, informing me that I owed two hundred fifty thousand dollars for transporting the aid from San Diego.

Sitting across from me, the Mafia man would not meet my eyes. "Why won't you look at me?" I asked. He was staring at Nathaniel, who seemed more interested in the green crocodile briefcase than the problem at hand.

I addressed the man trying to get his attention. "Sir, you don't know your own laws." I had just learned this one myself. "There's a law in your country that states that humanitarian aid must be brought without charge if space is available on any Russian aircraft." I got up and walked around the table. Looking him in the eye, I enunciated every word with clarity and emphasis. "You've made a mistake, sir. I don't owe you anything. Not-one-kopek!"

Still avoiding my gaze, the man flushed, loosened his tie, took a sip of water, and then scraped his chair back, muttering. "Your food released tomorrow. Papers to Soviet Peace Committee, eleven o'clock." He ran to the door, almost forgetting his briefcase. I thought we had won.

Back in Moscow, our spirits high, Sean, Leandro and Yan celebrated with us. Feasting at the hotel café, we ate only food we were sure wouldn't kill us: Beluga caviar with toast. As we told stories and laughed, releasing the tension that had threatened to overwhelm us, I noticed two men sitting at a table in the shadows, pretending to read *Pravda*. "Do you suppose we're being followed?" I whispered. Nathaniel assured me that the men were not paying any attention to us, a fact underscored when two flashy young women, obviously prostitutes, joined them. I sighed. Prostitution and other crimes had not been in evidence during the good old days of the Politburo.

Loading Sean and Leandro into a cab, we said farewell as they left for the airport. I was relieved to have them out of the Soviet capital. "Keep warm," I said, kissing my son. His shrug told me to stop the mothering.

"You may not want me to tell you anything, but this freezing wind means a blizzard. So button up!" Sean smiled.

When we awoke the next morning drifts of snow made sculptures of trees, hugged buildings, hid cars, and were banked in layers across the ice of the Moskva River. Wheedling a samovar of hot water from our floor lady by bribing her with a bag of perfume samples, I made coffee. While it was brewing, Nathaniel stared out the double-paned windows at Boris Yeltsin's White House, just across the river from our hotel. It bore charred windows from the attempted coup of 1991, when hard-liners tried to oust Yeltsin. It ended with Yeltsin ordering a tank attack on the White House, thus the blackened scars.

"I'll try to call the Gorbachevs when this Mafia thing is over," I said, getting Nathaniel's attention.

"Yeah? You really know them?"

"Yeah, I really know them. But the real question is: Do they still know me?" Three years had passed since our paths had last crossed.

We headed for the Peace Committee Building on Mir Prospekt without pausing for breakfast. A meal at the hotel could consume hours and was never worth the wait.

Precisely at eleven o'clock, we exited the elevator on the forth floor of the Peace Committee Building. Tatiana and Valrey, a man I had known for years, were waiting. "Patricia, dear, there's been a change in plans." Tatiana said, blushing furiously. "VEK wants you to come to his office, dear." She was wringing her hands. "They have a car and driver waiting."

"No way!" My voice was a hoarse whisper. "They promised those papers at eleven o'clock, here, in this office. I'm not about to go over there. Do you think I'm a fool?"

"No, dear, no. We'll call them. It's quite okay."

Over the next hour there were six phone calls from the elusive VEK trying to persuade me to pay them a visit. Between hypoglycemia from not having eaten, and frustration from the run around, I was on the verge of becoming a raving maniac. Finally, Valrey said he would go to VEK's office and get the papers. Even though Tatiana tried to dissuade him, Valrey was confident.

While awaiting his return, Tatiana regaled us with tales of grave robbers and soldiers murdering buddies to steal their weapons for resale. "Things were never so bad in our country before." She wiped a tear, sighing. "Communism was much, much better."

"You were never sent to a gulag, Tatiana, or you wouldn't say that." She nodded, but would not engage in further conversation. My friend, an old-line communist, was biting her lower lip to stop its quivering, making me wonder what unnamed fear caused such a reaction.

Valrey, full of bravado when he left, returned pale, shaking. He did not have the promised papers and did not utter a word.

"You've been threatened, haven't you?" I asked. He did not answer.

"Valrey, have you been threatened?" He stared into space, a zombie, not reacting to my query. Tatiana, too, had retreated into a shell I could not penetrate.

"We're hungry so we'll go get a bite and when we return I'll call President Yeltsin's office, to see if he can help us," I said as we headed for the elevator. Neither Tatiana nor Valrey acknowledged my words. It was as if they had been transported to another place.

Yan, even more anxious than usual, was waiting for us in the cold lobby. "Paytreeseeya, you have phone call at keeper's desk." The so-called keeper was an old-age pensioner who directed people to the correct floor of the building.

"A phone call? Who could be calling me here?"

"Tatiana," Yan murmured, handing me the receiver with perspiring hand, "from upstairs."

"Patricia?"

"Yes."

"Patricia, don't say a word, listen. Listen carefully." My ear was glued to the receiver. Tatiana sighed and took a deep breath, "Patricia, please listen carefully. You are in danger. A man called, wanting to know your height, weight, coloring, and what you are wearing. I told him you had gone to St. Petersburg on the train." I strained to comprehend what this Russian woman was telling me. "You must get out of Moscow, at once." Tatiana cleared her throat. "Also, Patricia, your son did not get on that airplane last night. I thought you should know." She hung up.

My mind reeled with images of Sean and Leandro being kidnapped, held captive in the Intourist hotel where they had found VEK. Without thinking, I propelled a startled Yan and confused Nathaniel out the double doors and into the snowstorm that was burying Moscow so that we could not be overheard.

Telling them what Tatiana had said, I turned to our translator, "Yan, take a taxi to our hotel, pack everything, even my laundry in the bathroom. Take the name tags off everything. Get our passports from the desk clerk. Bribe them with the coffee and cigarettes in my black suitcase. Do whatever you have to do, but make it happen. Try to find out about Sean and Leandro. Deliver everything to the American Embassy. Hurry!" I thrust a roll of wadded up dollar bills in his hand. "I'm counting on you. Oh, and Yan, if you want to immigrate to the States, you had better do what I'm asking," I bluffed.

"You can count, so, on me," he said, disappearing into the snowstorm.

Then a dazed Nathaniel allowed me to lead him across the driveway as fast as we could manage in the drifting snow. "We've got to find a taxi," I said.

Crossing Mir Prospekt, running now, we were soon on Sadovoye Ring Road, usually a good place to find a taxi. Almost at once, a dilapidated Volga pulled over to the icy curb. Propelling Nathaniel into the front seat, I climbed in back. "Give the driver cigarettes," I instructed. Nathaniel carried a stash of tobacco and small bottles of whiskey in a backpack. Handy for bribes.

As Nat fumbled with the zipper on his backpack, I told our grizzled driver to take us to the American Embassy. I wanted to get our passports from Yan before going inside the embassy. So we circled the red brick building for half an hour. But Yan did not show up.

"Let's go to the hotel. Maybe he's there," Nathaniel suggested. "No one knows me, so I can find out a lot more than you can." He had a good point.

"Okay. Let's go." Showing the taxi driver a scrap of paper with the hotel name and address written on it in Cyrillic, I indicated we wanted to go there.

"Da, da. Okay." With a quick grinding of gears, the man put the old clunker into action.

Among the few automobiles braving the storm, I soon realized, was a black Zill keeping pace with us.

"Nathaniel, we're being followed."

"Tell this guy to go faster. We'll be murdered, I just know it."

"Prajalsta, please, faster, speciba, thank you, escape." Trying to convey the gravity of our predicament, I mixed languages while pointing in back of us at the Zill now turning a corner. There was no reaction until I thrust a wad of dollar bills at the driver. Stuffing the money in his pocket with his left hand, his elbow on the wheel, he shifted gears with tobacco-stained fingers.

Suddenly, the car became more powerful. Kicking up plumes of snow, the man skidded over the icy road, veered across several lanes of traffic, ignoring horns, whistles, and curses. After several dizzying turns, our driver cut the engine, and as if in slow motion, coasted through a clearing into a grove of thick pines, trees so weighted by snow they appeared to be a solid mass. The sudden quiet, when the car came to a stop, was more ominous than our dramatic ride across the Russian capital. Straining to see if I could recognize our location in the glimmering dimness, I marveled that our driver was calmly lighting up. We had lucked out by finding someone experienced in concealment.

The car trailing us was no longer in sight. I shivered from a chill not connected to the glacial wind. I was also uncomfortable. Broken springs jabbed as I crouched in a half twist while offering the driver vodka. I begged him to take us to the train station near the Leningradskaya hotel. "Prajalsta," I beseeched. "Please!"

He muttered, "Da," and after an unhealthy swig of alcohol, let the car roll slowly down the hillock behind the pine trees that had secluded us, onto Okhotny Ryad, the Hunters Row, just renamed from Karl Marx Prospekt.

From my restricted position, I could see a scarlet star glowing atop a red brick Kremlin tower; seat of power of the USSR, now the Russian Federation. It was a place where I had been honored—a lifetime ago it seemed.

Nathaniel's catatonic gaze had not changed since I pushed him into the car beside our talented driver. This, his first trip out of the United

States, made a case for never leaving the security of home. His full head of graying hair, outlined in the jaundiced glow of a streetlight, matched his attitude.

"Give it up, Pat. Let's get out of Moscow. Let the mob have that food and medicine." He coughed into a blue cotton handkerchief, "Damn, I'm catching a cold." Hearty nose-blowing followed another cough. "Patricia, listen up. I grew up in New York, I know Mafia, and believe me, this is stupid Mafia, the most dangerous kind. They'll kill without a second thought."

"Maybe you're right," I said, placating him. There was no way I would give in to thugs trying to confiscate the humanitarian aid donated for the country's starving orphans.

"After thirty trips to this godforsaken cesspool, you should have expected this," he fumed, adding a sarcastic toast. "Here's to the New Year 1993! Warm vodka in a paper cup, not exactly the way I pictured painting the town."

"I'm doing this to give you a chance to prove your manhood." I appealed to his depleted sense of humor. He did not laugh.

This was my thirtieth trip here, and eons away, it seemed from our televised arrival. For years, my meetings with powerful leaders in the former Soviet Union—from Andrei Gromyko to President Mikhail Gorbachev and Raisa Gorbacheva, writers, poets, artists, dancers, and especially children—had been given high-profile attention. It encouraged me to continue building bridges between our countries. How could I have anticipated what was happening now?

On this starless night, I was bereft. Corruption had become the norm in the former Soviet capital. Where were my friends who had made those flowery toasts, performed concerts, and danced ballets in my honor? I did not know friend from foe now and I was afraid to call any of them.

A letter from President Boris Yeltsin, thanking me for the donations of food and medicine, was folded neatly in my purse. The president of the Russian Federation had the missive faxed to my home in San Francisco shortly before I left for Moscow. A lot of good it was doing me, I thought.

Our car sputtered, and coughed, and skidded over a patch of ice before coming to a halt near the train station, and our destination, the Leningradskaya Hotel.

"Lie low, Patricia." Nathaniel opened the car door. "I'll check on Yan. I hope he got our passports and luggage." My lover was the perfect, if edgy, foil, as no one in Russia knew him or what he looked like.

"Be careful."

"I'll dole out a little money. We'll get what we need." Nathaniel handed our driver another pack of cigarettes and a small bottle of whisky, ensuring temporary loyalty.

"Speciba, speciba."

I could hear the driver remove the cellophane off the package of Marlboros, see the flare of a match, and then smell the strong stench of tobacco smoke, one of the better-known aromas in Russia.

"Ask Yan if he knows where Sean and Leandro are," I said to Nathaniel. Oh God, I prayed, let them be safe.

"Right," Nathaniel replied, disappearing into the frigid darkness.

To have Sean in danger was a possibility I did not want to consider. When Yan said the food was worth a million hard-currency bucks on the black market, I should have listened to him and not been so foolish, I thought.

I sat with our drunken taxi driver staring out into the gloom, waiting, hoping Nathaniel would be able to get our passports and have good news about Sean. My mind was drifting when a shadowy figure partially blocked the train station light. The Volga darkened. My heart was pounding so hard, I though it would pop out of my chest. I was sweating.

Abruptly, a man in a gray military overcoat pulled open the cab door. He reached toward me and took my purse pocketing what little money he found, and then threw my bag back at me. A large, decorative buckle hit my head, scraping the skin. "Get out of Moscova, Paytreeseeya," he said. "Now." Without another word, the man turned and walked toward a car idling nearby, headlights dim, motor smooth. Not the automobile of a robber, I thought. My driver was slumped over the steering wheel, either drunk or dead. He had not uttered a sound.

Moaning, hurting, scared, I hunkered down on the car floor, praying for help. What could I do to save my life and that of my son and his friend? How could I escape the Mafia and still get the food delivered to where it was intended? The discomfort of the crankshaft digging into my side awoke a memory of psychic suffering and how my meditations had guided me. Could I still access that higher power? I closed my eyes, willing myself to calm down, to pray, but there was nothing, except battering wings of fear engulfing my mind.

Kneeling, I peered out the car window into the black hole of night. In the distance, the sickly yellow glow from a street lamp revealed two dark forms. Fearing the return of "the robbers," I waited, ready to bolt for the train station. But it was Nathaniel and Yan. "Thank God," I whispered.

When Nathaniel and Yan were closer, I opened the car door and made a dash across the snow toward them, crying, babbling.

"Patricia, what happened?" Nathaniel dabbed his gloves at my head as we trudged toward the car.

I could hardly talk. "Sean . . . is he okay?"

"The boys are okay, Patricia, they're fine," Nathaniel comforted, as I staggered back to the car. "They didn't make the first plane because their flight was canceled, but they got the next flight out."

"Thank God. Thank God," I sobbed.

We collapsed into the cab. Nathaniel listened to my story of being mugged. Now that we were safe Yan was mostly concerned about his visa.

"Your suitcases . . . in car of hotel pimp. I gave dollars, coffee, cigarettes, and later more to deliver to American Embassy, yes? Your passports, Nathaniel has. Yes, now so, I will have visa?"

"Right now we've got to get to the American Embassy. Can you drive?" Yan nodded yes, well, maybe he could drive a car. I found aspirin in my coat pocket and swallowed two. I wanted to stop the throbbing pain in my head.

Pushing the driver over to the passenger seat, Yan attempted to start the Volga. After several tries, the old car coughed, sputtered, and finally started. Slowly, our translator eased the automobile along the snowy streets of Moscow and ever so slowly to the red brick embassy, while I filled them in on what had happened to me. Yan sighed, "Mafia for sure. Paytreeseeya, you must leave Moscova."

We inched our way to the embassy thanks to the gallant actions of a young man who only wanted to get a visa to the United States. Kissing him good-bye, I made a promise. "Yan, you can expect your visa. I promise."

Scott Bolterwitz, the Regional Security officer at the embassy, tried to make light of my experience at first. But he became very helpful when I showed him the manifest establishing that the aid had arrived and was able to tell him where it was hidden.

"Knowing this makes you extraordinarily vulnerable. You must get out of Russia at once," he advised.

"Not until I get that food delivered. I have an obligation to the people who donated it."

"The Russian Mafia is exceedingly dangerous. We can't assume responsibility for your safety." He looked at me with clear blue eyes, and declared, "But if you insist on staying, I'll make arrangements for you at a German hotel. You can also hire a safe driver from the embassy."

I had one more request. "Will you help our translator get a visa? Please. He saved our lives."

"I can't promise such a thing. But I'll be on the look-out for him."

We were soon ensconced in the Olympic Penta Hotel on Olympiskij Prospekt. The reservations listed the American Embassy as our address.

Yan's pimp contact delivered our suitcases to the embassy and their safe driver brought them to the Penta. Yan had removed all identifying tags from our luggage, as I asked him to. If one person, I reasoned, beyond the embassy, was aware of our whereabouts we could indeed be dead meat.

For three days, we holed up in the German hotel, watching the same TV shows over and over, eating meals delivered to our room while I hid in the bathroom. All the while I was trying to make a plan, and trying to keep Nathaniel from jumping out the window from anxiety.

"We've gotta get out of here," he kept saying.

"You can go anytime you want to. I'll pay for your ticket." Our return tickets had expired. It was a week past our departure date.

"Let's go outside for a while. You can hide your hair under a hat," he pleaded. "Wear my sunglasses. They're goggles, they'll hide half your face."

I laughed. "Do you think we've seen too many 007 movies?"

"That guy, VEK, brought a yacht to San Diego to enter in the America's Cup race, right?"

"Right."

"A yacht from St. Petersburg on a military airplane; does that sound like a person without connections?"

"No."

"And Tatiana said your food wasn't on the plane."

"Right."

"And then when you proved it was, that guy said you owed him $250,000 for bringing it over. Right?"

"Yes, but . . ."

"No buts. When Sean found their headquarters, VEK said you were dead meat. Believe me, this is not a movie."

"And they're stupid, right Nathaniel? So how smart do we have to be?"

"Smarter than we've been. Now let's get some fresh air."

"No. I'm smart enough to know we have to stay put for a while longer."

Giving up, pouting, Nathaniel turned on the television set and began watching a repeat of the news on CNN. "Well, Ms. Paytreeseeyaa Montandon, you've been meditating. These are your friends. It's up to you to tell me what we're going to do."

Suddenly I had an answer. Of course! It was simple. "We'll have a press conference so I can tell the Russian people what happened. I'll call Tatiana and tell her to call the news agencies. We'll have protection when the public knows of our predicament."

"Bad idea," Nathaniel scowled, "our phone is probably tapped."

"If our phone was tapped they would have acted by now. I don't think they know where we are."

When I called, Tatiana was effusive in her concern. "Patricia dear, where are you? We've been so worried about you. I'll send a car and driver right now, just tell me where you are dear. Your brother called. He needs to locate you . . . where are you?" (Years later I got e-mail from a distant cousin, Michael Montandon, who said he was working at the embassy at the time of my Mafia encounter. He said that Tatiana had called the embassy trying to locate me. The Marine Guard had transferred the call to him. But he didn't know where I was.)

I said, "I have a car and driver, and I haven't seen my brother in two years. He is not looking for me." When I told her I wanted a press conference at the Peace Committee office, with international reporters present, she agreed to set it up for the next day. "I'll check on you, so you had better follow through," I pretended.

"Of course, Patricia, dear. Of course. It is not a problem. Anything you wish."

"And, I want Galina, from the Soviet Women's Committee, to be my translator."

"Of course, Patricia, of course."

The next day, at the appointed hour we arrived at the Peace Committee office on Mir Prospekt. This was the building where we had first been received in 1983, ten years earlier. A flustered Tatiana met me at the insulated set of double doors as I was swept into the building on the heels of yet another blizzard.

"Everything is set dear, everything." She led me to the room where the kids and I had met with Mr. Kutnesov and six other people on that first trip, for what became a breakthrough in our relations with the USSR. Now, on January 8, 1993, thirty or so photographers, journalists, and television cameras in the round center of a doughnut-like arrangement of tables occupied the room.

Thankfully, Galina was there to translate.

Surveying the room, trying to suppress my apprehension and the churning feelings of fear and betrayal, I took a sip of water and then launched into my appeal. My goal was to get the food released, not to get myself killed. I intended to be diplomatic. My hosts needed to save face. I needed to stay alive and be sure the food got delivered.

"There has been a huge misunderstanding about the humanitarian aid I brought from the United States for Russian orphans," I said. "I want you to know this aid was not sent as an act of charity, but as an act of love. If our positions were reversed, if we were in need, I know you, the Russian people, would send food and medicine to children in America."

Reporters were scribbling fast.

"I've been told I owe two hundred fifty thousand dollars for transporting this humanitarian aid to Moscow from the United States. Perhaps Mr. Kulbida, the person making this request, does not know that the seventy tons of food and medicine we brought here was donated by people in America, for your children. No one has been paid one kopek for this aid," I said. "No one." I went on to say we had paid our own way to come to Moscow and distribute the aid and that a new Russian law said that humanitarian aid had to be delivered free of charge on a space-available-basis. "Mr. Kulbida knows that airplane was empty, that they had the space."

I took a sip of water, hoping my words were having an effect. "And now that you know the facts, I'm sure you will release the food so a few of Russia's orphans can be fed."

I answered questions hurriedly, anxious to get away for a meeting with the committee overseeing distribution of humanitarian aid in Moscow. A woman from the American Embassy accompanied me from the press conference to a moody old stone building in the heart of Moscow where we were to meet with the bureaucrats. As with everything in Moscow in the 1990s, the whole place looked seedy.

"I'm sorry we have no coffee, Ms. Montandon. Times are hard for our country at the present." The man was soft spoken and polite. His styled gray hair skimmed the collar of an expensive suit. This was the new Russian bureaucrat: In the money. "We very much know of your work. President Yeltsin knows. And we thank you." His conversation rambled along with pleasantries until I cut through the verbiage.

"How can I get the food released?" I said, not smiling.

"Ms. Montandon, we will negotiate." The embassy staff person gave me a cautionary look. But I was tired, ready to go home, not in the mood for dillydallying. I just wanted to curl up with a good novel, back home in my own bed, alone.

"Ms. Montandon, if you give half the foodstuff to our military, we will release the balance to whomever you say," the man said.

"I'm not here to negotiate," I said.

"Yes, well, the Russian military needs food, too, you see. They also have children."

I had not put my life in danger to feed the Russian military. The aid was for children of civilians. Suddenly I had an idea. I hoped it would work. "Excuse me," I interrupted his wheedling flow of words. "May I borrow your jacket?"

"You are cold, yes? I'm sorry . . . please." He put his designer jacket around my shoulders. "So, is that better? Yes?"

Leaning back in my chair I pulled his pricey clothing around me. Stroking the soft garment, I asked a question. "Which part of your jacket would you like to have returned?" The man did not understand. The embassy representative looked uncomfortable. Had I flipped out?

"Do you want a sleeve? The collar?"

"Uh . . ."

"Do you want to negotiate to get half of your jacket returned?"

Everyone got it at the same time.

The room with the overstuffed moldy furniture resonated with the sound of laughter. "Ms. Montandon, okay. Okay. What do you want? Where shall we deliver the food?"

"I want it released to Alevitina Fedulova at the Women's Committee. And I want photographs and letters from everyone who receives it. That's what I want."

"Okay." He retrieved his suit jacket. "Okay, you win."

A week after my return, I got a fax from retired Soviet Consul General Valentin Kamanev who now lived in Moscow. He wrote that a Russian television show had focused on me getting the humanitarian aid released. They had superimposed my image onto the military base where I found the food, and turned me into a hero. Valentin suggested we use my celebrity and nonprofit status to get prime space on Gorky Street to open a clothing store. I could import the goods and we could make a lot of money.

I turned down the offer.

Three months after my encounter with the Mafia, a large sack of mail was delivered to my home. It was from the Russian recipients of the aid so generously given by American people. The kids sent pins and pressed flowers, strings of beads and red-colored hearts. "I love you, Patricia. You are Godmother," a child had printed in English block letters. "My babies were hungry. Thank you Miss Patricia, you save my babies," wrote another in splintered English. It had been worth my few hours of fear.

How had I had the guts to do what I did? I often wondered. The Russian Mafia was murdering people with impunity. I had been very frightened, but I was outraged that people would steal donated food from the mouths of starving children. I couldn't let that happen.

A year later, I received a letter from our tense, but brave, translator Yan. He had gotten his visa and was living in America, going to school, and working at a McDonald's restaurant. "I love here freedom. I eat very many hamburgers, all with good meat," he wrote.

Two years later, a friend in Moscow told me that Tatiana was the one who had alerted the Mafia about my food shipment. My friend said the word was that Tatiana had not dreamed I was so stubborn as to find it and then to get it released.

Ha, I thought, Tatiana had a lot to learn about an Oklahoma preacher's daughter.

With little more than a hug good-bye, Nathaniel dropped out of my life. I was glad to see him go. I knew him much too well to want a romantic relationship with him.

# 27.

# OLD WOUNDS

Sean was back in the United States and, prior to attending The New School in Manhattan, was coming home for the summer. Making it clear that he did not want to stay with either his dad or me, he rented a small apartment on Page Street, a few blocks from my house. Thrilled, determined to be as good a mom as possible, I prepared his favorite foods and set aside things I thought he might need for his apartment.

Little by little, as the days went by, Sean began to hang out with me. A good cook, he prepared the Italian foods he had learned to make in Italy. Six feet tall now, he spoke, read, and wrote fluent Italian. With his dark eyes and black curly hair, he even looked Italian. But something was wrong. He was not his usual ebullient self, nor did he hang out with his old friends or tinker with the motorcycle he had bought off the street at an earlier time. He seemed morose. When I asked what was bothering him, he shrugged and said, "Nothing. I'm okay."

One day, a few hours before he was to leave for New York, we went for a drive. Sean, usually a speed demon who caused me to gasp and ask him to slow down, was dawdling along on Fell Street heading toward Golden Gate Park. Our ride was a silent one when he suddenly let go with a few expletives. "Fucking, fucking, bitch!"

"Sean!"

"Sorry." A short pause, "I was thinking about that woman, that so-called person who wrecked our family." His knuckles, tight on the steering wheel, were white.

"I know, Sean, I know."

"Not the way I do."

My son, in some ways a stranger to me, was deadly pale, his jaw clenched. "Mom, that woman, that . . . she . . ." The explosive eruption of his curse gave way to deliberate words. "Used me to get to dad! Like when I was a little kid . . . before they married, I actually, uh, thought I was in love with her!"

Heat flooded my body. I forced myself to act calm, gazing at the traffic continuing to travel smoothly along the street, the drivers oblivious to the drama being played out within our car. Adjusting the blue wool scarf around my neck, I covered my concern with a cough and moved cautiously ahead. "In love?"

"Mom, that woman, that sorry excuse for a human being, acted like we were peers, hanging out . . ." Sean's forehead was beaded lightly in sweat.

"Peers?"

He did not reply.

I asked the question again, louder. "Peers? What do you mean, Sean?"

"Yeah. Told each other secrets. You know, boyfriend-girlfriend stuff."

"She fed into your kid fantasies, Sean."

There were long minutes of silence. Sean made a left-hand turn. We headed back toward the Enchanted Cottage.

"Sean, please talk to me."

"Remember that expensive helmet she bought me for go-cart racing?" he said.

Oddly enough, I did remember the helmet because at the time I thought it was way too extravagant a gift for a child. "Yes, the one that cost about eighty dollars?"

"That's the one. She said you were a bad mother when you said she shouldn't buy me high-priced gifts."

Sean pulled into our driveway and parked. We sat there, the car windows down, not saying anything. A tendril of mist was creeping into my garden. I could hear the sorrowful sound of distant foghorns. Fronds on tree ferns trembled.

Sean leaned forward, not looking at me. "Mom, remember the time you threw away one of my drawings of a fire truck? It had been on our bulletin board for ages and when it got ragged, you threw it away. You said you were cleaning up the clutter."

I nodded as he turned toward me. "My feelings were hurt," he said, continuing, "I told Dede. She hugged me and said you were a mean awful mother to do such a thing. I was so innocent. I guess I fell in love with her, sharing secrets like a couple of kids. Thinking back now, it makes me sick."

I thought my heart would burst from my chest and splatter. "You were nine, ten?"

"Nine," he said.

"She was a grown woman, almost thirty years older than you, with sons your age. She set you up. Got to you after making me believe she was a friend so she could get your father. And then made sure you were sent away to boarding school."

"Yeah, like a bag of trash. Made me hate you, too."

"Have you told your dad about this?" My mouth was dry.

"Yeah." We got out of the automobile. "Yeah, I told Dad. You know what he said?" Sean leaned against the car door as if his legs were too weak to hold him up. "You know what Dad said? He told me to talk to her about it."

"Talk to her!" I said, as we made our way up the steps and inside the house to the kitchen. "Oh, Sean, I'm sorry, so sorry." Pain shot down my left shoulder. My arms ached.

"Yes, Dad said to talk to her. That's how much he cares about me." Sean slouched against the kitchen stove.

"Sean," I put my arms around him. "Listen to me, please. You've got to get psychological help."

"I don't want to spend my life in therapy . . . it's okay . . . I'll . . ." He looked tired, defeated.

I moved away from him and sat down on a kitchen chair. "Without help, you might not have a life, Sean."

"How can I ever trust women? After what you did too, Mom."

"Me? What did I do?"

"You know. When . . . when . . . you said you were going to kill yourself. I felt responsible. For years . . . it was awful and I . . ." He stopped talking, and then resumed a softer tone. "I was scared of you . . ."

Scared of me? "Sean, I would never hurt you, you know that," I said. "And you are not responsible for me in any way. Please listen to me, hear what I'm saying. You are not responsible for me. I am responsible for myself in every way."

"It's okay, Mom."

"It's not okay, Sean. It was terrible for me to talk about killing myself and asking if you wanted to go with me. I'm so, so sorry. Can you ever forgive me?" I said, wringing my hands. I stood up and began to pace back and forth. "I have big gaps in my memory of that time. Linda reminded me that your cousin Patrick spent the whole summer with us in 1981. I don't remember it at all," I said, still pacing. "I think nature has a way of numbing us to extreme trauma. There are lots of things I can't remember. Lots. But that's no excuse for what I said to you."

"Mom, it's okay."

"No, it's not okay. But what can I do about it, now? When your dad deserted me for Dede and then you chose to be with them instead of me, I was out of my mind with sorrow. I'm so sorry. I wish I could have been stronger. I hope you can forgive me."

"It's okay, Mom." Sean wiped his eyes with the back of his hand. He began to walk toward the front door. "I love you, Mom. I didn't want anything bad to happen to you."

"I love you, too. I pray for you every day." I was determined not to cry. "If I could turn back time . . . but, as someone once said, what is, is. Now we have to get on with it."

"It's hard for me to trust my feelings. I'm afraid to like a girl too much, afraid it will all go away."

"Sean, please, please, you must get help."

A car honked. It was a school chum taking him to the airport. Sean picked up his backpack from where he had dropped it near the entrance to my home.

"I love you, Sean."

"Love you too, Mom."

A quick hug and he was gone.

I was shattered. Had my self-absorbed angst caused me to overlook a vulnerable little boy who needed me? I wondered if Sean would ever forgive me, just as I could not imagine forgiving the woman who destroyed our family.

What kind of mother was I if I could not face down the female who had smashed our lives, as if we were nothing more than cheap glass? And Al was as guilty as she was. Neither exhibited qualities that showed they cared about anyone or anything outside of themselves, except when it served their purpose.

My mind wandered back through the years of humiliations to which they had subjected me: my constant begging for my own money, the public relations campaign they launched against me, the way they caused my young son to turn against me, and then dumped him at a boarding school.

Now I had the burden of knowing from Sean how they had used him. I loathed my ex-husband and his wife with a passion that caused me to lose all perspective. I thought about driving my car at top speed up the driveway at River Meadow Farm, crashing through the front door, and killing them. Fantasy. It was not in me to harm anyone.

I knew I was better off than many divorced women, but comparing myself to others did little to ease my suffering. What it did do was give me a sense of empathy and connection with women and children who most often bear the brunt of divorce.

Meditation was impossible. I was as barren as the Ethiopian plains.

Over the next weeks I decided to put all my plans on hold so I could go to New York and camp on Sean's doorstep until he got into therapy. I wanted to make sure he was getting the help he needed. Before I could act, Sean called. He told me he had thought about what I said, and was now in therapy with Doctor Leopold Caligor. Bringing me up to date on other matters, Sean said he was living in a historical boat on the Hudson River where he had to work on weekends for the privilege. He was unusually talkative and said he wanted to be a writer, and was enrolled in journalism classes at The New School. He did not yet want me to come and visit.

In an effort to come to terms with the past, I went to San Antonio,

Texas, to talk to our former cook, Geri Crumpler; and our driver, Clifford Mooney, who no longer worked for Al, and his wife Thuy, who for four years had helped care for Sean. They had seemed devoted to my husband and to Sean, and to me, too, I thought. But when our breakup took place, they all went with Al, except for Thuy, who became a hair stylist. It was a crushing blow. I had considered them members of my extended family.

Geri, Clifford, and Thuy met me at the San Antonio airport, acting happy to see me, insisting I stay in their homes. My emotions were in turmoil upon seeing the people who had played such an important role in my life. I felt resentment, happiness, anger, and love in equal measure. But soon the years fell away as we caught up with each other.

Geri, a gourmet cook, had retired. We sat on a brown sofa in her living room surrounded by framed photographs of her children and grandchildren, talking.

"I'll never forget cooking for all those famous people at your Roundtable lunches," she said. "Remember when Alex Haley came? It was right after *Roots* was published. He brought a dozen copies of his book and signed two for me."

"You cooked southern fried chicken, collard greens, corn bread, and black-eyed peas, foods he grew up eating. He said it was the best meal he had eaten since leaving Tennessee," I said, laughing. "Why Alex even took a doggy bag back to Los Angeles."

"We laughed so much about that." Geri chuckled now at the thought. "I've often wondered what Jacques Pepin would have thought about that meal. You sent me to study with him, remember? I learned so much."

"You're a terrific cook, Geri. Why did you retire?"

"Well, I have kidney problems. I couldn't stand on my feet so long anymore." She glanced at a framed photograph of Al and me with our arms around Sean. "You were such a happy family," she said. "I love that boy of yours, Ms. Montandon, you know I do."

"Yes, Geri I do know that. You and Sean always acted like a couple of kids together.

"When he visits me, we still act silly. I send him cooking recipes. He likes to cook."

"Are you okay, Geri, financially, I mean? You should have had a good amount of money in your retirement account."

"Mr. Wilsey said I didn't have any retirement coming, Ms. Montandon."

"Why, that's not true. You earned plenty."

Her voice was soft. "Mr. Wilsey said I didn't have any retirement. But when I asked him he finally let me sign a note for two thousand dollars, so I could move to Texas to be near my son, Lonnie." She smiled. "I paid him back. It took me four years, but I did it. Every penny."

"Oh Geri, I'm so sorry. That's awful. You should have had a comfortable pension." Geri, gentle and forgiving, took my hands in hers. "Ms. Montandon, the good Lord doesn't give us more than we can bear. When I'm not on dialysis I've been able to work in fancy houses in San Antone. And Lonnie takes good care of me, too."

"Sean was lucky to have you in that dressed-up fake house," I said. "He thinks of you as his mother, or wishes you were."

"I say prayers for you and Sean all the time. I keep telling him you are the only mother he has," Geri said.

After two days with Geri, I went to stay with Clifford and Thuy. Unsure about Clifford's loyalty to Al, I treaded cautiously. "Clifford," I said one evening after supper, "Sean told me something that has me greatly concerned." I did not know how to word my question. "Do you know of anything that happened, that you saw, to make Sean think Dede was his peer?"

"Oh, yes." Clifford, a giant of a man with a slashing scar across his face and a collection of silver stars from the Vietnam War, also has a keen wit. There was no humor in his voice now, only disgust. "You know, before they got married, Dede would be at the Brockelbank apartments where Mr. Wilsey was staying, every cotton picking minute. She was so dad-gum afraid he would get away from her. She would put Sean on her lap and kiss and nuzzle him, giggling as if they were playmates. She was trolling, you know, making sure all her bases were covered. Sean was the key. Get him and she had his dad. She would take Sean out for the whole afternoon, not with her boys, mind you, but by himself." The ex-Marine paused and looked me in the eye, "Ms. Montandon, the best part of being a Marine is when you take your pack off. You'll feel better when you do."

"I'm trying, Clifford, I'm trying."

"Me, too, Ms. Montandon." Clifford shifted his weight in the chair and rubbed his hands across his face; hands that had fired guns in Vietnam, driven our cars, piloted our helicopter, and comforted me when my marriage first broke up. "You know, I thought Mr. Wilsey hung the moon, that he was a doggone saint."

"He's good at saint shit!" I said. My crude expression caused Clifford to smile.

"Yeah, for sure. You know, I knew Mr. Wilsey was having an affair with that woman, but I thought he would wake up. He didn't. It was as if he let a parasite devour him. The man I knew disappeared. I can't tell you how sad that makes me." Clifford cleared his throat and stood up. "Gotta get some air," he said. The big man got up and walked toward the door, limping a bit from an old war wound. The screen door slammed behind him and he disappeared into the warm Texas night.

I sat at the table a few minutes and then I got up and walked outside, too. Clifford was leaning against a porch pillar. I leaned on the opposite side of the same support. We stood gazing up at the stars in the big sky of the Lone Star State. Lightning bugs flitted about, crickets and frogs called to mates. The heavy scent of new-mown grass in the humid air ignited childhood memories.

I touched Clifford's hand. "In the long run, even though it nearly killed me at the time, they did me a favor, Cliff. I wouldn't change places with them for any amount of money. I hope you feel that way, too."

"Sometimes," he said.

"An Irish poet, Patrick Kavanagh, said 'God enters through a wound.' I believe that's true. My work with children has given me treasures beyond counting. And look at you. You have a lovely home. You are respected in your community. You work with the disabled. You have loads of friends."

"Yeah, but you know it hurts to find out that someone you thought was a saint is a fraud," Clifford said.

d beside each other for a few minutes longer, not saying any-
sorbing the gentle quiet. "I love you Clifford," I finally said.
nd Thuy, and Geri are like family to me. I'm glad we've made
peace with each other."

"Me, too, Ms. Montandon, me, too." He patted my hand.

The three of them, Clifford, Thuy, Geri and her handsome son, Lonnie, took me to the airport for my return to San Francisco. We hugged
good-bye as if parting from well-loved family members.

"Now you write to us, hear?" Geri said. "Come back to visit soon."

Six months later, I went to New York and, with Sean's consent, met
with his psychologist. Doctor Caligor told me that my son had been betrayed in a brutal way, by his dad and by Dede. As a vulnerable child Sean
had even thought he would marry Dede someday. The therapist was
working hard to restore his belief in himself and in women. He said he
would not talk to Sean's dad about his son, even though Al had asked.
"He doesn't deserve to hear about Sean," the doctor said.

Back home, my neck began to ache in spasms of agony, sending me to
a doctor who prescribed muscle relaxants and antidepressants. My
thoughts about what had happened to Sean threatened to swamp me
back into the bitter past.

Then one evening I stumbled across something I had written in a
notebook while at Sai Baba's ashram in Puttaparti, India.

The quality of our lives is made by us, by how we choose not to bog down
into becoming a victim or a survivor, but rather, a thriving aware contrib-
utor to our own lives. Forgiveness isn't for the one you think you're forgiving. It's for you. Forgive for your own sake. Only God can forgive
those who have sinned against you.

Okay, I'll try to do that, I thought. After all, Sean was strong and intelligent. He had found a good therapist and he would solve his problems
his own way. There was nothing I could do about past wrongs. It was
time for me to stop feeling responsible for my son's misery.

# 28.

# EMBRACING
# THE VISION

While still at The New School, Sean began working in the mailrooms at *Newsweek Magazine* and then the *Ladies Home Journal*, all the time with his sights set on *The New Yorker*. Then in the fall of 1994, when he was twenty-four, Sean achieved his goal. He began there as a messenger and after graduating from The New School, advanced to the poetry department and before long became a junior fiction editor. I was so proud of him.

On a trip to San Francisco, Sean went with me to an opera. We had been to the mezzanine bar, an old hangout from a previous life, and were going down the marble staircase to the orchestra level when I saw my ex and his wife coming up the same steps. As a suddenly hushed crowd watched, Al and Dede, who also saw us, turned their backs to Sean and me, and swept past.

Wheeling around, Sean ran up the stairs after his father. Facing him, Sean put the flat of his hand on Al's stomach. "Remember me?" Sean said, his face pale and pinched.

The sad old man, the rich stranger, the unrepentant betrayer, stared at his son, the baby he had said was the greatest miracle of his life, the child he would always care for, then murmured a faint "Hi," and moved on.

When I tried to commiserate with Sean he said he didn't want to talk about it, but I could feel his suffering. Yet, when Al had heart surgery, like a good son, Sean came from New York to be with him. For several days, he hung around my house waiting for Dede to grant him permission to visit his dad. Sean said he was afraid to go on his own because Dede would have a fit.

Finally, Dede called and said that Sean could come to the hospital for one brief visit, during which she never left Sean and Al alone together. Although I was dying to know what happened, Sean didn't discuss it.

Sean loves his father.

He loves me, too. But I wasn't sure he loved me until a friend called and asked if I had seen the May 1996 Mother's Day issue of the *Nob Hill Gazette*.

"No, not yet."

"Well, you should read it because Sean wrote a whole paragraph about you."

I knew Sean had been asked to write something. Finding the magazine, I turned to the Mother's Day feature. A sweet photo of the two of us topped the page. Holding my breath, I read what my son had written.

Maybe I'll never be as impressive as my mother is when it comes to charging into uncharted regions—be those regions the offices of a large publishing concern, or the Kremlin in 1982—and demanding with poise and agility to be taken seriously.

She's my Mom: the notorious activist, hostess, and Bolshevik Pat Montandon, whose initials have mirrored her life as a blonde bombshell Pre-Madonna, a Press Member, a Prolific Mentor, a Pricey Marriage, a woman who 'Pleases Myself,' and is all these things at once in Perfect Measure. My Mom has instilled in me the belief that anything is possible. I think those eponymous initials of P.M. really stand for Paternal Mother, who, in her fusion of nurturer and role model, has taught me how to live.

By the time I finished reading Sean's piece, I was crying and I called Sean to tell him how touched I was. We had a pleasant conversation. He told me he was in love and all he wanted to talk about was his girlfriend, Daphne Beal, who was also a writer. They had met at *The New Yorker* and had a lot in common, Sean said. "She's beautiful, Mom, inside and out. She lived in India for a while and speaks several languages. Russian, too."

"I can't wait to meet her."

A few months later, the two of them came to San Francisco for a friend's wedding. Daphne Beal was beautiful, tall and slender with auburn hair and a flawless complexion. They were involved in their friend's nuptials, so I hardly saw them.

And then I didn't hear from Sean again for two years.

"You don't have the money, Pat, his dad does," my friend Jane Robb said. I refused to believe Sean would forfeit our newly minted connection for money.

"You know the saying, 'A daughter is your daughter for all your life, but a son is your son until he gets a wife.' " Jane tried to console me. "Maybe he's acting this way because of his girlfriend."

I didn't think so, although everything about our relationship was conjecture. Many of Sean's chums seemed almost proud of their estrangement from their parents, and I knew for a fact that for years Al had been badmouthing me to our son. I could only assume that Sean believed what his father had been telling him about me, whatever it may have been.

In 1998, I began writing "Sunday Night Supper," a column for the *San Francisco Examiner*. Guests such as Danny Glover, writer Herb Gold, artists, preachers, scientists, carpenters, feminists, and housekeepers gathered at the Enchanted Cottage for supper and good conversation. I was also working on my memoir. But what I was really doing was trying to come to terms with growing old. I wanted my remaining years to count for something—to live, really live, and embrace every opportunity fully.

In the dark of night when I could not sleep, I would think of the kids who had trekked around the world with me, lived with me, won our peace prizes. Had I really had a vision? Had my work made a difference? In spite of honors, nominations for a Nobel Peace Prize, and hundreds of letters from young people telling me my work had changed the course of their lives, I questioned myself.

"I'm too young to be this old," I said to Glendora on my sixty-ninth birthday. Christmas had been hard, as were most holidays for the past seventeen years, except when I was traveling with children. Those had been the good times. Every year I received a faxed holiday greeting from Mikhail and Raisa Gorbachev, which was nice.

I had hoped to be with Sean and maybe Daphne, too, but Sean had sent me a note saying that he would be somewhere in Italy for the holiday.

I also missed Star. It had been two years since I had last seen Starling Rowe. She had lived with me on and off for four years, crisscrossed the world with me, and offered her Prayer for Peace ballet without hesitation to presidents and prime ministers. Trying to find her had proved daunting until I'd asked local street artists where she might be. Star called me that very night and came to see me the next day. I hardly recognized the delicate young woman, now with cropped hair dyed jet black and a diamond stud in her lip. The same vulnerability she projected at ten was still evident, though.

"Do you regret not accepting the offer to study with the Bolshoi?" I asked after we had gotten reacquainted.

"I was scared," Star said, as she twirled a silver ring round and round on her right index finger, spotlighting purple polish on nails bitten down to the quick. As she talked, nervous, not wanting me to ask questions, her gaze wandered toward the front door, the exit. But street acquaintances had told me her secret, and in an effort to get it out, to acknowledge there was a dragon in our midst, I decided to lance it with truth.

"Star, I was told that you're a stripper," I said, my tone a studied neutral.

Star blushed. "Yeah, but I only do topless," she said. "I don't do lap dancing. And I don't work weekends, when it's really rough, you know." Her pale green eyes, fringed by lashes heavy with black mascara, stared at the carpet.

Star's explanation was meant to appease me, not to ring the alarm that I was hearing. But who was I to judge this girl who had moved twenty times in two years? A girl whose definition of "peace" was when a man, supposedly her father, stopped knocking holes in the walls with his fists and battering her mother. Perhaps we all do the best we can in this life, trying to survive, I thought.

When Star and I said good-bye, I told her that I would pay her tuition if she wanted to go back to school.

"Okay, Pat, sure, I intend to go back to school. Thanks a lot," Star replied.

"Well, let me know when. Okay?"

"Yeah, okay for sure, and thanks for everything you did for me Pat. I think about those years a lot. You're the only mother I've ever known," she said.

"I love you Star."

"I love you, too," she said.

Star told me whatever she thought I wanted to hear. Her words were like mist rising off a lake. There was no force behind them. Somewhere over-the-rainbow: Family. Hearth. Prince Charming, Security . . . Home. Starling, a wounded butterfly, a golden child caught in a slimy web of abuse, not having whatever that quality is—backbone, confidence, drive—to extricate herself.

After disappointment came delight: Win called from Canada where he was interning. He asked if I would be around for my birthday.

"I'll be here unless you know of a difficult place I can go," I said, with a laugh that Win shared.

"Maybe I'll pop by and see you, okay? I might be coming your way."

"I would love to see you, anytime, you know that," I said.

On my birthday, the day after Christmas, I was purging the CATP files, reliving special moments. Although it was past noon, I was so engrossed that I had not gotten dressed, and I had just read a note I had written to myself years earlier. *"You will not be punished for your anger, you will be punished by your anger, so say all the spiritual leaders of the ages."* A good enough reason to finally let go of that emotion, I decided.

When the intercom sounded, startling me, I pushed aside the curtains and saw someone at the gate. It was Win! Then I saw Rachel. Good heavens! There was John Valesquez, Alison Chosen, Barbara, and for heavens sake, Anita Gullassen from Norway, Dr. Sheila Krystal, and Marilyn Rose, as well as a number of other people from my past. Wishing I had gotten dressed, I ran outside to greet them, thrilled beyond measure to see them. Piling into the Enchanted Cottage, throwing their coats on the bed, they were exuberant. "Happy birthday, Pat!" they said. Soon we were eating chocolate cake, drinking champagne, and having a wonderful time.

The young adults looked the same as they had when they were children, just broader and taller. Do we ever really change? So far as I could tell, these young people held the same values, and acted as they did when they were eight, nine, and ten. It gave me pause. Had Sean always been the way he was now? Was I the same as when I was nine, running to the altar, trying to atone for imagined sins? Is everything we are to become, our life path, established by the time we are six or seven? Or even before birth?

Laughing, catching up with each other, we began to reminisce. "Remember that time in Belfast, when I ended up with the blender you used to mix that diet stuff?" Barbara asked.

"Yeah," I laughed. "They held you up at the airport thinking the thing was a bomb."

"They couldn't believe anyone would travel with an electric blender."

"How about East Berlin when the hotel people covered the banner box with a tablecloth, put flowers on it, and were using it for a table?" Win said.

"It took us all day to find it. We thought, for sure, the banner was lost," I laughed.

Our laughter was contagious. "Or . . . or . . ." Rachel was giggling so hard she could hardly talk. "The time we were in Rome and Martha Lyddon had six Italian guys knock down the door to our hotel room. Her key wouldn't work and I was sleeping so soundly, I didn't hear her knock. Martha was afraid I had died or something."

"I'll never forget the first trip we made to China," I said. It seemed unbelievable that fifteen years had passed. "Before our meeting with Premier Zhao was over, you kids were acting really goofy. I couldn't figure it out until I bit into the candy you were eating. You had been given chocolates with liqueur centers." I laughed. "I should have been more wary since the kids on the first trip to Moscow were served vodka."

"I was present at the birth of Pat's vision," Sheila Krystal offered. "It was an authentic experience. But the important thing is that all of you acted in concert, as concerned citizens, not doubting that you could stop a nuclear catastrophe."

"Our meditations were powerful," Rachel said. "Even now, when I have a problem to solve, I close my eyes . . ."

Laughing, the others joined in. . . . "Take a deep breath of sunlight . . ."

The Buddha, ensconced nearby in a bower of ferns, the enigmatic rock still nestled in his hand, seemed to be smiling.

John Valesquez, a law student in Washington, D.C., was itching to speak. He remembered our trip to Hiroshima for the fortieth anniversary of the dropping of the atom bomb. He talked about the thousands of people who brought little plywood boats with colored paper sails to Peace Park that night. "They wrote the names of their dead family members on the frames and lit a candle on their boat, then set it on the water. The river was covered with them, bobbing up and down, their candles reflecting in the dark current. It was magical, and sad, somehow beautiful and awful all at the same time," John said, the experience seemingly still alive for him. Even as a child, John had spoken somewhat stiffly but eloquently, planning his every word.

"I'll never forget the ninety-five-degree heat, or the unceasing sound of a gong being struck for the dead, the church bells, and the fragrance of incense," I added.

John was a handsome young man, tall, sure of himself, and smart. As a student, he had been chosen to help oversee the voting process in Bosnia. "Those trips, meeting kids from across the planet, talking to world leaders and being listened to by them, affected the course of my life. It made me see that a small band of people, united for a cause, can change the world. That's why I'm going into politics, to create positive change."

It was Rachel's turn again. "Traveling with you, being able to speak my mind, at a young age, has given me the confidence to tackle anything." Rachel's voice was so soft, I could hardly hear her.

"Speak up Rachel, honey," I reminded her. "Let your light shine out."

Rachel grinned, speaking louder now. "Pat, since my Mom died, you've been like a second mother to me. I love and appreciate you."

Her lovely mother Glenda had died at age forty-five from a botched hysterectomy.

"Rachel, you are like a daughter to me. You are so intelligent. You have high ideals and integrity. Your Mom would be so proud of you." We embraced, holding on to each other for a few minutes.

The young people gathered in my living room that day had initially been brought together by the universe, the result of a vision, a whisper from God. Now, I felt like we were related by blood.

Win hit a spoon against his coffee cup, to get our attention. "Pat, we have something to tell you." My mind flashed back to the terrified boy who had been forced off the train during a frigid trip through Eastern Europe. "All of us who have benefited from your work have something to tell you," Win said. Studying to be a pediatric cardiologist, he was wearing tortoise-framed eyeglasses.

He smiled. "Pat, we know that you value justice and beauty highly, which is more than just to side with the most powerless group in society—the children." Speaking as if he had rehearsed, Win talked about "the power of one," of how what I had done had "a lasting impact, so children's voices could be heard."

"We fully believe," Win continued, "that the lawyers, businessmen and women, teachers, scientists, artists, and doctors we have become will work to safeguard peace and human rights. Thank you for taking a leap of faith for us, for our future. Now it's our turn to help the next generation."

My heart overflowing, I started to reply.

"Wait, we're not through." Rachel took over from Win. The talented young woman stood up, and in a voice just above a whisper, gave me a stunning present.

"Well, Pat," she giggled. "You're not going to believe this. But, well, we want to take a trip, retrace our steps around the world, and take little kids along."

"Kids? You want to take little kids?" It was a delicious moment.

"Yeah, we want people to see the value of listening to children, showing them respect, giving them an opportunity to shape their future." Rachel's luminous brown eyes reminded me of the eight-year-old who had asked, in East Berlin, if we could be present when the Wall came down six years before it had happened. "And if you'll put the trip together, we promise to take care of you, you know, carry your suitcase and all." She laughed. "And, we'll buy you a first class ticket."

With total clarity, as if a murky haze obscuring the view of my own life had been magically ripped away, I saw that what I had been longing for was right in front of me. I had a family. Not a "let's pretend family," but a family gestated in the womb of my inner sight, birthed through the travails of a divorce, given that first gasp of oxygen by an unanticipated vision. Here they were—the children of my longing—gifts from God.

How tragic to have forgotten that I was loved.

"We'll have a heck of a trip." I stood up, ready to roll. Then, singing a rap song I had written for our peace clubs, I tried to tap dance across the floor.

*"Come on kids no jive,*
*We've gotta keep this planet alive*
*Listen here, we've got lots to say,*
*Peace ain't nerdy, it's the only way*
*We'll survive . . ."*

The "children," my family, stumbled along with me, trying to remember the words. We made a curious chorus line, different ages and hues, carrying on like little kids.

After my unexpected and welcome company left, I stood at the window, looking out at the cypress trees, thinking about the mystical journey of my life. In 1982, when I was in the depths of despair, I had a vision and an awakening. I awoke to the reality that all things are connected, and to the certainty that there is indeed an invisible force, and a number we can reach, after which we attain critical mass. All the rest automatically lines up.

I thought about the fall of dictatorships after the Berlin Wall had come down. Vaclav Havel, a man who was imprisoned for his political views, became the president of Czechoslovakia. Lech Walesa, imprisoned because of his Solidarity movement, became the president of

Poland. In Nicaragua, Violetta Chamorro decided to run for president against a dictator and won. South Africa's Nelson Mandela was freed after twenty-six years as a political prisoner, apartheid was abolished, and Mandela became president of that country.

At the beginning of our work in 1982, during the Cold War, President Ronald Reagan was making speeches about the Evil Empire. Now the United States was working in space with the Russian Federation, whose leader, Vladmir Putin, a former KGB agent, was struggling to establish a market economy. In China, Premier Zhao, who had signed the Children's Declaration of Dependence, made human rights history by being on the side of the students during the Tiananmen Square massacre, and was placed under house arrest. On a subsequent trip we made to China, attempts were made to discredit our organization, and Ambassador Lilly had to rescue us, but we were beginning to work together again.

Still, it was a different world than when I began my work, scarier even. I realized this was not the time to let go of my vision, but to embrace it further. This was the time to validate the power of children to effect change, and to acknowledge the grace of an invisible, collective mind. We could not allow the unspeakable consequences of using nuclear weapons to fade from the public psyche. Somehow, I had to get to the current crop of kids, an international delegation, go to the leaders of nuclear power nations, and get them to sign the Children's Declaration of Dependence, and commit to . . . *"clasping hands with the children of the world in a global effort to preserve the planet."*

# 29.

# LETTING GO

After so many years of travel, international breakthroughs, danger and excitement, and with my own family turmoil still unresolved, it was difficult to settle down to a more placid life. Socializing and cocktail parties were no longer satisfying. I had long since lost interest in conversation about the latest fashions or who was sleeping with whom. When I got a request from a writer at *People* magazine asking me to participate in an unauthorized biography about my friend Danielle Steel, who had married Dede's ex-husband John, it seemed like an alien request.

I scrawled "denied" across the fax and sent a copy to Danielle. She wrote a note thanking me and congratulating me on my work.

When a copy of *The Lives of Danielle Steel*, with its shocking pink-and-gold-heart cover arrived in the mail months later, I thumbed idly through it. Becoming more curious when my name jumped out at me, I was startled to read that my ex-husband said Danielle had wanted to marry him. It would have been at the same time Al was bedding Dede and still married to me. I could not believe Danielle would also betray me. Angry, I wrote her a hot little note, but regretted it as soon as I mailed it. I no longer cared what my ex did or did not do or to whom. I should have called Danielle and asked her about it instead of writing.

Danielle's handwritten reply ended with a cautionary note, one I should have realized after all the negative press I had endured. She wondered how I could believe such garbage and assured me that she would never betray a friend.

I wrote back, recapping that time in my life and laying out a scenario of how the rumor, fed by Al and Dede, probably got in the book.

She responded with a thoughtful three-page letter. She said that I had come out ahead where it really counts: as a human being. She went on to say that family means everything to her. "Sean will someday recognize the truth about what happened, and what a good mother he has," she wrote.

Danielle was right about family meaning everything. That is what I missed most. Letting go of my son, realizing I was not responsible for his heartache, was not as easy as I thought it would be. I reflected on the psychological injuries Sean had been subjected to, the cruelty, and wished I could rock him in the old green rocking chair as I did when he was a child; tell him fairy tales, and reassure him that everything would be okay.

How shortsighted I had been to have lashed out—expecting him to pay attention to my suffering—when his own pain must have threatened to overwhelm him at times. In spite of it all, he was doing well at *The New Yorker*.

One morning Sean called and mentioned in an offhand way that he had experienced a health scare a few days earlier. Slowly, inch by verbal inch, he told me he had lost his vision one day and had been taken to an emergency hospital. Alarmed, I said I was coming to New York to see about him.

"No, Mom, it's okay, please, no. The emergency room doctor said it was probably an optical migraine, it happens."

"Have you seen your own doctor?"

"Yeah, Mom, yeah. I'm having an MRI next week."

"Like it or not, I'll be there tomorrow, and I'm staying until I know you're okay."

Sean's MRI was normal, thank God, but I learned something significant about the day of his eyesight scare. Sean was to join his dad, Dede, and her son Trevor at the St. Regis Hotel for dinner that evening. During the meal Dede had turned to Sean and said, "You were an unwanted child, you know. Your father was fifty. He didn't want another kid." Sean said Dede's cruel words had not bothered him, but I wondered how much the tension he felt that day affected his eyesight.

"Sean," I looked into his beautiful hazel eyes, remembering how they sparkled as a child when he was up to mischief, "you were a planned baby. I've told you that before and it's flat-out true. When you were conceived, I was forty, your dad forty-nine. We thoughtfully and lovingly discussed the prospect of having a baby, and then decided we wanted a child together. We wanted you."

Kissing the unshaven cheek of my son, I marveled at how grown-up he was. "Sean, we were gaga over you. As a baby, your dad would put you in a backpack and take you on his morning walk every single day, pointing out trees, telephone poles, teaching you about the physical world." I put my arms around my son, swallowing tears. "I'm deeply sorry, more than you will ever know, that you've suffered because of our divorce. I thought the foundation of our family was erected on bedrock, not quicksand."

En route home, my neck pain became so intense I took a prescription pain medication. My physical discomfort always increased during emotional times. Sean's eyes, my neck. Would we ever be well again?

Staying in touch with the hundreds of young people who as children had traveled with me or won a Peace Prize gave me comfort. A new generation, they were taking over the programs and management of CATP. Win was writing the foundation newsletter while studying at Emory University to become a doctor.

But Star was the child I worried about. One evening she had brought her boyfriend Jay Bradshaw over to meet me. A handsome and broad-shouldered young man, Jay was an organizer for the carpenter's union. They both seemed uncomfortable and Star was faintly hostile. But it wasn't until we were saying good-night that I understood why. Just as I was closing the door my surrogate daughter told me that she and Jay were going to Las Vegas to get married the next day. "You mean to tell me that you've been here all this time and you're only now giving me such big news?"

"Well, I already told you," Star said. "No, no you didn't Star." "Yes, I did," she said, belligerently. "Okay, darling. In any case I wish you and Jay the very best, you know that," I said. But my heart sank. Star had been drinking, I was sure. What would happen to my lost daughter, I wondered.

My small garden, with its glorious profusion of pink-and-white camellias, purple wisteria, fern trees, and a waterfall, had become a refuge, a place to meditate, just to be. But it was becoming increasingly difficult to enjoy because of chronic neck pain, which I learned was caused by two disintegrated discs. When I decided to have cervical spine surgery, Sean came home and took me to the hospital. It was almost worth the months in a cervical collar just to have him with me for a few days.

"I'll be home for Christmas and your birthday, too," he said, surprising me.

"I would love that. Bring Daphne too!"

"I'm not quite ready for that. But is it okay to invite Leandro to join us? He lives in Los Angeles now."

"Sure, I like Leandro."

"He's my best friend. Stood by me when it was rough, you know?"

"I know. It will be fun to have you both here to help celebrate my birthday. I can't believe I'm almost seventy. Your Mom is old enough to be your grandmother," I laughed.

It was also hard for me to believe that I was considered a senior citizen. Like almost everyone else, I imagined, I thought of myself as young with the future ahead of me. Somewhere over the rainbow . . . I would find love; I would have a family; I would get my books written; I would . . . but the years were slipping inexorably away and I felt the pressure of time, the urgency to accomplish things, just as I had after my death dream.

When Leandro joined Sean and me for the holiday, we told anyone who stopped by the story about our life-threatening brush with the Russian Mafia.

Later, Sean told me he would like to meet Armistead Maupin, the author of *Tales of the City*, so I invited Armistead to dinner. The caustic things he had written about me no longer mattered. I had come to realize that nursing old wounds did not offer joy, only bitter, cold gruel.

"Mom," Sean said two days before he was to go back to New York, "Do you think I could meet Mel Belli? I think he was the most interesting man you were ever married to."

"More than your dad?"

"Yeah, more than Dad."

"It's been thirty years. He doesn't want to see me any more than I want to see him."

"Oh, come on, Mom, help your would-be-writer son out."

"Well, all right, but you'll owe me." Laughing, I picked up the phone and called Mel's office. Yes, he would love to see me, his assistant said.

When we arrived at the famed barrister's financial district office, I was nervous, giddy. "You're acting like a schoolgirl," Sean teased.

According to news stories, my Thirty-Seconds-Over-Tokyo-almost-spouse was as flamboyant as ever. In his eighties, broke and sick, he was nevertheless a force to be reckoned with.

"Mel's excited that you want to see him, Pat." His secretary showed us into a cramped room where bottles of Scotch and half-eaten sweets tottered atop piles of documents. This space would have been the size of a closet in his former spacious and historical offices. That place had been a regular stop on bus tours. I missed the rows of apothecary jars from his grandmother's drugstore in Sonora, masks from Katmandu, the joke coat of arms that bore the words "Rex Tortuous" and featured crutches and dollar signs in its corners.

"Mel will be along any minute. Just have a seat." The secretary flounced out of the room, wide hips swinging, charm bracelets jangling, long earrings swaying. She was a one-woman band accompanied by the heavy scent of Opium perfume.

Sean raised his eyebrows.

Edgy, waiting for Mel, trying to quell rumbles of disquiet lurching in my stomach, I was not prepared for the doddering and grossly over-weight man who appeared in the doorway. He bore little resemblance to the handsome John Barrymore look-alike from thirty years earlier. Mel peered at me, ignoring Sean, eyes sunken inside a bloated face. It seemed the devilishness that had been so much a part of him had been erased, with nothing discernable having taken its place. But, after a cursory greeting, he became the Belli of old, spinning a yarn calculated to impress.

"I've got this big silicone breast implant case going, you know." The stentorian rumble was intact. "My firm disclosed the whole mess when we filed a class action lawsuit against the Dow Corning Corporation." He glanced up to be sure he had the jury's attention. "Those girls have silicone in their vaginas, coming out their nipples, and from under their fingernails." Glancing up again, he continued, "Those bastards knew what they were doing. They knew the implants could kill those girls. They had a reckless disregard for the truth. We've been awarded a $200 million settlement."

Just then Mel's secretary walked back in, and plunked herself down on Mel's lap. When she ran her fingers through his thick white hair, I laughed out loud. Nothing had changed.

Sean grinned and raised his eyebrows, ready to go.

"Do you remember our Shinto wedding ceremony?" I asked, as we rose to leave.

A rapscallion look crossed the old man's face. "I remember a girl who didn't know how to cook a bear."

"But I knew how to get away from a crazy Leo," I shot back, referring to his birth sign. Even after thirty years, I still felt a tinge of irritation from that nonmarriage.

My almost-husband died a year later. His death sparked lawsuits from three of his previous wives, two of his children, and five of his law partners. In death as in life, a reporter said, Mel was center stage of a soap opera. A bona fide, wisecracking, stunt-pulling, headline-generating, deceitful, one-of-a-kind character wrapped inside a lawyer, he undoubtedly planned it that way.

# 30.

# TILL DEATH
# DO US PART

A few days before Easter in 1999, I had an exciting phone call from Sean.

"You're the first person we've called," he said, his voice was filled with excitement. "I've got something important to tell you." His laugh conveyed his joy. "Mom, Daphne and I are getting married!"

"You are?"

"Yes, in September."

"How wonderful!"

"We're being married on a pier in Brooklyn. How's that for a son-of-party-girl idea!" he laughed. "And, Mom, I want to walk you down the aisle to your seat. I've checked it out. It's traditional. Okay?"

The lump in my throat threatened to choke me. "Are you sure?"

"Yes, I'm sure. We're both sure."

"I'm overwhelmed."

"You're the best."

"I love you, Sean."

My cup runneth over.

"Faith, faith, faith. Never give up," my dad would have said. "Always remember that you are part of a great cosmic symphony, Patsy Lou. We each choose the part we want to play. The notes, both sour and sweet, make us who we are."

A friend, Leonard Perillo, who as a child had watched me on the tube, said he would fly with me to New York and also attend the rehearsal dinner. Leonard had known Sean since he was ten so I was especially happy to have him along. I was also glad to have him on the flight with me as Hurricane Floyd was sweeping across the East Coast and the trip was proving to be a scary one. I kept squeezing Leonard's hand.

"It's okay Patricia, we're not going to crash," my friend said as we bumped across the sky. And then in a transparent effort at distracting me, he asked about Star.

Six months earlier Star had called me, her voice a slur. "Oh, Star, I hope you're not drinking," I said after we had greeted each other. She assured me she wasn't drinking. "I love you," she said. "I love you too, Star," I said. But something was dreadfully wrong. Star was either drinking or on drugs or both, I feared.

The plight of my surrogate daughter weighed heavily on my heart. When I called her a few weeks later, I was relieved that Star's voice was clear and alert. She said that Jay was a good husband and she was happy, but, she said, she had realized she was going down the same slippery slope as her mother and would end up like her if she didn't do something about it. So she did. She and Jay were both in recovery. Star had gone back to school, too, after having dropped out at Mari Ellen's insistence so she could help her at the Wharf. Star was now getting her GED and intended to go to computer school. She wanted to be a writer, she said.

I was so happy I wanted to shout. "Oh Star, I'm so proud of you for taking that step. You are a lovely young woman, full of promise and so talented. I'm glad that you aren't throwing your beautiful life away," I said. "Call me if you need anything. And come to see me, soon."

"I will," she said. There were a few seconds of silence and then she continued. "Pat, you're the only real mom I've ever known. I love you. I'll always be there for you."

"You can count on me, too, Star darling," I said. "I'll help you in any way I can."

As the airplane bounced through the storm, I continued to ruminate on the past. Rachel Skiffer, who lost her mom when she was fourteen, had graduated from Harvard Law School, and was now a real estate attorney in San Francisco. Win, who as a child was forced off the train dur-

ing our trip through Eastern Europe, had completed his medical training
and was now a pediatric cardiologist. While interning at Oakland's Children's Hospital, he had lived with me. The afternoon he arrived from Atlanta, we sat at my dining table drinking oolong tea out of thin china
cups, and catching up on the news. Win, his black hair cut short, seemed
nervous, stirring spoonfuls of sugar into the hot beverage without
thought.

"What's bothering you?" I asked.

Sipping his tea, avoiding my eyes, he finally screwed up his courage.
"You might not like me after I tell you about myself."

"What did you say?"

He cleared his throat. "You might not like me any longer . . ."

"That's what I thought you said." I took his hands in mine and looked
into his eyes. "Win, you're gay," I said. "So if that's what's bothering you,
don't let it. The fact that you're gay doesn't change anything about you."

"I was afraid you might reject me the way some of my friends and
loved ones have," he said. "But, Pat, I'm a doctor and I know that if I'm
to be a healer I have to first heal myself by fully accepting who I am."

"Who you are, Win, is perfect. It's the way God made you."

But I hadn't always felt that way. When Sean was three, Al had become concerned because Sean wanted to wear my high heel shoes and
have me put his hair in curlers. Al was afraid I would cause our son to become homosexual so we had taken him to a psychiatrist. Now I was
ashamed that we had done that. The doctor, Lenore Terr, should also be
ashamed, of "treating" a three-year-old child when she should have
known he was okay just the way he was, whatever that turned out to be, I
thought.

The plane shuddered as it plowed through a wall of water, causing my
stomach to churn. Tightening my seat belt I crammed a pillow behind
my head, and thought about other things, about selling the Enchanted
Cottage. I had been considering it for quite a while.

The home I had created was worth a lot of money in the white-hot
housing market of a dot-com economy. It was an opportunity to sever
the control my ex still exerted over my finances. And I did not want to

become an old lady, hanging on to "things," afraid of change, not daring to risk. It was time for me to leave San Francisco.

I turned to Leonard and said I was glad he would be at the rehearsal dinner with me. "I feel like spitting in Dede's eyes," I said. "But I won't."

"Patricia," my friend said, "Dede is a pathetic person so don't waste good spit." We laughed, and then he continued. "And stop worrying about Sean. That son of yours will make a name for himself, a good name, as a good person, I'm certain of it. After all, he's the one who said you had to take those letters to Russia."

"I would never have thought to do such a thing," I said.

"Patricia, be proud of the job you did with Sean. He wasn't an easy child."

"I'd be a better mother if I could do it over again. I still cling to what I think a family should be, what I wanted mine to be. It's sad that I know so little about my son, who he is, where he is, what he's thinking, or anything."

"During that divorce shit you were so hurt you couldn't see what was happening to Sean. He was just a kid. He loved his dad and thought he loved his stepmother. But you took him all over the world and on a special trip to Japan and on a rafting trip. I saw you cook for him and laugh with him and teach him things. Stop beating yourself up."

A sigh escaped from a place more turbulent than the storm outside the airplane windows. "I hope his marriage will be a good one. A lasting one."

Sunshine was trying to pierce the overcast when, at last, we felt the thud of solid runway. A good weather omen, I thought as we headed for Manhattan.

The next evening in the restaurant where the rehearsal dinner was to be held, I scattered red rose petals on tables covered by white linen, and lit white candles. And then I arranged place cards. I seated myself on Sean's right with Leonard next to me and Al and Dede across from us.

I had just completed my share of wedding chores when Sean and Daphne, her bridesmaids, his groomsmen, and her parents arrived from the wedding rehearsal.

Our feverish greetings competed with the noise of the gathering crowd. Stephan, a pal from Sean's school days in Italy, soft-spoken and shy, edged toward me.

"Pat, I have the honor of walking you to your seat tomorrow," he said, in a tremulous undertone, and looked away.

"But, but Sean said he was going to do that," I replied, stunned by the news.

"No. Sean told me to tell you that I would do it," Stephan said, quietly.

"Sean," I tapped my son's arm and whispered into his ear, "I don't understand. You said you were going to walk me down the aisle. It was your idea."

"Oh, okay. If that's what you want," he said, not looking at me.

"No . . . it doesn't matter," I replied. My heart had sunk to my feet.

"I didn't want to hurt Stephan's feelings, Mom. I'll walk you to your seat if you're upset about it."

I sighed. "You built up my hopes, that's all."

Before I could say more, out of the corner of my eye, I saw Al and Dede enter the restaurant. My stomach did a flip-flop.

Fleeing to the restroom I used paper towels to blot the sweat from my face. I brushed my cheeks with color and then took a deep breath, preparing to face them. But just as I reached for the door, a flash of orange against red floor tiles caught my attention. It was a flower. A Lilly so intense in shading it seemed to burn like artistic interpretations of the heart of Christ. I picked it up.

Sai Baba! His color!

I hadn't thought of the avatar for a very long time. But here, in a Manhattan restroom on the eve of my son's wedding, memories of Vibutti, Mother Teresa, scribbles of forgiveness, a mystical rock, and reminiscence of an Ethiopian child flooded my mind.

"I love you. No, I love you. No, I love you. Selam. Selam. Peace. Peace. Love. Love."

Leaning against the wall, I closed my eyes, hoping for inner wisdom. I waited, and then in a rush I heard the singing of children. In capitals from Moscow to Beijing, on a rain-swept square in San Francisco, their melodic words played on the keyboard of my memory.

*"Peace is what we're after.*
*Love will be the seed.*
*React only with love."*

It was the message I had been given in 1983 in the USSR when I faced down Cold War bureaucrats. What did I most desire? Love. The way to be loved? To be loving.

So why now, after experiencing such rich and rewarding years, was I focusing on the negative aspects of my life? I had wanted to tell Dede and Al how their cruelty had damaged Sean. But all I had to do was remember a time, many years ago, when I called to talk to Al about Sean and Dede had answered the phone. Startled, I had lashed out, "Is this the bitch who stole my husband?"

"Yess it isss," she had acknowledged.

Whatever I might say or do, would not, could not, filter through to either of them. If it did, their view of themselves would shatter. They were shell people. Hollow people made of shells.

What was I made of? I did not know. What did I want to be made of? Love.

Perhaps I'll never know what I'm really made of. But on the eve of Sean's wedding, I was infused with love. Real love. Not a pink syrupy thing, sticky and false, but a gutsy thing, real and honest. And I realized with certainty that I knew myself. I liked the strong person I had become.

Opening the restroom door that evening, I walked directly into Al and Dede. It was as if all noise ceased and, for me, there was only silence. Everything moved in slow motion, underwater. I saw my former friends, now husband and wife, as if they swam sluggishly along the banks of a stagnant river. The woman held out a bejeweled hand to me.

"Pat!" Her voice registered a note I couldn't hear. What I heard were guns firing in Belfast, the cries of earthquake victims in Armenia, a Jewish child in a death camp shouting out, "Please don't shoot my mother."

Looking into the woman's eyes, I saw that they were empty. "Hello Dede," I said. Her golden necklace was without light or life. Leonard was right. Dede seemed pathetic.

"Diane, her name is Diane," Al said. His face was mask-like. "I've had a stroke, you know."

"I'm sorry."

"We're very happy." His declaration begged approval.

"Yes, we're very happy." Diane's smile was a grimace.

Sean raced across the room, tension showing in the square of his jaw. "Hi," he said, trying to forestall problems.

I gave him a light hug. "Your dad and I were saying how happy we are for you. Right Al?"

"I've always been proud of him," Al grumbled. "I've had a stroke, you know," he said once again.

"I hope you're saying your prayers," I said.

"I'm going to live a long, long time." His eyes stared past me.

"I still hope you're saying your prayers."

As clearly as I've ever known anything in my life, I saw that God, or the universe, or the angels, had surely taken care of me. Without the saving grace of that divorce, that betrayal, I could be standing here in designer finery and jewels, a shell person too, without an iota of understanding of my soul's purpose or who I really was. Empty. It was an empowering insight, a liberating bit of knowledge.

And Sean, so accomplished, with such a good heart, could easily have become nothing more than a rich man's heir. A shell person.

Later, Sean said I made everyone nervous because I seated Al and Dede across the table from me. "Mom how could you have done that?" he asked.

I sighed. Sean and I would be at odds with each other forever, it seemed. "Sean, please lighten up," I said. "It was the correct place to seat them. I wasn't nervous so you and your friends should relax."

The wedding day dawned crisply clear, the sky scrubbed clean by Hurricane Floyd. It was perfect weather for a romantic event on a pier in Brooklyn. Accompanied by the music of an accordion, my son, having apparently changed his mind, walked arm-in-arm with me past two hundred guests to where I was seated next to his father and stepmother.

And then, his smile wide, Sean waited, under an archway of yellow sunflowers, for his beautiful bride. Daphne, in a wedding gown of red silk, fabric she had purchased in India, was willowy and graceful. She and my son radiantly reached out to each other. Their love, for all to see, was as brilliant as the sunshine reflecting off the river.

Sitting beside the stranger to whom I had been married for eleven years, gazing across the water at the Statue of Liberty, as gentle waves hit the pilings of the pier, I was at peace.

As Sean and Daphne recited their vows, a soft breeze sprang up, reminding me of my childhood. Often, on hot summer nights, our family slept outside under a cottonwood tree. I would lie there covered by a blanket of stars listening to the sounds of crickets. Daddy would point out the Big Dipper, Venus, the Little Dipper, and various constellations. And beyond those stars and galaxies, far, far beyond, he would say, lies heaven. "Always remember little Chic-a-lik, this world is not your home, you're just passing through." I would chime in with the next line. "My treasures are laid up somewhere in the blue."

Before our evening prayers, we would gather around our black upright piano to sing. Mama would pound away at the keys and my siblings and I would harmonize, singing the old hymns. My father would turn the pages of the songbook and keep time by tapping his foot. Soprano, bass, alto, our voices merged:

*"We'll understand it better by and by,*
"Do you Sean, take this woman . . .
*When the battle's over when the battle's won,*
. . . to be your lawfully wedded wife . . .
*When all the Saints of God are gathered home,*
. . . to love, honor, and cherish . . .
*We'll tell the story of how we've overcome,*
. . . until death you do part?"
*And we'll understand it better by and by."*

# 31.

# OH THE MIRACLE
# OF IT ALL

In 2001 Sean had called to tell me he was writing a book about his child-hood, Amity School, and the divorce.

"The divorce that keeps on giving," I had laughed.

When Sean came to San Francisco to research his book he asked if I would help him. Of course, I had said. "I have court records, video tape, and Herb Caen clippings in an old footlocker stored in a shed." Sean was pleased.

On a day when thick fog softened the edges of buildings and sharp wind whistled around corners, Sean and I went to look at the ancient legal documents. When I lifted the lid of the rusty footlocker, the raw past came swirling up at me like ghosts in a Dickens novel. Court records spilling out from legal folders contained the most difficult years of my life.

"This is a treasure trove," Sean said, already reading a file.

Yellowed Herb Caen columns, bound with a bent paper clip, indicted me all over again. "Sean, it's hard for me to look at this stuff," I said, picking up one of Caen's missives. The paper crumbled in my hands. Everything can be reduced to ash except the soul, I thought.

I sat down on the floor oblivious to the dust, my head swimming with old memories. "Sean," I sighed, "did you know that your dad told anyone who would listen that our divorce was my fault?"

Sean glanced up at me. "Yeah, I know."

"We both know he left because of Dede, but your dad said something to me that was more disturbing. He said he warned you not to help me in any way or I would try to make you into a husband, whatever that means."

Sean didn't respond. But I took a deep breath and continued. "When your father left me, I felt guilty, as if somehow I had done something to drive him away—although I couldn't imagine what it was."

Sean was quiet, but he nodded, prompting me to continue.

"I thought your father was a saint and so did everyone else, including the Catholic Church. So, when he suddenly said he wanted to end our marriage, I figured I must have done something terribly wrong, that I was to blame."

Until now, I had been able to contain my emotions but I could feel everything building up inside. "Sean, what I want you to understand is that all the personal attacks and bad press caused me to lose my sense of self—as a person and as your mother. I allowed your father to turn me against myself, and then he turned you against me the same way he had turned Mike and Lad against their mother. It's so sad."

Sean still hadn't said anything. I took another deep breath. Inhale, exhale, I reminded myself. The last thing I wanted to do was to begin crying.

"You and Dad both said you would never divorce! What happened, Mom?"

"That's one of the big mysteries of my life," I said. "I still can't fathom it. Do you remember how proud your father was that I kept my own name? He traveled the state with me to educate women as to their rights, but in court he said not using his name meant that I didn't love him!"

"Guess you were ahead of your time, Mom," Sean said. "Daphne kept her own name. It didn't occur to us to do otherwise."

"It's common practice now," I said, taking a deep breath, and pausing for a moment before getting to the crux of what I wanted to say to him. "Sean, the very worst thing your father ever said was that I was a bad mother. And even though I knew that wasn't true, I guess that deep down I wondered if you'd be better off without me." Surreptitiously I wiped my eyes on the sleeve of my jacket.

"Sorry, Mom," Sean said, turning his attention back to the footlocker, and then abruptly changing the subject he continued. "Mom, did you see that news item about Dede? It said 'Dede Wilsey has a heart of gold,' " he laughed. "I thought, that's right, man, that's exactly right."

"Like King Midas," I said. We both laughed and then directed our attention back to the job at hand.

"Sean," I said, "I'm going to burn this stuff. It's not healthy to keep it around."

"Don't you need it for your memoir?"

"No, my book is almost finished. I'll give you a copy if you want it."

"Thanks, Mom."

Al Wilsey died on January 4, 2002. He left this world on the anniversary of the day he left me. I thought back on the dream I'd had just two short months before. It was Thanksgiving Day and I was with my niece Linda. We had eaten a big meal and afterward, feeling sleepy, I decided to take a nap. I fell asleep at once and immediately began to dream.

The dream was a snapshot. I was in a house with Sean, although Sean was not clearly defined. We were looking out a large window facing a house across the street. The street between the houses was silvery from the way the light fell on it. There was no traffic on the street. The scene was stark with the kind of loneliness one feels in an Edward Hopper painting. Sitting under an archway of the house across the street was Al Wilsey. He was wearing a pink shirt, the only bright color in the dream. He waved. We waved back. I love you, he said. And then a black cloud that was Dede pushed him away.

The dream ended. I awoke.

When I talked to Linda about my dream, she kept saying, "That pink shirt means something. Pink is the color of love, you know."

"Not likely," I answered. "Funny, I never knew Al to wear a pink shirt."

I called Sean and told him about my dream. I wanted him to know that on some level his dad loved him. I also called Dr. Sheila Krystal and Dr. Michael Kirsch, a psychiatrist I had begun seeing while I was writing my book. Having to relive my divorce had thrown me into another depression.

When Sean and Daphne came to San Francisco for the funeral, they hardly had time to change their clothes before going to the funeral home to view Al's body. Sean said Dede was going to have Al cremated so they had to rush to get there in time to say good-bye.

I was confused. Al was being cremated? When we were married he said he didn't believe in cremation.

I paced the floor, waiting for their return. But when they got back I was not prepared for what I was told. Sean said, "Mom, sit down." I sat. "Mom . . . Dad was dressed in a pink shirt, like in your dream."

It took me a moment to grasp what he had said. "Do you think that dream could have been a message of some sort?" I asked.

"Maybe so, Mom, maybe so." Sean was uncomfortable with my intuitive side. Sometimes I was, too. I had no idea why I had such dreams, just as I couldn't really understand why I had had the vision that impelled me to create a peace foundation.

Al was dead. I felt a mixture of relief and sadness; relief that he could no longer cause me problems, and sadness over the end of the life of the man I once loved. It was a pitiful ending. He no longer had meaningful relationships with his children, or with his long-time friends either. It was as if he had been walled off from reminders of any part of his life before his marriage to Dede.

After the funeral I asked Sean when the reading of the will would be.

"There is no will, Mom. Dad's entire estate was already in Dede's name."

"You can't mean that. Your dad was worth over $200,000,000, maybe even $300,000,000 for all I know. He must have left something to you and his other children!"

"No, Dad didn't leave me so much as a cuff link."

"You can sue, you know. Have you considered that?"

"Mike and I talked about it, but I don't want to give Dede any more of my life than she has already taken."

"Sean, your grandfather would have been very proud of your attitude."

Before Sean's book was published, I moved to Southern California. I had found an old house, where purple bougainvillea blooms and palm trees sway, the land of sunshine, movie stars, casual dressing, and for me, anonymity . . . and another remodel.

One day Sean called, sobbing, to tell me that Dr. Caligor, his therapist, a man who had become like a father to him, had been killed in an accident. Dr. Caligor had held Sean's memories, his pain and his secrets, for ten years, and now he was gone. I wept with my son over his tragic loss.

"Mom," Sean said, "Dr. Caligor felt very strongly that your love was one of the only things that kept me from going over the edge in those difficult years."

What a bittersweet message that was.

In 2003, Sean called to tell me that Daphne was pregnant. I was elated. The baby, a boy, was born on July 17, 2004. They named him Owen, for a lake Daphne loves, and Taylor, for my maternal granddad.

When Owen was four months old they invited me to come see him for the first time. Holding my beautiful grandbaby, I wanted desperately to feel connected to him, to feel the same surge of love that I felt when Sean was born, but the connection was not there until I began to talk to him. "How was your trip to Earth, Owie?" I asked looking into his eyes. The baby began to babble, his voice getting higher and higher as I kept asking him questions about his journey. Holding my gaze he continued to "talk" until Daphne called Sean to come see us. Owen had never responded that way before, they said. I felt joy. I hoped this would be the beginning of a familial connection between Sean and Daphne and Owen and me.

When Sean sent me a copy of his 564-page manuscript, *Oh the Glory of It All*, I began to read it at three in the afternoon and finished it at four the next morning, and then I collapsed. My son had been through hell, let down by his parents, seduced by his stepmother into supporting her nefarious plans, and then abandoned by us all, in his mind, at a young age. As his words flowed across the pages and his suffering became evident, it was hard to continue reading. The weight of his words, his ferocious anger at me, his ultimate tenderness toward his father, and Dede's cruelty to him, was distressing to read about.

I knew Sean wanted to know what I had to say about his book, but I couldn't talk to him. I sent him an e-mail saying how sorry I was that his childhood had been so horrific. I also told him how very much I admired his writing ability, his literary flare, and his masterful way with words, but I was crushed by his negative feelings about me.

*Oh the Glory of It All* was published and became an immediate *New York Times* bestseller. I was so proud of him. Reviewers loved Sean's book, his writing skill, and his way with words. On the other hand, critics described my work with children as "small," I was "certifiable," "unhinged," I "dragged children all over the world," "Sean's mother is a hick gold digger and will always be a hick," one critic said. It was Caen and Maupin all over again.

Friends tried to console me. "Rise above it," they said.

"I'm beginning to feel like a hot air balloon, I've had to rise above so much," I replied.

A spark in me died. I realized that if I wanted to continue living I had to pull away from Sean, and stop trying to get him to love me. Al had won.


I searched for something to cling to, for someone who loved me and needed me. I thought of Star. When I called her and told her I was feeling downhearted because of Sean's book, she said she would come to see me the next day. At the Burbank airport Star threw herself into my arms just as she had as a child. We held each other and cried. Star was beautiful, with black hair and a creamy complexion, and best of all, clear green eyes.

"Pat, I'm so sorry about Sean. I know he loves you, he just needs time to sort it all out the same way I did," she said.

We sat at the kitchen table in my Beverly Hills home talking about our lives. She was doing well in computer school and was beginning to write about her life. As our time together unfolded and we shared our deepest feelings, Star told me that when she was five, she had been molested in her home while Mari Ellen was away. After the incident, Star had been locked in a dark closet for the rest of the day. "I still have to sleep with a light on," she said.

My heart ached for the lovely young woman who was sitting in my kitchen and pouring out her heart to me. "Star darling, I'm so sorry about the abuse you endured. I'm more proud of you than I can say for how you have taken hold of your beautiful life and not let that horrific experience define you."

"One of the hardest things I had to deal with was Mari Ellen telling me she wasn't my 'mammy,' that I was adopted, that she didn't want me," Star said, wiping the tears from her eyes.

"I think your mother loved you very much, Star. She let drugs and alcohol blind her to all that was good and that included you. I love you and I'm happy to be a mother to you."

"Pat, Mom, I love you so much. I hope you won't let Sean's writing about you the way he did define your relationship with him either," she said, hugging me.

"You've mended my heart," Star said, when she left.

"You've mended my heart, too, Star," I said, kissing her.

We plan to spend holidays together and we correspond regularly. This e-mail message from Star is now tucked away along with the note and rabbit stickers she left for me in 1984.

Dearest Mom:

Yesterday afternoon while I was waiting in the hall for classes to begin a woman walked up to me and said "Zdravstvuite," the Russian word for hello.

I said "Zdravstvuite" and asked the woman, in Russian, if she spoke English.

"Da, da. You are Russian?"

"No, I'm American," I said. "But when I was a kid I traveled with Katya Lycheva when she came to the United States and then to Russia several times."

"Oh, yes, I remember Katya and that special trip. Spasiba, thank you," she said and moved on.

After she left I got to thinking about the many opportunities you brought into my life.

As you know I've led a turbulent life, through it all, though, I have had those wonderful moments you brought into my life. Even at my lowest points some part of me felt special because of that. I know I have told you before, but I am so happy to be sober and to have you in my life. You were my mom when I was very young and at a point where I so desperately needed mothering and now again and always. I want you to know I am here for you whenever you need me.

Love to You,

Star

Star's visit and her wise counsel led me to think that maybe Al hadn't won after all, maybe I was the winner and maybe, just maybe, Sean would someday realize that I had also been a good mother to him. Just as I had in the past, I began to send love and positive thoughts to my son.

Sean and I had not communicated with each other for three months when I got an impassioned letter from him. He allowed himself to be vulnerable with me for the first time I could ever remember. He said he became physically sick whenever I pulled away from him, which I had tried to do one other time. He said that it interfered with his ability to be a good husband and a good father. He needed to talk to me.

I did not want my son to be in pain. I called him and said I would be staying overnight at an airport hotel in New York en route to Beslan, North Ossetia Russia (where twelve hundred people were taken hostage on the first day of school and three hundred fifty, mostly children, were murdered) if he wanted to see me.

Sean and I met on a dull August morning, in a dreary coffee shop in a dreary hotel. I held both of Sean's hands and looked into his eyes and told him I would always love him, but I could no longer cope with the push-pull of our relationship. "Sean I want you to be well, and to have a fulfilling and happy life," I said. "But I need to be well, also."

"Mom, I want the same for you," he said. Sean was pursing his lips exactly the way his father had. His beautiful smile had disappeared.

"We need to be kind to each other, Sean. You are thirty-five, a grown man, and I'm seventy-seven. I want the rest of my life to be a blessing, not heartache. I want peace."

"Me, too, Mom, I want all of that."

He asked me to visit his family on my way back from Beslan so that I could see my grandson and we could talk about what we needed from each other. I said I would.

In Beslan, Russia, we created a memorial to show our compassion for the survivors of the tragedy and then wrapped the bullet-riddled school, the scene of unimaginable suffering, with our World Banner of Hope. That's when I had an epiphany.

The wrenching sobs of the Mothers of Beslan brought tears to my own eyes and caused the thousands of names of children killed in wars written on our scarlet banner to blur in my vision. The names began to merge into one name: Sean. Suddenly I realized that for nineteen years I had been mourning not only the loss of other people's children, but the loss of my own child, as if his name was written on that red silk memorial. It was a startling insight.

Back in New York, Sean called as soon as I was settled into my hotel room. He had sent a bouquet of pink roses and peonies, and said he would come right over. Daphne and Owen Taylor would come later. We sat in my room sipping room service tea as we began to talk.

"Mom, I didn't write my book to hurt you. I had to write it so that I could get on with my life," Sean said. "I'm sorry you were hurt."

"Sean, for the five years you were writing your book, you lashed out at me the way you did when you were seventeen," I said, looking out the window. "You couldn't let me be close or you wouldn't have been able to write about me the way you did."

"Mom, I can't imagine letting the things that happened to me happen to Owen."

"I wouldn't have been able to imagine such things happening to you either," I said.

"Every boy wants his dad to love him. Didn't happen and now it never will," Sean said. "I guess we always want what we can't have."

"Every mother wants her child to love her, too, and to show her respect," I said.

"Good point," Sean said, looking directly into my eyes. "Mom, I love you. I need you in my life."

"I need you in my life, too," I said, "but not just during grudging visits or when you want something. In your book you made it clear I'm a bur . . ."

I almost began to list my complaints when I suddenly stopped. What was I doing? Sean's life was his own. And his book had nothing to do with me. Sean's book was about him. *Oh the Glory of It All* was a scream for me to pay attention to the hell he had been subjected to as a child. I had let my ego get in the way of our relationship. What he had written about me did not matter. His life did.

I looked into his beautiful eyes, told him I loved him unconditionally, and I would do anything to help him cope with the loss of his childhood.

"Sean," I said, "what we focus on expands until that's all we can see. There's lots of good in both of us and it seems to me that we need to start focusing on the good things about each other."

"I agree, Mom," Sean said.

"There is so much I like about you, Sean. You have a compassionate nature, you're sensitive, and a first-class father," I said. "When I get home I'll write you a letter about the numerous kind and thoughtful things you've done for me over the years."

Sean smiled with his old radiance.

When Daphne arrived with Owen Taylor, she kept saying to him, "This is your grandmother, Owie."

Owen didn't know me but he kept glancing my way. He was walking now and into everything, fascinated by the telephone, standing on his toes to look out the windows, not being still for one second.

Sean and Daphne were talking on the other side of the room when my grandson crawled up on a chair to sit next to me. He smiled Sean's smile and then stretched a small hand out to me. I leaned toward him and touched my fingertips to the tips of his. A tiny jolt of electricity surged between us. Owen giggled and looked up at me.

"Hi Owie," I said. "How did you get here? Tell me about your journey into this world." He gazed at me, unwavering, his hazel eyes revealing all those whose DNA he shared. There was Mama and Daddy and Granddad Taylor and Al and Sean; cards in an endless deck shuffled in a blur of time now revealed in the eyes of my grandson.

My beautiful grandson and I quietly sat with the tips of our fingers touching, our eyes locked, sharing the secrets of our ancestors for an eternity, it seemed. Owie leaned toward me. "Grnma," he said.

"Yes, Owie, I'm your grandma!" We both giggled.

"What's going on with you two?" Sean said.

"We're planning a peace trip, aren't we Owen Taylor?" I laughed. "Peace to the planet."

Owen said, "Da, da, Grnma!"

"Sean, Owie said yes. In Russian, too!" I laughed.

"Da, Grandma," Sean said. "We'll both go with you." He kissed my cheek.

Imagine that you hear monks chanting "Let My Prayers be Counted," Pavarotti hitting the high Cs with "Ave Maria," Johnny Cash belting out "There Will Be Peace in the Valley Some Day." And then imagine you hear the voices of children in Iraq, Afghanistan, New Orleans, The Sudan, Darfur, Rwanda, Chernobyl, Sierra Leone, Israel, Palestine, Lebanon, Beslan, Chechnya, their voices pleading . . .

*Let there be peace on earth . . .*

And . . .

Let it begin with me.

# EPILOGUE

It's February 2007. Owie is two and a half years old. Sean brought him to visit me two times last year, which made me very happy. In March, Owie will have a baby sister and I will become a grandmother for the second time. I joked that the baby should be named Patsy Lou knowing full well that one Patsy in the family is enough.

And Star? What a joy she is. Star will travel with me on my book tour, thereby reversing our earlier mother-daughter roles. One morning Star came bursting into my kitchen with great news. She was beaming. "Mom," she said, "I was meditating the way we did on the trips and I had an epiphany!" Star paused, caught her breath, and went on. "When the time is right, and if you agree, it came to me like a vision that I'm to take over the work of the foundation." She was shining with an inner light, so happy, so sure, reminding me of myself after the vision that led to my work with children.

And so we have come full circle. Star is already planning an international children's letter-writing campaign called *"Peace to the Planet."* And so. . . . Hope Abides.

> *"Hope abides; therefore I abide.*
> *Countless frustrations have not cowed me.*
> *I am still alive, vibrant with life.*
> *The black cloud will disappear,*
> *The morning sun will appear once again*
> *In all its supernal glory."*
>
> —*Sri Chinmoy*